THE IMPACT

OF STRIKES

PUBLICATIONS IN THE YALE LABOR AND MANAGEMENT CENTER SERIES

Mutual Survival, The Goal of Unions and Management
by E. Wight Bakke

Union Challenge to Management Control
by Neil W. Chamberlain

Job Horizons, A Study of Job Satisfaction and Labor Mobility
by Lloyd G. Reynolds and Joseph Shister

Workers Wanted
by E. William Noland and E. Wight Bakke

Steel Town
by Charles R. Walker

Bonds of Organization
by E. Wight Bakke

The Structure of Labor Markets
by Lloyd G. Reynolds

Social Responsibility and Strikes
by Neil W. Chamberlain

Executive Leadership
by Chris Argyris

The Impact of Strikes
by Neil W. Chamberlain and Jane Metzger Schilling

LABOR AND MANAGEMENT CENTER
YALE UNIVERSITY
New Haven, Connecticut
E. Wight Bakke, Director

Directors of Research Projects
Chris Argyris
E. Wight Bakke
Neil W. Chamberlain
Lloyd G. Reynolds

Assistants in Research
Jane Metzger Schilling
Cynthia H. Taft

Administrative Staff
Mary B. Clark
Dorothy N. Loucks   Grace J. Waite

THE IMPACT
OF STRIKES

Their Social and
Economic Costs

BY

NEIL W. CHAMBERLAIN

ASSISTANT DIRECTOR, LABOR AND MANAGEMENT CENTER
AND ASSOCIATE PROFESSOR, DEPARTMENT OF ECONOMICS

AND

JANE METZGER SCHILLING

ASSISTANT IN RESEARCH, LABOR AND MANAGEMENT CENTER

YALE UNIVERSITY

GREENWOOD PRESS, PUBLISHERS
WESTPORT, CONNECTICUT

Library of Congress Cataloging in Publication Data

Chamberlain, Neil W
   The impact of strikes.

   Reprint of the 1st ed. published by Harper,
New York, in series: Yale Labor and Management
Center series.
   1. Strikes and lockouts--United States.
2. Strikes and lockouts--Social aspects.
I. Schilling, Jane Metzger, joint author.
II. Title. III. Series: Yale University. Labor
and Management Center series.
[HD5324.C42 1973]   331.89'2973   73-11841
ISBN 0-8371-7066-4

Originally published in 1954 by Harper & Brothers, New York

Reprinted with the permission of Harper & Row, Publishers, Inc.

Reprinted in 1973 by Greenwood Press, Inc.,
51 Riverside Avenue, Westport, Conn. 06880

Library of Congress catalog card number 73-11841
ISBN 0-8371-7066-4

Printed in the United States of America

10 9 8 7 6 5 4 3 2

CONTENTS

PREFACE

This book is an outgrowth of another study, *Social Responsibility and Strikes*. In that study social responsibility was related to public opinion, and analysis indicated that unions and managements failed in only one aspect of their relations to measure up to the social responsibility created by public expectations. That exception was the strike relationship. The hypothesis was suggested that public antipathy to a work stoppage is closely correlated with the real costs which it imposes on the public, and a method was devised for measuring the real costs of any strike by "rating" its impact on consumers and industrial users of the struck product and suppliers of the struck firm. That device was then applied to a number of strikes in several industries.

Measurement of the costs of a strike to the public was only a preliminary to the study of social responsibility, as it bore on unions and management, but as the measuring scales were applied the resulting material soon developed an interest of its own. It became evident that here was an instrument for ascertaining the differing pattern of strike effects in the various industries of the American economy and for building a body of knowledge directly pertinent to the problem of public policy concerning strikes. The result was the present volume.

Chapters 2 and 3 reproduce the strike rating procedure as originally presented in the social responsibility study. The remainder of the book is devoted to the use of that procedure in analyzing strikes in three industries and to the conclusions which emerge from the analyses. The statistical data on which we have had to rely have often been imprecise and incomplete, so that the conclusions must necessarily be tentative. Nevertheless, the results have a logical appeal which suggests that the inadequacies of the underlying data have not been seriously distorting. It is to be hoped that the members of the industries examined, who may have access to more accurate and precise information than was available to us, will assist in making any corrections that will improve the reliability of the ratings.

We share another hope. The device which has here been used to examine the public effects of strikes in only three industries is applicable to any other industry. The method of using it is carefully set forth. We should like to believe that the members of other industries will see the value of undertaking an examination of such strikes as have involved them and will make their own independent analyses. These would have their immediate practical usefulness to those in the industry—at the least as guides to public relations policies during the course of strikes. But they would also contribute to a cumulating body of knowledge that would ultimately make possible a more systematic and penetrating understanding of strikes as they affect our society.

THE IMPACT
OF STRIKES

CHAPTER 1

The Problem of Strikes: To-Do or What to Do?

THE end of World War II marked the beginning of the greatest industrial crisis in American history. With the fighting over, organized labor was released from its wartime no-strike pledge. The preceding years of wage restraint were compensated for by a rash of demands for increases ranging up to 50 per cent of existing rates. Backing up these demands was a strength that had been only newly acquired before the war, that had been repressed during the war, and that now was restless for assertion. The situation was made to order for explosive union-management relations, but few expected the magnitude or duration of the explosion.

It was the oil workers whose stoppage initiated the pattern of industrial disputes in the year 1945. On September 17, 43,000 of their number, in twenty states, struck to enforce a demand for the equivalent of a 30 per cent wage increase. After twenty days of idleness a third of the nation's supply of gasoline had been cut off. A threat to the return of servicemen from abroad was imminent. The President ordered the Navy to seize and operate the struck properties while a fact-finding board considered the issues.

Only four days after the oil industry had been hit, a substantial percentage of the nation's coal mines was closed, as 200,000 members of the Mine Workers left the pits in support of the efforts of their supervisors to obtain collective bargaining rights from the owners. For a month this dispute continued and then was abandoned by the union until "a later, more appropriate date." Other strikes—their importance dimmed only by the magnitude of what was to follow—came in quick succession.

The Northwest lumber industry was struck by 44,000 members of the AFL's Brotherhood of Carpenters on September 24; the east coast longshoremen went out for nineteen days beginning October 1; the CIO Glass Workers began a 102-day strike against the major part of the flat glass industry on October 16; close to 40,000 machinists and shipyard workers in the San Francisco Bay area opened a 140-day strike October 29; the New England textile industry went down November 1 and stayed down for 133 days; 10,000 truckers in twenty Midwest states began an eighty-one-day strike November 12. But all these represented only the preliminary bouts before the main events.

Mindful of the growing crisis, President Truman on October 30 addressed the nation on the problems of reconversion. "Like most of you," he said, "I have been disturbed by the labor difficulties of recent weeks. . . . There is no room in our economy for unfair dealing or for greedy individuals or groups on either side who want their own way regardless of the cost to others. The people will not stand for it. Their government will not stand for it." Executive orders were issued somewhat easing wage and price controls, to facilitate negotiated settlements. Price increases were to be allowed to accommodate approved wage increases, within a flexible stabilization program. On November 5 there opened the President's National Labor-Management Conference, from which it was hoped to obtain some agreement between leaders of both camps on policies that would smooth postwar readjustments. The conference rejected the CIO's plea that attention be focused on the substantive matter of appropriate wage policy and adjourned without offering any suggestion for procedural solution of the wage controversies that lay ahead. The arena was set for a power struggle with few holds barred and with a referee—the government—operating under no explicit authority.

On November 21, after weeks of fruitless negotiations, Walter Reuther of the Automobile Workers led 200,000 General Motors employees in a strike that was to last four months and provide some of the bitterest in-fighting of the period. The President moved without waiting for Congressional action on the labor legislation which he had proposed, appointing a fact-finding board to investigate the dispute. The company withdrew from the hearings in protest over the board's consideration of "ability to pay," but the proceedings continued and on January 10 the board recommended a settlement of 19½ cents an hour. The union accepted. The company refused. The strike went on, and within ten days the Automobile Workers were joined in the wage movement by more than a million other workers. Across the nation plant after plant was shut down.

On January 9 more than 140,000 Western Electric employees went out, returning after a week, however, under orders from the parent union. Approximately 180,000 electrical workers on January 15 closed General Electric and Westinghouse, along with General Motors' electrical operations. Some of them (the Westinghouse employees) were not to return until May 10. The next day 125,000 packinghouse workers joined the strike procession. Five days later came the severest blow of all, as 750,000 steelworkers left their jobs, and the basic industry and hundreds of fabricators' establishments suspended operations for what dragged on into a minimum of one month and in some instances ran as high as six months. The farm equipment industry was staggered as its major companies went down successively on January 21 (International Harvester), January 29 (Caterpillar), and April 30 (Allis-Chalmers).

The crescendo of the postwar strike activity was reached in February, 1946. In that month some 23,000,000 man-days of idleness were attributable to the direct impact of strikes, with unmeasured secondary effects in industries relying on the output of the struck units. Two more major stoppages were precipitated in the months immediately following, however. On April 1, the nation's soft coal mines were closed by a walkout of 340,000 miners, remaining closed—except for a fourteen-day truce period—for almost two months. And on May 23 there occurred the first nation-wide railroad stoppage in the country's history, as engineers and trainmen struck. Only swift and decisive governmental intervention brought the rail tie-up to an end in its third day.

The strikes identified above were only the most important of a total of almost 5000 work stoppages occurring in the year following victory in Japan. About 5,000,000 workers were directly involved, and their loss of working time amounted to 120,000,000 man-days. This strike activity coincided with the period when consumers were impatiently awaiting the promised flow of goods—particularly of consumer durables such as automobiles, refrigerators, stoves, washing machines, radios, television sets, and housing—which had been denied them during the war. One consequence was to focus public attention upon what came to be known as "national emergency" strikes. The feeling became widespread that special procedures were required to deal with labor disputes that threatened to work unusual hardship upon the community at large.

An analysis of public opinion polls taken by the major polling agencies suggests how general was—and still is—this concern for some "corrective" to the problem posed by strikes. A detailed examination of all polls dealing with union-management relations suggests that strikes are in fact the one aspect of these relations about which the public is exercised.[1] There is rather clear evidence that large sections of the public would welcome almost any substitute for the strike, particularly in those cases dealing with services deemed "essential" or involving the large corporations. This sentiment predates the strike wave of 1945-1946, but it was intensified by the events of that period.

Public support of strike-control legislation became manifest in the year following the great industrial upheaval. In 1947 the Taft-Hartley Act incorporated provisions granting the President permissive authority to restrain strikes or lockouts which would, in his judgment, "imperil the national health and safety." In that same year ten states—Florida, Indiana, Massachusetts, Missouri, Nebraska, New Jersey, Pennsylvania, Texas, Wisconsin, and Virginia—enacted legislation limiting the right to strike in certain industries, with nine of them providing for seizure or compulsory arbitration if needed. The connection between these federal and state acts and public disquiet over the turn of events the preceding year seems clear and direct.

The sentiment for protection of the public against the repercussions flowing from certain kinds of strikes does not appear to have diminished. Bills continue to be introduced in state legislatures. Proposals for amending the Taft-Hartley law to make its "emergency" provisions more effective continue to be offered. (Experience under the provisions of that act has been mixed. In several instances strikes have only been postponed, resuming after the government has, in accordance with the act's terms, stepped out of the picture at the end of eighty days. The functions of the fact-finding boards provided for in the act are vague and probably even unnecessary. Court interpretation suggests that the act's enforceable provisions operate against the "official" union only and are powerless with respect to unofficial strikes which the union's officers have sought to terminate.) In the presidential campaign of 1952 the candidates of both political parties admitted the need for strength-

[1] For details of this analysis the reader is referred to *Social Responsibility and Strikes*, by Neil W. Chamberlain (New York: Harper & Brothers, 1953), especially chaps. 3-5.

ening the strike-control provisions of this federal legislation. There thus seems to be a continuing belief that a problem is posed by strikes which seriously affect the public, even though uncertainty remains as to how that problem can best be resolved.

This conclusion has not gone unchallenged, however. There are some who believe that the strike as a social problem has been exaggerated out of proper proportion. They argue that the events of 1945-1946 have colored our thinking and that there is little likelihood that such a sequence of strikes will ever be repeated. To adopt restrictive legislation to meet emergency situations which are likely to arise only rarely is to sacrifice important freedoms to a falsely conceived need for public "protection."

One of the most effective spokesmen of this latter group is Edgar L. Warren, formerly director of the federal Conciliation Service, who has made an investigation of strikes which were serious enough to have commanded front-page newspaper attention on both East and West coasts over the thirty-six-year period from 1914 through 1949. Disputes which failed to receive a total of two columns in the *Los Angeles Times* and of six columns in the *New York Times* were considered of insufficient importance to be included in the analysis. This left a total of 104 strikes, of which forty-six were classed as "more important" in the sense of having been given a total of at least six columns of space in each of the papers mentioned. Of these forty-six, some 60 per cent occurred in the two postwar periods 1919-1922 and 1945-1949. There were none at all in the seven-year period from 1923 through 1929. Even among the "more important" strikes there have been few which threaten to "imperil the national health or safety." "Vital services have never been completely curtailed because of strike activity," according to Warren, who suggests that the availability of substitutes, the presence of some stocks of the struck good, the willingness of the striking union to continue "emergency" functions rather effectively manage to remove any "peril" from the situation.

Warren concludes:

Forty percent of those strikes which have attracted nationwide attention during the past thirty-six years were in industries where "necessary goods and services" were not involved. Another 24 percent did not result in a "dangerous curtailment of supplies" because they were in industries where the product could be stock-piled and stock piles were never entirely exhausted. Of strikes in those industries producing necessary goods and services where a dangerous curtailment of supplies might have been created, there were no more than twenty of extended duration; and it may be assumed that in most of these situations the strikes were not entirely successful and substitute facilities were available. Only in the field of public utilities and transportation do we find instances of strikes which come within the definition of national emergencies, and even these industries produce few real crises.[2]

His recommendation is to provide special machinery to deal with strikes in only two kinds of situations: (1) strikes involving public utilities and transportation, and then only when substitute facilities are not available, and (2) in time of war.

The issue of whether the strike problem is real or false, of whether the cries of alarm are greater than the cause warrants, of whether "something" needs to be done, largely revolves around how seriously the public is affected by strikes. If there are only a few types of strikes which have a significant impact on the public, and if these recur infrequently, then one may reasonably expect that public resentment over strike-caused inconvenience is ephemeral and does not call for ameliorative action. On the other hand, if the public is more profoundly affected than analysis such as Warren's suggests, the issue cannot be laid to rest so readily.

Few studies have ever been attempted to estimate the impact of any given strike on the public. A special committee of the Chamber of Commerce of the State of New York prepared an estimate of the loss to business concerns and workers in the manufacturing and distributive trades of New York City resulting from the 1945 elevator operators' strike. The Research Department of the National Association of Manufacturers published a case study of effects of the 1949-1950 bituminous coal strike.[3] Other less intensive surveys have been made, as by newspaper reporters, but the available information is thin indeed.

The purpose of this book is an exhaustive examination of the impact of strikes on their publics. By "public" is meant all of those who are not themselves party to the strike relationship but who are affected by that relationship, all those whose welfare is influenced by the strike except the union and management members directly involved in it.

[2] Edgar L. Warren, "Thirty-Six Years of 'National Emergency' Strikes," *Industrial and Labor Relations Review*, Vol. 5 (1951), pp. 12-15.

[3] *The Economic Impact of an Industry-wide Strike*, Economic Policy Division Series No. 27 (1950).

Publics thus change with each strike: the affected public in a coal strike is a different one from the affected public in a rail strike. We are interested in who are affected by any given strike and how they are affected.

We shall proceed by first developing a comprehensive scheme for rating any strike in terms of its relative impact on the public. This rating procedure is discussed in Chapters 2 and 3. We shall then investigate the impact of a number of strikes in three selected industries—coal, railroads, and steel. In the case of each industry the effects of its strikes on variously situated members of the public will first be described, in terms of experience, and then we shall differentiate among the strikes analyzed in terms of their relative impact, making use of the rating scales previously developed. We shall be particularly interested in discovering the *pattern* of strike effects which characterizes our three selected industries.

On the strength of these investigations we shall then be in a position to draw certain conclusions relevant to public policy. We shall be better able to judge whether sentiment for restraints on strikes constitutes only a noisome to-do about a relatively minor problem or whether it recognizes a more basic issue which demands resolution.

CHAPTER 2

How Strikes Affect the Public:
The Urgency Rating

I F THE one aspect of union-management relations to which there appears to be general opposition is the strike, we may reasonably inquire why opposition arises here. What is there about strikes (and here the term is used broadly to include lockouts as well) that arouses public resentment?

The simplest answer is that a strike is likely to injure not simply the party against whom it is directed but the public as well. Before a strike leads to agreement, the public may have been subjected to substantial inconvenience. Indeed, at times the "innocent" public seems to be regarded by the parties only as a weapon or bludgeon to be used against each other to force surrender; each side proclaims its sympathy for the public, which is being abused by the other's adamant refusal of concession, and seeks to align public support for its own position by expressing sympathetic concern for public welfare. But what is the basis for the public's involvement?

The whole structure of economic relationships in our society is based on the principle of specialization of services. In general, each individual becomes attached to a unit which is geared to produce services or goods of a particular, specialized type. So familiar are we with this principle of specialization of labor—which forms the basis for our mass production industries, on which our rising standards of living have largely depended—that we have taken certain of its corollaries for granted. One important corollary of specialized production is the mutual dependency of producers. Each individual can afford to specialize only because other specialists will make available goods and services which he demands. A worker can afford to be a full-time assemblyman in an automobile plant only because he knows that other workers will build his house for him, provide him with electric power, gas, and water, produce food and clothing for his use, and so on. In this relationship of mutual dependency, individuals come to experience a right of expectancy of the provision of the goods and services on which they rely. Indeed, our material culture has built into it an expectation that electric power, telephone service, fuel for heating and cooking will be with us each morning on rising just as surely as daylight, and without any personal responsibility other than the payment of bills. In similar fashion if lesser degree, we all carry expectations that the local transit service will pick us up in the morning, that schools will take care of our children, that restaurants will feed us, theaters and movie houses entertain us, and so on.

While division of labor establishes our dependence as consumers on other producers, and it is this that we are most inclined to consider, it is equally true that the economy of specialization leaves us dependent as producers on other consumers. The lathe operator who expects to buy the goods of other specialists must himself have a market for his services. The trucker who is to enjoy the fruits of the work of others must be able to market his own skills. In the integrated pecuniary economy, our consuming capacity is largely dependent on our producing capacity. From our functions as suppliers of specialized services we derive the income permitting us to purchase the product of others' specialized work. All this is a familiar story, but it must be retold as a reminder that we develop rights of expectancy in the marketing of our own services no less than in the buying of the services of others. We entertain an expectation of continued income as long as we do our jobs adequately and as long as consumers demand our services. The strike sometimes frustrates such an expectation, however. When the struck firm suspends operations it ceases to buy materials, and the repercussions may be felt by many suppliers beyond the struck firm itself. The effects can spread by chain reaction. Each producer who is no longer able to sell to the struck firm and who, therefore, reduces his own operations curtails his purchases from others, and so on in almost indefinite regression. Numerous individuals whose livelihoods depend on continued earnings, and who have been performing their duties as required, and whose services are still desired by ultimate consumers, may thus suddenly find themselves cut off from a market for their labor because of a strike. In some types of strikes—notably coal and steel—the number affected as producers may actually be greater than the number affected as consumers. Once again, the expectations on the basis of which we assume our specialized producing roles are frustrated. Not only may a strike deprive us of the flow of goods and services on the use of which we depend; it may also deprive us of an outlet for our own goods or services, on the sale of which we equally depend.

To the extent that a strike inconveniences us, then, it frustrates our rights of expectation, rights which are just as surely built into our culture as if they were matters of law. It is only the fact that serious frustration of such rights is sufficiently infrequent that has permitted us to accommodate over the years two essentially conflicting rights—the right to strike and the right to expect continued provision of specialized services. Yet there can be little doubt about the inconsistency of these two rights, expressed as absolutes, and depending on the nature of their conflict some resolution may emerge, over time, which will reduce the content of one or both rights. One may interpret the critical content of public opinion polls on this matter as evidence that a rather large portion of the population recognizes an inconsistency between the right to strike (by others) and its own expectations and that it would approve a resolution of this conflict which would modify the right to strike.

Nevertheless, although this may represent a satisfactory generalization on a high level of abstraction, there is some room for believing that the public does not regard all strikes in the same light. Strikes in wartime are condemned more unreservedly than strikes in time of peace; strikes in "essential" industries are viewed with less sympathy than strikes in general; strikes in large corporations are more frowned on than strikes in small enterprises. This discriminatory approach is, of course, a reflection of the fact that strikes affect the public in varying respects and degree, or to put it more precisely, each strike affects differently a different public. To the extent that a strike affects a larger public or affects it more drastically, it arouses greater public opposition.

These commonplace observations must be set down as a preliminary to the much more difficult problem of distinguishing between strikes on the basis of their effects on the public.

Any strike has a potential effect on the household consumers of the product involved. It is this effect that we primarily have in mind when we speak of the impact of strikes. Yet this initial consequence is only one of a chain of effects and indeed may be the least important. In addition to household consumers, other individuals are affected in their capacity as producers or because of a relationship to producers. First, there are the families of the parties themselves, a group so intimately associated with union and management that we tend to identify them as one of the parties. Actually, they are party to the dispute only by relationship and deserve consideration in their own right. The striker's wife who struggles to make ends meet when her husband's income has been cut off and the manager's wife whose home may be picketed are entitled to independent identification as an intimately affected strike public. Their views with respect to the acceptability of the strike technique (in distinction to the specific issues of a strike) may well differ from the views of their husbands. Second, there are the employees of the struck plant who are not actually party to the dispute—the clerical or sales force, possibly the maintenance employees, foremen, members of "middle" management. Third, there are the suppliers of goods and services to all the individuals who are members of the struck plant. These would include the local merchants, landlords, churches, outlying farmers, and so on, and their employees, for all of whom employment or income, or both, may be reduced in consequence of the strike. Fourth, there are the firms which supply goods and services (primarily materials, equipment, and transportation) to the struck plant, whose members (from owners to employees) may likewise be affected income-wise. Fifth, there are the firms which use the struck product in their own productive operations, whose output may have to be curtailed if another source is not discovered. In all these cases where the strike has its impact on producers, the effect is transmitted not only to the producer as an individual (and "producer" includes, of course, all employees engaged in production processes) but also to his family. The number may run high of those who are thus involved not as household consumers of the struck product but as producers whose operations are somehow affected by failure of supply of that product.

But where can the line be drawn? The indirect effects of a strike may ramify and spread throughout the economy. The producers whose operations are curtailed because of the strike likewise market goods and services. These too have their household consumers, their suppliers, their commercial users. The cycle continues. Each of these suppliers has its own suppliers. Each of these producers has its products, shortage of which affects their particular household and commercial consumers, as well as suppliers. There is an almost infinite regression of effects—potentially. Whether these effects appear, or the degree to which they appear, is dependent on such factors as the characteristics of the product, the extent of the bargaining unit which is struck (single firm or industry), and the duration of the strike, as we shall shortly see.

There thus emerges the notion of constructing a scale on which strikes might be rated in terms of their impact on the public, a scale which would take into account—for any given strike—the total effect on (1) household consumers of the struck product; (2) the "direct" producers, by which is meant (a) nonparty members and families of all members of the struck unit, (b) commercial users of the struck product, and (c) suppliers of the struck unit and its members; (3) the "indirect" producers, who are (a) the suppliers of the commercial users of the struck product and suppliers of the suppliers of the struck firm and (b) commercial users of the products of the commercial users of the struck product; and (4) household consumers patronizing any of the "indirect" producers, whom we will refer to as "indirect" consumers. The construction of such a scale has several uses. It requires an examination of what factors actually determine the impact on the public of any strike, which in itself is a useful task and one not as simple as appears on its face. It also permits the ranking of strikes to show which are more public-affecting than others. Finally, it suggests the changing nature of public-affectedness of any strike as the strike continues, thus providing an answer to such a question as, What will be the impact on the public of a coal strike (which begins now) on the first day, the tenth day, or the fortieth day of the strike?

Another interest in the construction of such a rating scale is that by establishing the extent of a strike's impact on the public it reveals the "real basis" for public opinion concerning the strike relationship between unions and managements. It helps in understanding why public opinion should regard particular strikes as conflicting with rights of expectation of a continued flow of a product or service more seriously than in other cases.

In rating strikes by the extent of their effect on the public, we shall first evaluate separately a strike's impact on consumers and producers. Later we shall have to break these two broad categories into finer categories, in accord with the groups identified above, but for the moment let us concentrate on these two major subdivisions. In the case of each, we shall try to set up the principal considerations which determine how important the loss of the struck product is in the lives of those affected. These principal considerations will be set up in the form of continua, that is, scales on which any strike may be rated as affecting the public, in the given respect, anywhere from the least possible to the most possible degree, from 0 to 100 per cent (though here we shall use a scale of 10 to represent all possible values). The significance of such continua will become more evident as the discussion proceeds.

Let us, then, consider the impact of any strike on the household consumers of the product involved. That impact is a resultant of three considerations, which we shall here refer to as (1) the cultural necessity of the product, (2) the stock effect, and (3) the substitutability effect. We shall examine each of these.

By cultural necessity of the product is meant how important the product is in the lives of those who consume it, how vital the product is in their structures of living. Here the term "cultural" is meant to subsume not only the need which a given civilization has created for a particular good or service (though that is frequently the relevant consideration); it includes also the biological needs (as for water or food, without respect to form or variety). This cultural need for the product is easy to confuse with a consideration which we shall examine later—the substitutability of other products for the given one. It may be thought, at first, that no product is vital as long as there are adequate substitutes for it, so that how vital a product is, in fact, depends on how satisfactory are its substitutes. To avoid this confusion it may be worth while to think of cultural necessity as how vital in the lives of its consumers is a given product *or any satisfactory substitute for it.*

Examples may further help to clarify the significance of cultural necessity. Let us say that the only newspaper in a town, and the local transit service, and milk delivery, and grand pianos, all have no very acceptable substitutes for most of their consumers. Although resort may be had to radio news or out-of-town papers, walking or private cars, canned milk or other beverages, upright pianos or harpsichords, none of these provides a close enough approximation of the services of the primary product to be counted as an adequate substitute. Despite this common degree of substitutability (or lack of substitutability), we could not say that all these products are equally important in the lives of their consumers. Milk delivery and local transit services are evidently more vital than a newspaper or a grand piano in the material culture of most consumers. We would, then, say that a strike in either of the former services affects a public more importantly than a strike in enterprises providing the latter two. They would be rated higher on our continuum.

The element of deferrability of consumption enters into this conception of cultural necessity. Regardless of how necessary a product is

in the lives of its consumers (if one thinks dichotomously of having it
or not having it at all), the consumption of certain kinds of items may
be postponed, making them less immediately necessary. Two products
may be equally necessary in the culture of a group of consumers, but
one must be had now if its value is to be realized while the other retains
its value even if consumption is deferred. Admittedly, it is not always a
simple matter to determine what consumption is deferrable and what
is not. Suppose there is a strike of the movie houses in a community.
Consumer A, who particularly wants to see the picture "West of the
Smokies," may be able to postpone seeing this film. The picture may be
shown after the strike is over, and the timing is not important to him
as long as he sees the picture *some* time. But consumer B, who during
the strike simply wants to go to the movies as a form of relaxation for
which the need is felt *then*, cannot postpone this consumption; a picture seen later is no substitute for a picture seen now, under the circumstances. If this pleasure is to be realized at all, it must be realized
in the present. Despite such difficulties of determining whether or not
consumption is deferrable, the principle is evident. Cultural necessity
has two characteristics, then: it refers to the *dispensability* of the product in the lives of the consumers and also to the *deferrability* of consumption of that product.

The cultural-necessity continuum may be thought of as ranging
from products which are unnecessary (dispensable or deferrable) even
for pleasure, with a value of 0, to products which are absolutely necessary to health and safety, valued at 10. In between these extreme values
any product can be placed. The actual placement of any product is
largely a qualitative judgment by the observer, but it would be entirely
feasible to elicit—by opinion polls, for example—consumer responses
providing a more objective determination. Tentatively, certain grada-
tions of cultural necessity may be suggested, as guide points along the
continuum, not as classifications.

Cultural Necessity to Household Consumers

0 1	2 3 4	5 6 7	8 9 10
Unnecessary	Necessary for pleasures and conveniences of varying degrees of importance	Necessary if hardship (physical, mental, pecuniary), in varying degree, is to be avoided	Necessary in varying degree, for health and safety, ranging up to "absolutely necessary"

The second factor determining how a strike affects household consumers is what we shall call the stock effect. Strikes differ in their impact because there are differences in the extent to which stocks of services yielded by the struck products are available for consumption during the course of the strike. A coal strike which begins with high coal stocks in consumers' bins and in retail yards holds less concern to the consumer than a coal strike which finds both bins and yards relatively empty. How large is the stock of any product depends in part on the physical "pileup-ability" of the product (railroad services and electric power do not readily lend themselves to stock-piling, while coal, clothing, and some foods do), on the economic "storeability" of the product (some products, while physically capable of being stocked, involve excessive cost of storage—size 17 shoes, for example, for which demand is slight), on the "extendability" of products already in the hands of households (razor blades can be made to provide additional services even though normally they would have been scrapped, while food eaten once cannot be re-used) , and on normal accessibility (beehive coke ovens located close to coal mines do not carry large supplies of coal because the source of replenishment can be easily tapped). It should be underscored that it is the *services* of products rather than the products themselves which are important here. Dial telephones, for example, can store up service for consumers in a manner which manual phones cannot, so that effects of a telephone strike differ depending on whether dial or manual service is involved. Similarly, a railroad strike is less damaging if there are large stocks of all types of goods which have already been moved to their destinations, thus providing a stock of railroad services already performed.

Stocks by themselves are not enough to give us the "stock effect," however. Alongside the services of goods which are available during the course of a strike we must place the amount of those services which are being used up during the course of the strike. A given stock of coal has different meaning to consumers depending on whether they are then consuming coal at the rate of 5000 tons or 50,000 tons a day. This relationship of stocks to consumption is typically expressed in the stock-consumption ratio. A ratio of twenty-eight days for bituminous coal, for example, indicates that enough stocks are available to provide for normal consumption for a period of twenty-eight days.[1]

---

[1] In the case of durable goods (for example, automobiles), the stock-consumption ratio may be computed by either of two methods. (1) The number of new automobiles available for use may be regarded as the stock, while the number of automobiles withdrawn from use (services completely exhausted, for which replacements may be presumed to be needed)

The stock-consumption ratio is obviously affected by anything modifying the size of stocks or the amount of consumption. The most important modifications of amount of stock occurring during a strike are depletion due to consumption and additions due to increased production. The former is self-explanatory: the days of the strike pass and consumers continue to use up some portion of the stock pile, leaving less for the period over which the strike may continue.

The possibility of additions due to increased output takes into account primarily two factors: the proportion of the industry which is struck, and the proportion of industry capacity being utilized prior to the strike. If one firm contributing only 5 per cent of an industry's output were shut down, the remaining firms would be able to make up the resulting loss of product more easily than if the struck firm had contributed 50 per cent of industry sales. If the whole industry is struck, the possibility of additions due to increased production is virtually eliminated.

Nevertheless, it is possible that in times of high production levels the non-struck firms in an industry may already be operating at peak capacity, so that they are unable to expand output at all. Regardless of the fact that the struck firm may contribute only 5 per cent—or less— of the industry's output, the remaining firms may be totally unable to offset the loss of output by expanded operations. This is likely to be the case for many firms during wartime, though capacity operation is not confined solely to such emergency periods.

Modifications of the amount of consumption during the course of the strike are primarily a reflection of whether consumers, in anticipation of shortages, either voluntarily or compulsorily ration their use of the service. In the course of a coal strike, for example, households may heat their homes at lower temperatures to conserve dwindling stocks; local governments may establish priority lists for sales from coal yards, on the basis of need; apartment houses, schools, and other institutions have at such times limited their use of fuel.

It would indeed be convenient if we could use the stock-consumption ratio itself as a basis for reflecting the impact of a strike on consuming

plus the expected net increase in demand for automobiles would be considered as consumption, the two giving the stock-consumption ratio. (2) Alternatively, the total amount of services available in all cars in the hands of private owners, sales agencies, and producers would be considered as stock, with the total amount of services of cars consumed during the course of the strike plus net new demand for cars constituting consumption. Either method of computation is satisfactory, and choice can rest entirely on convenience.

households. Large stocks relative to consumption would make a strike less severe than low stocks relative to consumption. The continuum would be set up to give increasing values for decreasing stock-consumption ratios, with a maximum of 10 for a ratio of 0. Such an approach is untenable for two reasons, however. (1) In many instances consumers will not feel the effect of a strike until stocks are exhausted or nearly exhausted. Whether the stock-consumption ratio of coal is 50 or 10 is not likely to affect a consumer's habits. Not until the ratio falls to a very low figure is rationing likely to be instituted in many homes. If we use stock-consumption ratios, then, the effect on consumers is less correctly expressed as a continuum than as a turning point: up to some ratio, consumers have been unaffected; past that ratio they are affected. Increasing values for continuously decreasing stock-consumption ratios are clearly erroneous. (2) On the other hand, at the time that consumers' habits are affected, so that they institute rationing, it is conceivable that stock-consumption ratios will conceal rather than reveal the nature of the effect. As rationing is instituted, consumption falls so that a given stock will last for more days. The more severe the rationing, the less will the stock-consumption ratio suggest the effect of the strike. Stocks will decline less slowly due to conservation, so that stock-consumption ratios (even though based on normal consumption) will similarly decline more slowly, concealing the actual impact which conservation may be having on the consumers. Consequently, we use a different basis for our continuum designed to show the stock effect.

Stock Effect: The Extent to Which Consumption Declines Owing to Diminishing Stocks

0	1	2	3	4	5	6	7	8	9	10
0%	10%	20%	30%	40%	50%	60%	70%	80%	90%	100%

On this scale the effect of rationing is expressly indicated, and the lack of effect which diminishing stocks may actually have on consumer habits is provided for. Nevertheless, the stock-consumption ratio need not be discarded as useless. As a practical matter, it seems likely that a conversion table may be developed, showing—for a given product— the extent to which consumption declines are influenced by stock-consumption ratios. On the basis of experience, we may find that, with coal at a stock-consumption ratio of five days (consumption being computed in terms of normal use), consumption may decline by 20 per cent, while with stocks at three days consumption may be reduced to 50 per cent of normal. From such experience we would be able to estimate, from stock-consumption data, the actual stock effect on household consumers.

There is one admitted weakness with this continuum: it does not take into account what economists refer to as declining marginal utility. The least important uses of a good or service are eliminated first; as long as some stock remains it is always the most essential uses which are satisfied. Increasing cuts in consumption of a good, then, result in more than proportionate hardship. A 100 per cent cut in the use of electricity creates more than twice as much hardship as a 50 per cent cut, yet we rate these as 10 and 5, respectively, on our scale. Ideally, the rating should increase more than proportionately with the reduction in consumption, where all individuals are affected alike by the strike. On the other hand, most strikes do not affect consumers equally. Some have large stocks and others none. In the first instance the proportionate hardship is considerably less than in the second instance. There appears to be no adequate way of estimating "average" hardship on a nonproportionate scale. Because we have been unable to accept any scale as indicating the effect of diminishing utility satisfactorily, we have retained the less satisfactory but simpler method of rating the stock effect as though hardship is equiproportionate to the reduction in consumption of the good.

We come now to the substitutability effect. By this is meant the extent to which consumers find another product acceptable as a substitute for the struck product. A strike at a theater is not likely to weigh heavily on its consumers since they can turn to movies, finding these perhaps not as satisfactory as their original choice but sufficiently acceptable so that the strike imposes no hardship. On the other hand, a strike in the local utility supplying electricity leaves its consumers relatively helpless, not simply because they are dependent on electricity for so many essential services (cultural necessity) but because its substitutes are relatively unsatisfactory. Local transit services probably fall somewhere between the two extremes of these examples. Increased use of private automobiles and cabs or walking provide acceptable substitutes for a substantial number of consumers but are not available to others, for whom no satisfactory substitute exists.

The measure of substitutability which ideally should be used here is perhaps the economist's concept of cross-elasticity of demand, which shows the proportionate change in the demand for one product (its price remaining unchanged) resulting from a small proportionate change in the price of another product. Thus if the price of theater tickets is increased and the resulting increased demand for movie admissions is proportionately greater than the resulting increased demand for night-club entertainment (the price of both remaining constant), we can say that movies are better substitutes for theaters than are night clubs. A small proportionate increase in the price of a given product has caused a larger proportionate number of consumers to switch to one alternative rather than the other. On the other hand, if the local transit fare is increased but there is no perceptible increase in the amount of gasoline sold or downtown parking space rented or in the use of cabs, we can say that the latter are not considered satisfactory substitutes for public transportation.[2]

Unfortunately, no empirical estimates of cross-elasticities of demand exist, so that cross-elasticity is useful to us only conceptually, clarifying what we are interested in measuring. There is one deficiency which cross-elasticity, even as a concept, has for our purposes, however: it indicates nothing concerning the availability of the substitute products.[3] Goat's milk may be a reasonably satisfactory substitute for cow's milk for those who can obtain it, but it is not available in sufficient quantities to make it a practical substitute for most milk consumers. We are therefore forced to fall back upon an impressionistic judgment about the substitutability of other products for the struck product. Our scale, running from 0 to 10, simply reflects varying degrees of substitutability, ranging from very high to none.

Substitutability of Other Products for the Struck Product

0	1	2	3	4	5	6	7	8	9	10
Completely acceptable substitutes										No acceptable substitutes

[2] The stock-consumption ratio requires a delimitation of "the industry," in order to determine the proportion of the total amount of any given product which is withdrawn from the market. This is not a simple matter, in the face of product differentiation. We speak of the automobile industry, for example, but it is questionable whether we should include Cadillacs and Packards as well as Fords and Chevrolets in estimating the percentage of "the industry" struck, since the industry concept has implicit in it the notion of a very high degree of homogeneity among a line of products. In elasticity terms, an "industry" would be composed of companies producing products having a very high (nearly perfect) cross-elasticity of demand in terms of each other.

Once it has been decided what firms compose the industry (that is, the units where products are considered homogeneous), then the acceptability as substitutes of all other (nonhomogeneous) products is, conceptually, measurable, and it is the adequacy of the "best" substitutes that is measured on our third continuum.

[3] Availability of alternative producers of the struck product has been taken into account in the stock effect, it will be recalled.

These, then, are our three principal determinants of the impact of a strike on household consumers: cultural necessity, the stock effect, and the substitutability effect. But what of a strike's duration? Surely the length of time over which a strike extends is a principal ingredient of its impact on the consuming public.

Duration is, of course, vitally important in determining the effect of a strike on consumers. But duration is significant only because it affects each of our three continua. It is not a separable measurement but, rather, something that enters into the measurements of cultural necessity, stock and substitutability effects. How long a strike is protracted would be of no importance if the struck product were rated o on all three scales—as unnecessary (dispensable or continuingly deferrable), with loss of production having no effect on consumption of the product, and with highly substitutable products available in any case.

What we must do, then, is to measure the *changing* effect of our three principal considerations over the period of the strike. In some cases we must even extend our measurements to the period after the strike has been settled: declining stocks may have no effect on consumption during the course of the strike, but before depleted stocks can be replenished consumers may be deprived of the good or service even though production has been resumed.

The rating which is derived from our three continua is thus the rating of the effect of a given strike on the consuming public as of any given day of the strike. As the strike progresses, the cultural necessity of the product, the stock effect, the acceptability of substitute products —these are likely to receive changing values. (1) Cultural necessity need not remain the same over the duration of the strike: failure of garbage collection may be only a matter of inconvenience in the early days of the strike but a threat to health as the strike continues. The importance of milk to the consumer on any given day will depend in some degree on the availability of milk on previous days; the cultural necessity of milk to a housewife on the eighth day of a milk strike will be different depending on whether she started the strike with no quarts or a dozen quarts of milk on hand. It should be noted that this is not the same thing as the stock effect. It takes account of the stock effect on *previous* days of the strike, to be sure, but our stock-effect continuum is designed to show only the effect of the consumer's stock position *on the given day* of the strike. (2) The stock effect changes with the prolongation of a strike. Rationing effects are likely to be less noticeable in the early days of the strike but more significant as stocks decline. On the other hand, stocks may be limited in the early days of a strike but may subsequently expand after non-struck producers of similar products increase their output. (3) Substitutability may change: what was acceptable early in the strike may cease to be acceptable with continued use, or what was unacceptable as a substitute at first may become acceptable with continued need; goods or services not available at the start may become practical alternatives when a little time has been allowed in which to organize their production.

The effect of time on the ratings is suggested by the following tabular form:

Day of the strike	1	2	3	4	5	6	7	8	9	10	11	....
Cultural necessity												
Stock effect												
Substitutability												

On each day, the cultural necessity, stock and substitutability effects would be separately rated to show these effects as of that day. This does not, of course, provide any measure of the cumulative impact of the strike. A given day's score does not reveal, for example, how long consumers may have been forced to curtail consumption. To show such cumulative effects, ratings would have to be added. As yet, however, we have not had occasion to discuss how the scores based on our three continua are used; we must still defer that question for a few paragraphs.

A rating of the changing impact of a strike on consumers, as it continues and as it is measured by these three continua, would presumably be made at or just before the start of a strike. Certain of the data might be difficult to acquire—such as stock-consumption ratios or the experience data necessary to convert these to percentage declines in consumption as a strike progressed. Judgments must reflect opinion where data are not available—as in the case of substitutability of other products. Nevertheless, there is no real barrier to establishing approximate ratings for all three considerations over any given duration. Such a rating would facilitate calculation of what strike duration is "tolerable" before public intervention is "compelled."

Up to this point we have been talking about the strike effects on household consumers. We have now to consider the effects on producers, if we are to observe the total impact of a strike on the public. For present purposes, let us distinguish between producers using the struck product (or some product of which the struck product is an ingredient) and producers supplying the struck firm (or supplying firms which use, directly or indirectly, the struck product). In both cases the same kinds of considerations apply as to household consumers, though with slight variations.

In the case of producer-users, it is not the cultural necessity of the struck product which determines need, but the production necessity. Some products are vitally necessary to a production process, so much so that without them operations must be suspended. Other products, while ingredients of the production process, can be more readily dispensed with. Floor brushes (or some substitute for them) are materials used in the course of production; the sweeping up of debris from factory floors is not a matter of aesthetics but one of production efficiency. Nevertheless, most plants could continue operating for some time without benefit of cleaning apparatus. A steel mill could hardly get along so easily without coal (or some substitute). Our first continuum is therefore converted to measure the importance of the struck product (or some suitable substitute) to the production process.

Production necessity is compounded of dispensability of the struck product in the production process (indicating the extent to which production will be lost owing to lack of the struck product or some substitute for it) and recoverability of the affected production (indicating the extent to which production lost during the strike can be recovered by make-up operations after the strike). Even if steel production is suspended because of a coal strike, for example, there remains the possibility that steel output lost now might be made up later. This possibility is best realized when the user of the struck product is operating at less than full capacity (so that operations subsequent to the strike can be expanded to recover lost production), when the user's sources of other necessary supplies can be expanded as needed, and when the user's customers are themselves willing and able to defer their purchases, the latter condition being most nearly met if there are no good substitutes for the user's product.

The assessment of recoverability is one of the most difficult aspects of estimating the real costs of a stoppage. There is frequently an uncertain connection between orders unfilled because of the strike and orders filled after the strike. Moreover, to some degree subsequent production is not an exact equivalent for strike-interrupted production. It may not forestall the need for resort to credit which would otherwise have been unnecessary, it may allow a time advantage to competitors which affects future business performance, it may not prevent customers from giving more serious consideration to alternative sources of supply or alternative products; for user employees it may not forestall hardship during the strike, and the lost output may be made up by fuller production schedules without a necessary accompanying recapture of wages. For these reasons it is not easy to determine to what extent recoverability should be viewed as mitigating the impact of a strike. Nevertheless, some judgment must be attempted in the light of all these considerations. Throughout this study whenever the term "recoverability" is used it should be understood in the special sense of the extent to which postponed operations are an offset to losses suffered during the strike, and we shall limit the period of make-up operations to the six months following the strike to avoid thin-spinning the result.

It will help to keep more clearly in mind the meaning of "production," in connection with production necessity, if it is identified with employment in the producing firm. We are interested in the extent to which output of the industrial user depends on the struck product on any given day, but output does not refer simply to the flow of finished goods from a plant. It includes no less the various maintenance and clerical services without which the plant could not, over time, operate. Even if a steel plant were deprived of coal, for example, so that the actual flow of iron and its products came to a halt, not all employees of the plant would be laid off. Some would be retained to keep plant and equipment in good condition, others to repair equipment, perhaps others to modify plant layout or to expand facilities, still others to continue to make out invoices, take care of continuing correspondence, keep records up to date, make payments, and so on. All these are aspects of the production process, over the long run. Nevertheless, such ancillary or facilitating operations cannot be continued indefinitely in the absence of the basic production process. Hence, production necessity like cultural necessity is a function of time, that is, the duration of the strike. During the first week, services such as those just mentioned may be continued even if the strike has shut down the plant, but as the strike progresses fewer clerical and maintenance employees will be required, until—if the strike lasts long enough—the user firm will reduce its employment to the bare minimum, the fixed labor charges that cannot be avoided giving rise to services which, however, from the long view, must still be regarded as part of production.

There remains one final consideration under production necessity. If we think of production in terms of user employment, then such employment may be sustained by resort to temporary alternative jobs *outside the user firm*. To the extent that the decline in production employment in the user firm is thus offset by an increase in production employment elsewhere, the impact of the strike on producer-users is minimized.

To summarize, then, in the production-necessity continuum we take account of the degree of dependence of producer-users on the struck good, as if no stocks of or substitutes for that good are available, a dependence which is reduced by the extent of continuing sustaining operations, by the availability of temporary alternative employment, and by the amount of recoverability of strike losses.

The remaining two continua are virtually unchanged. The stock effect indicates the extent to which use of the struck product declines owing to diminishing stocks (or the nonexistence of stocks). As in the case of consumers, producers sometimes ration their use of materials in short supply. Such rationing may be undertaken for several reasons. With a given stock of materials and no immediate source of replenishment, a producer may choose to allocate supplies primarily to high-profit or low-inventory lines, restricting their use in items which have a lower margin of profit or in which a substantial inventory has been accumulated. Complete shutdown may damage equipment (as in steel) or suspend production of goods or services deemed essential (as in railroads), so that partial operation over a longer period is preferable to full operation for a shorter time.

Finally, the substitutability effect measures the adequacy of other products as substitutes for the struck product in the production process.

The tabular form on which we rate the effect of strikes on commercial users is then:

Day of the strike	1	2	3	4	5	6	7	8	9	10	11	....
Production necessity												
Stock effect												
Substitutability												

With producers who *supply* materials or services to the struck unit or to other firms using the struck product, the same three criteria of affectedness are used, again with slight changes. The supplier is concerned over outlets for its goods, rather than with materials to make them. The struck firm ceases to be a customer, with repercussions upon its supplying firms. If the struck plant does not resume operations within a short time, production in the supplying firms may have to be curtailed for lack of markets. "Market necessity" therefore replaces "production necessity" in our first continuum. Market necessity, like production necessity, comprises the two elements of dispensability and recoverability.

Dispensability relates to the dependence of the supplier on the struck unit—or on some substitute market—as an outlet for its production. The Chesapeake and Ohio Railroad is an important coal-hauling railroad, for example, supplying transportation services to coal-mining companies. Its dependence on the coal industry (or on some substitute for the coal industry) is great. The impact of a coal strike on it, because of market necessity, is more serious than for a railroad only 10 per cent of whose services are taken for coal hauling.[4] As with user firms so too with supplier firms do we equate production with employment; in consequence the dependence of the supplier's employment on the struck unit is reduced to the extent that temporary alternative employment is available outside the supplier firm. Recoverability measures the extent to which production not purchased by the struck unit during the strike will be bought by it after the strike, so that some portion of the supplier's output is not lost but only postponed.

Market necessity, like production necessity, is a function of the duration of the strike. A coal strike will not immediately affect all employees of a coal-hauling railroad, since even if coal is not carried some portion of the labor force will be retained for maintenance and clerical operations. The longer the strike continues the fewer such functions

[4] We take the ratio of purchases by the struck unit to total sales of the supplier as representative of dispensability in this sense. The procedure here would be as follows: First, we would break down the total purchases figure of the struck unit into its principal component categories, such as purchases of electric power, or of steel, or of railroad services, and so on. We would then take total sales of each of the supplier groups so identified and compute the percentage of its total sales which is normally taken by the struck unit. When reduced to our scale of 10, this would give us the first approximation of the market necessity rating, which would then be modified to reflect the other elements of dispensability and recoverability mentioned in the text. In practice, however, as will be explained later, we have modified this approach for convenience.

will be performed, however, so that the dependence of the supplier group upon the struck unit increases with the passage of time.

For the supplier, the stock effect indicates the extent to which his output declines owing to inability to accumulate as stocks that part of his product which the struck unit would normally take. In some instances a supplying firm may be able to continue production and stock-pile its product, while in other instances this is not possible. A railroad supplier cannot stock-pile transportation services which are not currently demanded. A coal company is better able, in purely physical terms, to continue operations even if its market outlets are currently shut down. Whether or not stock-piling is physically feasible, however, there are sometimes economic reasons why it is not attempted.

In some cases a struck unit may continue some of its purchases from a supplier. If the supplies are of scarce materials, the struck unit may be reluctant to give them up even if it cannot use them until the strike is terminated. In the case of coal-hauling railroads, coal already mined enables the coal industry to continue purchases of coal-hauling services for a time. To the extent suppliers continue to provide goods or services to the struck unit, to that extent, of course, is the stock effect reduced. To that extent is its output not reduced by inability to accumulate stocks of its products.

The substitutability effect measures the extent to which a supplier can substitute another outlet for the one which has been struck. This is partly an effect of the level of economic activity. If any one automobile company had been struck at almost any time in the decade of the forties, steel companies would have had little difficulty in substituting other outlets for their steel. In times of slack production alternative buyers may not be so readily found, however. Substitutability of markets is also a function of the degree of specialization. If one company is geared to supply a particular product to another producer, made to the latter's peculiar specifications, there is increased difficulty of finding another purchaser whose needs are precisely the same. Some suppliers are so closely linked to producer-customers that a strike in the latter's plants will force a shutdown in their own. One example of such a close relationship is that between Briggs and Chrysler, with the former geared to produce to the specifications of the latter. The result is that a strike at Chrysler can be predicted to have its effect on Briggs. Finally, it is not always as easy for one firm as another to find temporary substitute outlets. If the steel industry is struck, it is not as simple for coal companies to find alternative buyers as it is for meat dealers in the event of a restaurant strike, who—by lowering prices— might induce more home consumption. The ability to exploit substitute markets is thus a function of the short-run price elasticity of demand for the product being supplied.

For suppliers of the struck firm, then, our tabular form for rating the effect of a strike is as follows:

Day of the strike	1	2	3	4	5	6	7	8	9	10	11	....
Market necessity												
Stock effect												
Substitutability												

So far we have a set of three continua for each of three groups in the public which is affected by a strike. We must now consider the relationship of these continua to each other. The fact that each of our three primary determinants of the impact of a strike on the affected groups is expressed as a relative on a common scale facilitates the use of each with the others, on the basis of the rating given.

Our necessity ratings (cultural, production, and market) may be taken as indicating the maximum possible effect of the strike on the relevant public on the given day. They are a measure of what the relative effects of a particular strike on consumer and producer groups would be if there were no stocks of or substitutes for the struck good. Production necessity and market necessity have a statistical basis—they reflect the extent to which output would drop, in percentage terms. Consumer necessity has no such significance but simply measures, on a relative basis, the hardship to consumers if a particular good or service were withdrawn on a given day, without stocks or substitutes available.

However necessary the struck good or the struck unit is to the relevant groups, to the extent that stocks are available or substitutes are adequate the impact of the strike is reduced. An example may help. Suppose that on the given day of the strike,

Cultural necessity = 10 (the good is vital to consumers)

Stock effect = 4 (consumption declines by 40% due to diminishing stocks)

Substitutability = 8 (substitutes are inadequate to supply 80% of the "value" of the services of the struck good)

Substitutes will be called on only to fill the gap left by the 40 per cent fall in consumption due to declining stocks. We take 80 per cent of 40 per cent as the extent to which substitutes are inadequate to meet the effect of the decline in the consumption of the good, or 32 per cent. The substitution effect thus diminishes the stock effect. We then take 32 per cent of 10 or 3.2 (on our scale of 10) as the measure of consumer dependence on the struck good which neither stocks nor substitutes have been able to cushion. To this measure (which we have derived by taking the substitution effect as a percentage of the stock effect, and the resulting figure as a percentage of the necessity rating) we give the name *urgency rating*. The urgency rating indicates the degree of impact of the strike on the relevant affected public.

The Census Problem: The Number Affected
by a Strike

IN THE preceding chapter we constructed scales on which to measure the relative extent to which individuals are affected by a strike, a measure which we have called the strike's urgency rating. All strikes having the same urgency rating are not of equal importance, however. Obviously, the impact of strikes differs with the number of individuals who are affected. If two strikes have urgency ratings of 5, but one affects the city of New Haven while the other affects the city of New York, we would have to say that the latter has greater effect. From the point of view of the individual affected, of course, the number of fellow sufferers is not material, but if we are trying to calculate the effects of strikes we must take into account not only the character of the strike's incidence (as given by our urgency rating) but also the size of the publics involved. In each case, then, we are interested in the *number* of people affected, as well as in how they are affected.

In taking the absolute number of those affected, let us simplify matters by making the understood unit of account 100,000 people. Thus if a strike affects 5,000,000 individuals (both consumers and producers) we shall consider the number affected as 50. If the urgency rating of that strike, for all groups, was 2, then multiplying the numbers affected by the urgency rating would give us a score of 100 for that strike—a score which would represent the impact of that strike on the public, placing that strike relative to all other strikes with respect to public-affectedness.

For purposes of estimating the absolute number of individuals feeling the weight of a strike, it is necessary to segregate the public into categories. We deal here with seven major categories, as previously identified. Each of these involves something of a problem in estimation, and we shall have to make some tentative resolution of the problems presented. We shall briefly examine each of the categories for that purpose, but readers who are not concerned with this problem in estimation may prefer to skip this section.

First, we begin with the major subdivision of household consumers, under which we treat with direct consumers and with indirect consumers. By households is meant not only private family units but also all nonprofit institutions, such as hospitals, schools, churches, fraternal societies, service organizations, and so on. Direct consumers are those who normally would have used the product of the struck firm or industry. In the case of a strike at General Motors, for example, the direct consumers would be the absolute number of individuals who would have bought General Motors cars during the period of the strike. Indirect consumers are those who would have bought products which require the struck product in their making. If the coal industry is shut down by strike, not only may individuals be deprived of coal for residential heating purposes (direct consumption), they may conceivably be deprived of the services of coal-burning passenger trains or of the products which would have been shipped by coal-burning freight trains; they may be restricted in their use of electricity from utilities relying on coal-fueled generators; they may fail to get their local newspaper if its supply of newsprint is manufactured in a coal-powered paper plant. All these effects we refer to as indirect consumer effects.

Calculation of the number of direct consumers affected can be made in at least two ways. (1) We can take the expected number of sales of the struck unit for any given strike duration. "Expected sales" may be calculated on the basis of the sales of the same period in the preceding year corrected by trend and cyclical factors or they may be estimated from the sales of the month preceding the strike, corrected by seasonal and cyclical factors. (2) Alternatively, one might take the expected number of sales of the industry as a whole (the expected sales of automobiles, for example) and reduce this figure by the proportion of total sales normally supplied by the struck unit. (If 1,000,000 people could be expected to buy cars in a given three-month period, and General Motors normally supplied one-half the new car market, then the number of direct consumers affected by a three-month strike at General Motors would be 500,000 (or 5 when reduced by our unit of account).

A serious problem is presented by the fact that most companies produce not one product but a number of products. A company like General Motors, for example, may turn out literally hundreds of products, not all but a great many of them consumer items. If the company is struck, all these goods are withheld from the market. How shall we treat such multiple-product firms in estimating the impact of strikes?

There seems to be no escape from the fact that each product deserves its own urgency rating and its own estimate of the absolute number of consumers who would have bought it over the course of the strike. It may be, for example, that the urgency rating for General Motors' new car output is quite low, since adequate substitutes are available. On the other hand, the urgency rating for its output of automobile repair parts may be high. Ford and Plymouth parts may be far less substitutable for Chevrolet parts than a new Ford or Plymouth is substitutable for a new Chevrolet. We should have to make a separate rating for parts, to add to the rating for new cars, then, in each case multiplying the relevant number of consumers by the relevant rating, in order to determine the total impact on direct consumers of a strike at General Motors, adding in as well the scores for all other General Motors consumer items.

To follow this practice faithfully would involve, at least in the case of the large corporations, more of a search for obscure data than the results would warrant. As a compromise, which is not likely to lead to much distortion, we can group the output of multiple-product firms into major classifications, rating not single products but classes of products. It appears unlikely, even in the case of our largest or most diversified corporations, that their line of products would require more than ten product classifications, and in most cases fewer will be sufficient. To rate this number of "products" is not an unmanageable task.

The calculation of indirect consumers presents an even more difficult problem. With a product like coal or a service like railroad transportation, the number of possible indirect consumer effects is almost limitless. They would include all the products which consumers buy that are produced with the aid of the coal which is no longer available or distributed by means of the rail system which has been struck. Clearly we cannot consider all these. The solution which has been adopted here has been to limit ourselves to the two indirect uses of the struck product most obviously affecting consumers, unless the consequence is so to understate the indirect effects as to require consideration of additional indirect uses. Here too we can best proceed by defining user groups broadly. Moreover, if we are dealing with a strike at a multiple-product firm, then this requires consideration of the two most important indirect consumer uses of each of the struck products or product classes. In the case of all such indirect effects, we must first obtain the urgency rating for the "secondary" product and then multiply the number of affected consumers by this rating (using our unit of account of 100,000 persons). Those who are affected are the consumers of products which normally require the struck firm's output in their making.

If we encounter problems in trying to estimate the number of consumers affected by a strike, our difficulties are vastly increased when we seek to estimate the number of ·producers affected. Indeed, the effort would seem scarcely worth while except for the fact that it is precisely such producer effects that frequently magnify the impact of one strike over another. A strike in steel is likely to be so much more public-affecting than a strike in meat packing not because consumers feel the effects more tellingly—the reverse would be true; when steel goes down, it is the number of producers affected which makes the strike so costly to the public.

The term "producers" is used here to refer to all those involved in the production process, whether as owners, managers, or employees. Despite this inclusiveness, the most usable measure of the number affected in a producer capacity is the number of employees. This is the measure which has been used here. The primary justification for this simplified approach is that the urgency rating reflects the impact on production, and the immediate, most concentrated effects of any cut in production are felt by the working force rather than by owners and managers. There is no intent here to minimize the impact of a strike on these latter groups, but it is believed that, in terms both of strike-affectedness and of the numbers affected, employees provide the most significant single measure of the importance of a strike to the producing groups.

Producers—thus defined—can be divided into five categories: the direct users of the struck product; indirect users; direct suppliers of the struck firm; suppliers of the direct and indirect users, and non-party members of the struck unit. Each presents its own problems in estimation. Some of these problems can be resolved only expediently, with not very satisfactory results.

In the case of direct producer-users, we first identify the principal uses of the struck product. We then take the total number of employees in each industry so identified, reduced by the proportion of the industry which the struck firm or unit normally supplies, to obtain the number of direct-user producers affected by the strike. For example, if the railroads constitute one of the chief users of the coal industry's products, and if total railroad employment is 1,000,000, and if a strike in coal shuts down a portion of that industry which normally supplies one-half of the railroads' needs, we would say that 500,000 direct-user producers were affected.[1] We multiply this number (5, when converted to our unit of account of 100,000 people) by the relevant urgency rating to obtain the score for the direct-user effects of the strike on railroads.

Indirect producer-users are those who use products which in turn require the use of the struck product, as in the case of a processor of foods who uses electric power which requires struck coal, or the farmer who needs a new motor for his truck or tractor which is made by an automobile company which uses struck steel. In the case of these indirect users we face the same problem we encountered in dealing with consumers, and we treat it the same way. We select those two groups (broadly defined) most obviously affected. (If this procedure too grossly understates the effect, then additional categories may be added.) We calculate the urgency rating of the product which they lack because of the strike (which in this case is not the struck product itself—or products, if multi-product operations are involved—but rather a good or service of which the struck product is a component). We estimate what proportion of the tertiary product (processed food, for example) is normally dependent on the output of the secondary producers (electric power suppliers) and take the same proportion of the total number of employees in the tertiary (processed food) industry against which to apply the urgency rating to determine the effect of the strike (in the primary industry, coal) on indirect production users.

[1] For our purposes, it would be immaterial whether the struck coal firms normally supplied one-half the needs of all railroads or all the needs of one-half the railroads. In the first case, unemployment would be spread among all the roads, while in the second case it would be concentrated in half the railroad companies. The actual amount of unemployment is likely to differ in the two cases, but not by enough to warrant a distinction.

If the problem of estimating the number of industrial users affected is more troublesome than that of estimating the number of household consumers, the difficulties in calculating the number of suppliers affected by a strike are scarcely less. Assume, for example, a strike at General Motors. That company normally maintains relations with close to 13,000 subcontractors, all of whom—with their employees—must be counted as suppliers. To these must be added the number of suppliers of nonprocessed materials—like steel and electric power—which General Motors itself uses. Moreover, since we include employees as an integral part of the struck unit, we must include as direct suppliers all those merchants who provide goods and services—food, clothing, entertainment, gasoline, and so on—to General Motors' workers.

The procedure for calculating numbers affected which corresponds to that which we have adopted for other strike-affected categories would be as follows: First, we would identify the principal suppliers of the struck unit. For each of these supplier groups we would calculate an appropriate urgency rating, the market-necessity component of which would reflect the ratio of purchases by the struck unit to total sales of the supplier group. This urgency rating would then be applied to the number of employees of the supplier firms in each group. Unfortunately, however, we have no way of estimating the total number of employees in those firms actually supplying steel to the coal industry, for example, or coal to the railroad industry. We have therefore adopted the expedient of using the ratio of purchasers by the struck unit to total sales of the relevant supplier *industry*, and applying the resulting rating to the number of employees in the whole supplier industry.

Further, we have a choice of two possible methods of calculating the direct supplier effects of a strike. Overlooking for the purposes of exposition the fact that the stock and substitution effects must modify the market necessity effect, let us consider that the urgency rating (by which we multiply the number affected) is given solely by market necessity, and that market necessity is unmodified by any other considerations of recoverability. Our strike effect for the supplier category would then be given by the formula

$$\frac{\text{struck unit's purchases}}{\text{total supplier industry sales}} \times \text{total employment of supplier industry.}$$

But this would be the same thing as to take the equivalent of the number of full-time employees who are wholly engaged in producing for the struck unit and for whom market necessity would then be at a maximum (100 per cent or 10 on our scale). The equivalent formula would be

$$10 \text{ (that is, } 100\%\text{)} \times \frac{\text{struck unit's purchases}}{\dfrac{\text{total supplier industry sales}}{\text{total supplier employment}}}.$$

By adopting this latter formula in preference to the former, we avoid the inconvenience of having to work with minute fractions. The expression, $\dfrac{\text{total supplier industry sales}}{\text{total supplier employment}}$, we call the employment divisor. It gives us the volume of sales of the supplier industry which is attributable to one employee. By dividing the purchases of the struck unit by the employment divisor, then, we obtain the equivalent of the number of full-time employees wholly engaged in servicing the struck unit, which we use for our number affected. (The market-necessity rating must then be 10 except as modified by other considerations of dispensability or deferrability.)

Next we turn to the indirect suppliers, which consist of those business firms supplying goods and services to direct suppliers of the struck unit (in the case of a coal strike, for example, a telephone company supplying communication services to a coal-*hauling* railroad);[2] those supplying goods and services to direct commercial users of the struck product (for example, a telephone company supplying communication services to a coal-*burning* railroad); and those supplying goods and services to indirect commercial users of the struck product (for example, a telephone company supplying communication services to manufacturing firms which ship goods and receive materials via coal-burning railroads).

How seriously indirect suppliers are affected by a strike depends largely on how vitally affected are their commercial customers in all three of these categories. We cannot assume that the urgency rating of indirect suppliers is equal to that of their customers, however, for there are the possibilities of stock-piling of, and substitution of markets for, the supplier's own product, which are likely to cushion the effect, and of further reducing market necessity by diverting employees with

[2] Moreover, since our term "producers" includes employees, "indirect suppliers" embraces, too, those who supply goods to the local merchants supplying the strikers.

reduced production work loads to maintenance and improvement operations. We have no way of estimating the number of employees involved, even of judging whether it is smaller or larger than the number of employees of their customers. Nevertheless, our best expedient appears to be to make the indirect-supplier effects of a strike a direct function of the strike's effects on their customers. The following procedure which, though arbitrary, is probably conservative, has been adopted. We arbitrarily enter a final score for indirect supplier effects equal to one-fifth of the combined scores of their three customer categories. This reduction should be adequate to allow for the possibilities which indirect suppliers have of cushioning the strike effects and for the contingency that total employment in the supplier firms, as a group, may be considerably smaller than employment in the user firms (relying on the struck product) which normally are their customers.

The final strike-affected producer category is that of nonparty members of the struck unit itself. Obviously this includes all the employees who are not themselves striking but whose employment or income is curtailed because of the strike. A walkout by a key group of workers may force a shutdown of all production operations. A strike of railroad engineers, for example, may mean the layoff of many more nonstriking employees than the actual number of strikers. Since the nonstrikers are not parties to the dispute, they must be included as part of the affected public. While properly they are direct suppliers of labor services to the struck unit, we have segregated them because of their peculiar status.

The three continua from which is derived the urgency rating applicable to other suppliers cannot be transferred to nonstrikers. For other suppliers, market necessity reveals the maximum potential effect on the assumption that production for and sales to the struck unit (or some substitute market) are completely discontinued. This maximum potential effect is reduced to the extent that production designed for the struck unit continues to be produced either for inventory (stock effect) or for alternative markets (substitutability effect). But when it is the struck unit itself which is the market for nonstrikers' services, these latter two effects lose their meaning. The relevant consideration is the extent to which the struck unit continues to produce—not for stock, not for substitute markets, but simply to supply as much of its normal trade as possible. In the case of nonstrikers, then, our urgency rating will constitute a measure of the extent to which their employment is reduced by the strike, on the assumption that no final production is undertaken (an estimate which takes into account that some of their number are retained for supervisory, clerical, maintenance, and stand-by operations, that others may obtain temporary jobs elsewhere, and that some portion of strike losses are recoverable), an estimate which is modified in whatever degree output is actually maintained. In most instances the struck unit will make no effort to produce; firms closed by a walkout attempt to continue operations more rarely now than formerly. Nevertheless, in a few important cases —notably, the supply of electric power or the running of trains— supervisory employees are called upon to keep some essential service functioning, and to the extent that output is maintained the potential impact of the strike on them is not fully realized.

One remaining step must be taken to make our estimates of producer effects comparable with those for consumer effects. In considering the number of consumers involved, each individual consumer counted for one. If in a family of five each is a consumer of bread, we count five consumers. A coal-heated house sheltering three people would give us three consumers of coal. In considering the number of producers affected, however, we have counted only the number of employees, without respect to dependents. Yet it is apparent that loss of income or employment makes itself felt not only on the breadwinner but on all who eat the bread that he wins. Consequently, it is necessary to multiply all our previous estimates of numbers of producers affected by some figure which will reflect this additional impact. Let us use 3 as our multiplier, thus allowing for spouse and one other dependent—child or parent—for each producer.

Moreover, as soon as family effects are introduced it becomes necessary to take account of strike effects on the families of strikers themselves, since the families are not themselves a party to the strike relationship even though intimately affected by it. This group may be viewed as another component of the category, "nonparty members of the struck industry": we have included the families of nonstriking employees in this category because of their relationship to members of the struck unit, and we may reasonably include the families of striking employees in the same category, by virtue of their relationship to members of the struck unit. By taking twice the number of strikers, we thereby allow for two dependents for each striker.

Those family members are dependent on strikers' employment income in the same manner that the families of nonstrikers depend on the latter's job earnings. The urgency rating, like that for nonstrikers, simply shows the extent to which strikers' employment has declined owing to the stoppage, an estimate which takes into account the possibility of temporary alternative work and of recoverability of strike losses. (Partial employment by the struck unit ceases to be relevant, of course.) There is one major modification, however. The families of strikers are distinguished from other component groups of a strike's public in the respect that they are party-oriented in a way that none of the other groups are. They are not parties to the strike, since the members of a striker's family do not initiate strike action, may have independent views with respect to its conduct, and, in general, are involved only through association with the strikers themselves, just as in the case of nonstrikers. But though members of the public, they stand on a different footing from the other identified public constituencies. They are intimately concerned in the strike's success or failure. While not parties, they are peculiarly involved, in that its *outcome* is of immediate concern to them, whereas other parties are concerned only with its *termination*. As has been previously noted, there may be some who believe that the intimacy of association is so close that families of strikers should be classed with the parties themselves. The view adopted here is that such intimacy lessens but does not remove their nonparty characteristics. We would be unwarranted, then, in regarding strikers' families as affected to the same degree as the families of others idled by the strike. Unique compensating factors are present in their case. Such special offsets to the losses inflicted by the strike are sufficiently akin to our concept of recoverability (offsets to strike losses) to suggest the method of allowing for the peculiar status of this group: their recoverability of strike losses is set greater than that for nonstrikers. The nonrecoverable losses of the latter are, in the case of strikers' families, further reduced by 90 per cent. By this procedure we cut drastically any score for the impact of a walkout on unionists' families but at the same time retain the recognition that this group is not actually a party to the strike, but a nonparty, even if unique in its nature.

We have now considered all the members of the public affected by any given strike.[3] The accompanying diagram recapitulates the groups involved. For each of the affected groups we obtain a score derived from the urgency rating applicable to that group multiplied by the number in that group. But what weight shall we give to each of these affected groups relative to the others? How important is loss of goods and services to the consumer categories relative to loss of employment and income to the producing categories? We see no basis for attaching unequal weight to these groups.[4] We consider that the scores for all the affected groups, when added, give a measure of the total effect of a strike on the public. This measure has no meaning in itself, however. It simply places one strike relative to other strikes in terms of

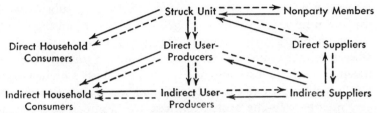

(Solid arrows show the direction of flow of goods and services between the related groups, while broken arrows show the direction in which strike effects are transmitted.)

its impact on people, wherever and however they are situated. It enables us to say whether one strike imposes more hardship than another, taking into account both the degree of hardship and the number subjected to it.

One important limitation which lies upon this strike rating system is that it is inapplicable to wartime periods. In time of war popular antagonism to strikes arises not simply from the real costs, as they have been described in the preceding chapter, but from psychological costs that cannot be similarly measured. The feeling of potential danger to national security, the resentment over workers' laying

[3] Because of the manner in which the criteria of strike-affectedness have been developed, an individual may be "counted" more than once in determining total strike effects. In the course of the same strike he may be counted as a consumer of the struck product (perhaps, indeed, of several products of the struck firm) as well as a producer. We believe that this "multiple counting" is desirable: presumably the more ways in which a person is affected, the more intensely is he affected.

[4] Especially in view of the fact that in the producer group we include the dependents of producers. Thus if there are three consumers in the family of a wage receiver (himself, his wife, and one child, let us say), there are, for our purposes, likewise three in the producer group, since we include those who are dependent on the producer's income.

down tools when other men are shouldering arms on battle fronts, the possible danger to the security of loved ones—these are effects vastly different from loss of income or inability to secure some product or service. This limitation of the rating system does not appear to be a serious one, however. In time of war, it is not public costs which are crucial but military costs. Even before a public begins to experience the psychological costs mentioned, the federal administration will have moved to avert or end any strike which threatens military effectiveness. General strike-control programs will have usually been enacted, in support of a general economic mobilization.

We could perhaps enter a supplementary category to make the strike rating system applicable even to periods of war, with an urgency rating determined by military necessity, a stock effect, and substitutability, and with the number of persons affected graduated more than proportionately to increases in the urgency rating. Thus with a low urgency rating, we might presume that a relatively small number of the general citizenry would be psychologically affected. With a higher urgency rating, reflecting a greater threat to national security and to the safety of family members in the armed services, the number of the general public psychologically affected would increase more than proportionately, until with an urgency rating of 10 we consider the entire nation to be affected. But such a procedure appears to be cumbersome and unnecessary. The fact is that when war is declared, any strike carrying any potential threat to the military program will fall under government proscription, with governmental sanctions becoming operative on its inception, without respect to relative strike ratings. It appears to be common sense, then, to admit that in time of war strike effects on the public are likely to be vastly different from those in time of peace, but that governmental sanctions operating on the parties are likely to render needless a rating system such as has been presented here.

Relative Strike Effects

This measure of the "public-affectingness" of strikes is based upon absolute numbers of individuals involved, whether as consumers or producers. For this reason it would be quite possible that a power strike which "cripples" a local community would rate lower than a national strike, say in automobiles, that actually affects people much less severely, simply because the latter affects more people. Such a result is, however, entirely consonant with the purpose of showing the total effects of any given strike. Similarly, it might also be true that on the rating scales here presented a railroad strike today would be more public-affecting than a railroad strike of twenty-five years ago, simply because the population served by the railways had grown and not because railways were any more necessary at the later date. The earlier strike may have, relatively, created hardships quite as great—perhaps even greater—than the later strike, but fewer people would have been affected, in absolute numbers. Again, this result is consonant with an effort to show the total effects of any given strike, since total effects are compounded of two elements, only one of which relates to the product itself (the urgency rating), the other being the number of affected consumers.

There are occasions, however, when it is desirable to calculate the relative impact of strikes that may occur in different communities, with populations of disparate size, or of strikes that have occurred at different times, with a population base of different size at each time. Such comparisons may be made by converting the population base from one of absolute numbers to one expressed in percentage terms. If we are interested in the relative impact of a power strike in New York City as opposed to a similar strike in Los Angeles, for example, we could calculate the urgency ratings for each of the strikes and then express the number of consumers and producers affected as percentages of the total consumer and producer populations of each community. We assume, as before, that all consumer effects should be weighted equally with all producer effects (both user and supplier) and the scores of the two categories added to obtain the total relative effect of a given strike.

Thus if a New York City power strike with a hypothetical urgency rating of 9 (let us say for all groups, to simplify the example) on the fifth day of the strike affects, hypothetically, 70 per cent of the consumers in New York City and 60 per cent of the producers (or 7 and 6 respectively if for convenience we use a scale of 10) , our rating of the New York power strike will be 117. On the other hand, if the Los Angeles strike gave an urgency rating of 7 on the fifth day of the strike, with only 60 per cent of the total consuming population affected and 50 per cent of the producing population (or 6 and 5, on a scale of 10), the Los Angeles strike would have a rating of 77. The two ratings of 77 and 117 could then be directly compared, to give an approximation of the relative impact of a power strike of given duration on the respective communities. The same procedure would be followed for strikes separated in time. By thus converting our ratings into proportionate terms, we might say that a power strike of given duration is as public-affecting to a local community as a railroad strike of specified duration is to the nation, or that a local transit strike now inflicts proportionately less hardship on a community than a local transit strike of equal duration inflicted ten years ago, even though many fewer are affected in the former case and even though many more are affected in the latter case.

In making such relative ratings for local communities we do indeed drop out of the picture some of a strike's effects. Many local strikes do have their repercussions beyond local boundaries. Not all of a firm's consumers, both domestic and commercial, are located within a single city's limits, particularly when goods rather than services are involved. And the suppliers of a firm are likely to be spread, quite literally, throughout the nation, even though the amounts which they supply may be small. When, therefore, we concentrate on a strike's *local* effects we necessarily lose sight of the consequences which it has beyond the locality. We take into account only the consumer, producer-user, and supplier effects *within the local area.* Our justification for so doing is simply that, for some purposes, we are interested only in the local effects. One such purpose might be to gauge how a local strike stimulates public opinion.

For the purpose of indicating the state of public opinion in *local* strike situations, it is the relative rather than the absolute effects of a strike which are important. A strike of the same absolute magnitude *may* affect opinion quite differently depending on whether it occurs in a small community where its impact is concentrated or in a large metropolitan area where its impact is relatively slight. A strike in the Meriden, Connecticut, plant of an automobile parts manufacturer, for example, may affect no more people than a strike in a similar plant in Cleveland, in absolute terms, but in the former case a more substantial element of the town is affected, since the plant represents a larger proportion of its industrial operations and employs a higher percentage of its labor force, who constitute the principal customers for its merchants, while in the Cleveland case the operations affect only a very small proportion of the city's population. Public opinion in Meriden is therefore likely to operate on the parties more effectively in the case of a strike than in Cleveland.

The rating scheme which has been presented in this and the preceding chapters is the tool with which we propose to examine the impact of strikes. Turning from the abstract to the specific, we shall investigate strikes in three major industries, ranking them relative to each other on the strength of the criteria described above and gaining insight into what factors, in actual experience, have made some strikes more public-affecting than others. The industries selected for examination are bituminous coal, railroads, and steel.

Several factors contributed to the choice of bituminous coal. (1) It has been characterized by frequent strikes. Between January, 1939, and January, 1952, there were fifteen occasions on which more than 75 per cent of the nation's soft coal capacity was idled by union action. No other industry approaches this record. (2) Public interest in coal stoppages has been great. To some extent this is a function of their frequency, but it is also attributable to the colorful leadership of John L. Lewis, who has epitomized union power. (3) Bituminous coal is one of our most basic raw materials, the principal single source of inanimate energy and the principal single source of heat.

The dependence of the modern economy on steel largely dictated the choice of that industry. Steel products directly or indirectly enter into virtually every production process. We should here, then, obtain considerable insight into the ramifying effects of some strikes. Railroads were selected not only because of their significance in the economy but because they constitute an industry which is often included in the public utility category and for which special strike treatment is prescribed. All three industries employ substantial numbers of workers who are geographically dispersed over large sections of the country.

In each case we shall first describe how each of the segments of the industry's public—consumers, producer-users, and suppliers—has been affected by its strikes. This analysis, which cuts across a number of strikes to give a composite impression of their impact on the variously situated groups, serves two purposes. It sharpens our understanding of the nature of the industry's strike effects, and it provides data which will be useful when next we rate the several strikes.

From this qualitative analysis of the impact of strikes in the industry we will then turn to their quantitative analysis, rating each of the several strikes independently to determine its relative importance. This comparative, quantitative examination should provide further clues to the forces determining the impact of strikes.

CHAPTER 4

When the Mines Shut Down: Coal's Publics

HOW many members of the American public actually feel affected, financially or physically, by a "typical" industry-wide bituminous coal strike? A comprehensive and systematic listing of the types of persons who *may* feel injured by such a strike is different from even a reasonably accurate quantitative estimate of the number who actually *are* affected. In the first place, no coal strike is "typical." Between January, 1939, and January, 1952, there were fifteen industry-wide or near industry-wide bituminous strikes.[1] The combination of factors which

[1] These include all work stoppages which at some time, according to the Bureau of Labor Statistics, involved 250,000 or more bituminous employees. They are: spring, 1939 (April 1-May 15); spring, 1941 (April 1-April 30); fall, 1941 (Nov. 15-Nov. 23); May, 1943 (May 1-May 4); June, 1943 (June 1-June 7); June, 1943 (June 21-June 23); November, 1943 (Nov. 1-Nov. 3); spring, 1946 (April 1-May 29); fall, 1946 (Nov. 21-Dec. 7); spring, 1947 (April 1-April 13); summer, 1947 (June 23-July 11); spring, 1948 (March 15-April 23); spring, 1949 (March 14-March 26); summer, 1949 (June 13-June 19); winter, 1949-1950 (Sept. 19-Nov. 8, 1949; Dec. 1, 1949-March 5, 1950). The dates for each strike are those given by the B.L.S. where available, and where not, the dates of the beginning or end of the "hard core" of the strike are as reported in the *New York Times*.

In most cases, duration was computed simply by counting the days elapsed between the dates. Three strikes, however, presented special problems. In the spring, 1946, strike, which began officially on April 1 and ended officially on May 29, a truce was in force from May 13 through May 26. But because resumption of mining operations was only partial during the truce, the period of the truce has been included in computing the duration of the strike, that is, May 13 has been considered the forty-third day of the strike, May 14 the forty-fourth day, etc.

The summer, 1947, strike actually covered three different stoppages: from June 23 to June 27 over 200,000 bituminous employees were made idle by stoppages in protest of the Taft-Hartley Act; from June 28 to July 7 the industry was shut down for a scheduled vacation period; from July 8 to July 11 over 300,000 employees were idle while contracts were being negotiated and signed. Because in respect to effects these three consecutive stoppages are similar to one nineteen-day continuous stoppage, they have been treated as such.

The 1949-1950 strike extended across an even greater variety of situations. From September 19 to October 3 all sections of the country were involved; after October 3 only the area east of the Mississippi; from November 9 through November 30 a truce was in effect; beginning December 5 a three-day week (which for technical reasons permitted only one or two days of actual coal extraction) was imposed on all mines which had not

strongly determine the effects on the country of any one stoppage—percentage of capacity shut down, initial size of coal stocks, season of year, status of war or defense mobilization, level of business activity in the nation as a whole and in the bituminous industry in particular, duration of the strike and expectations as to the duration, attitudes and expectations of governmental authorities (as embodied, for example, in rationing orders) —has never been duplicated in another strike.

As a further difficulty, the data on which estimates of the total number of persons affected could be based are meager and incomplete. The authoritative source of strike figures, the U.S. Bureau of Labor Statistics, furnishes no relevant data other than estimates of numbers of employees "directly" involved. Information gathered from contemporaneous newspaper accounts, while fragmentary and sometimes contradictory, provides our best single source. These accounts are supplemented by data from government and trade association sources. Even with such limited material it is possible to give considerable content to the empty categories in answering the questions of who are affected by a strike in the soft-coal industry, and how.[2]

Those Affected Through Association with Striking Employees

According to government figures,[3] the most nearly complete peacetime shutdowns of the bituminous industry since 1939 have made between 320,000 and 340,000 coal employees idle during the central period of each strike. (Smaller numbers customarily are idle for several days before and after the "official" period of the stoppage.) During the

---

signed the new standard contract of the United Mine Workers (the non-contracting mines accounted for around 90 per cent of the employment in the industry). In addition to the restriction of output caused by the three-day week, production of bituminous was cut by "wildcat" complete shutdowns beginning January 3 with 15,000 employees involved and growing until by February 1 over 100,000 employees were idle. From February 6 to March 5 some 370,000 employees were involved in stoppages. For purposes of this study the entire period from September 19 to March 5, with the exception of the November 9-November 30 truce period (during which resumption of mining operations was nearly complete), has been treated as constituting one continuous partial strike. Thus the period from September 19 to November 8 encompasses the first to fifty-first days of the strike; the fifty-second day of the strike is December 1, the fifty-third day December 2, and so on through to the last (146th) day on March 5.

[2] Unless otherwise noted, all of the factual material has been taken from issues of the *New York Times*. In most cases the information appeared in the issue of the day following the date to which the information pertains.

[3] U.S. Bureau of Labor Statistics' annual reports on strikes in the United States covering the period 1939-1950: Serial R. 1114; Serial R. 1282; Bulletin 711; *Monthly Labor Review*, May, 1943; Bulletin 782; Bulletin 833; Bulletin 878; Bulletin 918; Bulletin 935; Bulletin 963; Bulletin 1003; *Monthly Labor Review*, May, 1951.

war about 360,000 employees were made idle by the more extensive shutdowns. The *New York Times* estimates (presumably less authoritative) for the same strikes have consistently been higher: around 400,-000 in peacetime, 450,000 during the war.

Of the total number made idle, the strikers themselves, being parties to the labor-management relationship, are not members of affected publics in the sense in which that term is used in this study. Nonstriking supervisory and office personnel laid off as a result of the stoppages *are* affected members, but no precise data as to what proportion of total idle these categories constitute are available. The families of all idle employees are presumably affected in some manner. The members of a miner's family are indeed likely to be so intimately affected that one might almost construe them as being parties to the strike relationship. Strictly speaking, however, the family members—since they are individuals in their own right—are affected only through their relationship to the striker himself and are therefore considered here as part of the affected public. According to a *New York Times* report, most of the miners in one western Pennsylvania coal town have from three to five children, but even if we estimate total dependents as only two per idle employee, then in the most nearly complete shutdowns in the postwar period some 680,000 persons have been affected by virtue of their family relationships to idled employees.

For the most part, family members are affected because of the financial problems, actual or potential, caused by idleness, though psychological considerations may be important, especially in war and defense periods. (Coal miners' families have a more difficult time during strikes than do workers whose unions pay strike benefits; on the other hand, unlike workers who live in congested urban areas, miners can and do keep livestock and raise considerable amounts of food for home consumption.) The strength of the financial effect varies, of course, from family to family. For bituminous employees as a group it depends to a great degree on (1) their savings position and income expectations, as determined by how full their employment has been in the preceding months and how full it is expected to be in the succeeding months, (2) the continuance of credit during the strike, and (3) the duration of the strike. Thus the spring, 1946, stoppage followed a long period of steady, high employment in the bituminous industry; the war had provided a sustained demand for coal and there had been no extended industry-wide strikes since May-June of 1943. Miners in western Pennsylvania, it was reported, were in good shape to stand a prolonged stoppage, possessing bank accounts and war bonds. Even so, many miners were forced to take on debts during this fifty-nine-day stoppage, debts which had not yet been completely liquidated at the beginning of the fall, 1946, strike.

In strikes subsequent to 1946 the financial position of the miners has been more tenuous. When the summer, 1947, stoppage began there had been, since April 1, 1946, three industry-wide and two partial stoppages which had resulted in a loss of from 80 to 100 days of work for each miner. Moreover, from June, 1946, on, a shortage of coal cars had limited production in almost every bituminous area in the country. Among the hardest hit districts was northern West Virginia, where around 25,000 miners had been averaging only slightly more than three days of work each week since June 5, 1946. These car shortages with resulting short work weeks continued in northern West Virginia into 1950. By the spring of 1949 the accumulation of abnormally large stocks aboveground, resulting from a mild winter and a falling off of exports, was exerting pressure on prices and wages and causing layoffs and reduction of working time (to as low as one and two days per week) in many areas.

The role of previous strikes, layoffs, and reduced working hours in intensifying the financial effect on bituminous employees' families, by lessening financial reserves or necessitating the incurring of debts, is clear from the evidence. Reluctance to strike was reported particularly strong in June, 1947, and during the spring, 1948, stoppage northern West Virginia miners consistently lagged a few days in walking out and showed themselves extremely eager to return to the pits. But when financial stringency has been primarily the result of layoffs and reduced hours and these are expected to continue for some time the miners rightly feel that a stoppage will not materially worsen their financial positions. The wages forgone do not represent a net loss; much of the time lost during the stoppage would be lost anyway—a day or two a week. The stoppage merely concentrates the idleness and wage loss and pushes it forward in time. Thus a union official was quoted as saying near the end of the 1949-1950 strike that the strike had caused no wage loss, for the coal was still in the ground and the men would get paid for mining it.

It is true, of course, that by concentrating idleness at least some miners will be concentrating hardship. For some mining families a total loss of income throughout the period of the strike is no doubt a much greater burden than even substantially reduced weekly income spread over a longer span of time. Other miners may feel themselves more adversely affected by a strike when it means forgoing six full days of work each week, as was the case during the war and in southern West Virginia in the fall, 1946, stoppage, where enthusiasm for the strike was reported to be low. There is no assurance that all of such lost production will be made up—those who would have burned coal during the period *may* not burn it later—and, moreover, a present steady income is being sacrificed. Miners are therefore better able financially to stand a strike during a period of full and steady employment than during a time of recurring layoffs, but the possible financial loss to them is likewise greater. Under which circumstances hardship is greater— temporarily forgoing all of a much needed small income or permanently sacrificing some less vital portion of a relatively higher income— it is difficult to say.

It is the extension of credit by local merchants for the purchase of food and other necessities throughout the period of the strike that enables miners' families to survive the immediate financial consequences of fairly prolonged strikes. Independent merchants are prompted to carry their miner customers because they have few other customers to turn to as alternative markets; they face a choice of continuing miners' trade, with payment postponed to the future, or of losing substantially all trade for the duration of the stoppage. Company stores have the additional incentive of forestalling migration of miners out of the area, thus dispersing the mines' labor force. These considerations did not prevail throughout the whole period of the extended strike of 1949-1950, however. While it was estimated that between July 5 and December 1 independent and company merchants extended some $60,000,000 in credit to miners' families, on the ninety-ninth day of the strike several large companies, including the U.S. Steel Corporation, and most of the southern companies announced that they felt obliged to call a halt to further credit. By the 121st day many more stores had cut off credit or limited it to $2.00 a day. The consequence was an increase in applications for public assistance; by the 130th day, 18,000 Pennsylvania miners' families were on relief.

Other things being equal, the families of bituminous employees are affected more strongly, in number and intensity, the longer the strike. Variations in the availability of savings and credit, however, sometimes result in greater hardship during a shorter strike, explaining why enthusiasm during the nineteen-day stoppage of summer, 1947, for example, was reported to be lower than that during the fifty-nine-day spring, 1946, strike.

Suppliers to the Bituminous Industry

How strongly persons who stand in the relation of suppliers to the industry are affected by a strike depends on two factors: (1) whether their loss in revenues from the coal industry is a permanent or temporary loss, and if permanent, whether the loss in fact is due to the strike or represents merely a concentration in time of losses which would occur anyway because of a low level of employment in the bituminous industry; (2) the degree to which firms are specialized as suppliers, that is, the extent of their ability to substitute other outlets for those not available to them by virtue of the strike. By "suppliers to the industry" is meant those who sell goods or services to any who are party to the industry, including its employees.

Among the most specialized, and therefore hardest hit, of coal's suppliers are merchants in towns where mining is virtually the only source of livelihood, and railroads like the Chesapeake & Ohio, Norfolk & Western, Baltimore & Ohio, and Pennsylvania, a substantial proportion of whose revenues are derived from hauling bituminous coal and whose coal cars and lines running to mines cannot be used for other types of freight, even if the demand existed. Suppliers in such specialized positions may be contrasted with nonspecialized suppliers, such as automobile producers in the late 1940's. Although the sizable loss in wages due to the bituminous strikes occurring during this period must have caused some fall in the demand for automobiles, the proportion of the total demand attributable to miners was relatively so small and the availability of substitute customers, foreign and domestic, so high that the direct effects of the bituminous strikes on the automobile industry, as suppliers, must have been very slight.

A bituminous strike which lasts longer than a few days has a noticeable effect on the current revenues of coal-town merchants. It was estimated that by the sixth day of the fall, 1946, strike $4,000,000 in wage payments were being lost daily and that by the twenty-fourth day of the spring, 1948, stoppage miners were losing $27,000,000 weekly in wages. In the former strike a total of over $60,000,000 in wage payments had been lost by the seventeenth day. It has been estimated that approximately $370,000,000 in wage payments were lost during the 1949-1950 strike.[4]

Maintenance of credit by merchants preserves sales (though not immediate revenues) of "necessities," but purchases of many "luxury" items fall off substantially. Thanksgiving occurred soon after the beginning of the fall, 1946, strike, but in southern West Virginia storekeeper after storekeeper reported that he hadn't sold a single turkey all week. On the sixth day one store owner said that sales had dropped to almost nothing since the beginning of the strike. "People are buying only what they need and not much of that. They have turned from steak to bologna, and turkey is out altogether." For one company store in this area a sharp falling off of sales led to its closing at noon; half of its employees were laid off. The bulk of what sales remained consisted of meat, bread, and other foodstuffs. (The manager of a state liquor store, however, reported no decline in sales and expected none for another two weeks.) Moreover, the supply of credit which sustains sales even of necessities is not inexhaustible; the store owner quoted above pointed out that while he would extend as much credit as he could, his own creditors would limit him if he became too far extended and he didn't have much credit to start with.

Losses in revenue extend back to suppliers of local merchants; the producers of durable consumers' goods, the purchases of which are most easily postponable, tend particularly to be affected. On the 133rd day of the 1949-1950 strike it was reported that nearly twenty Pennsylvania home furnishing stores, located mainly in coal districts, had instructed suppliers to defer shipment of orders already placed.[5]

The loss of several hundred million dollars in wage payments would undeniably have, through the multiplier principle, a perceptible effect on the economy. It would require a value for the income multiplier of only $3\frac{1}{3}$ for a $300,000,000 loss of wage payments to cause, other things remaining constant, a fall in national income of $1,000,000,000.

However, losses in sales or declines in national income do not necessarily represent net losses or declines. The loss of sales during a short strike may be only temporary in time of high levels of employment in the bituminous industry: no visit to the movies this week but two visits next week; the refrigerator forgone in April purchased in May. During

---

[4] National Association of Manufacturers, *The Economic Impact of an Industry-Wide Strike*, p. 2.

[5] *Ibid.*, p. 8.

times of low employment in the industry, sales and income losses resulting from a strike may merely represent a concentration of effects which otherwise would have been spread over a longer period of time.

Stoppage of the flow of coal from mines to customers quickly reduces the need for coal-carrying services. Two days before the spring, 1949, stoppage was scheduled to begin, Eastern coal-hauling railroads announced layoffs for 45,000 employees; some of these, however, were made idle by the concurrent anthracite shutdown. By the eighteenth day of the strike some 70,000 employees of coal-hauling railroads had been furloughed. (Whether the idleness of these workers can be attributed entirely to the bituminous and anthracite strikes is not certain; a railroad union official claimed that some of the unemployment was seasonal.) In the 1949-1950 bituminous strike 32,000 employees of coal-hauling railroads had been laid off by the twelfth day; in the spring, 1948, strike, 15,000 by the fifth day. Other indications of the effects of bituminous strikes on employees of coal-hauling railroads are that by the forty-second day of the spring, 1946, strike 20,000 railroad employees in the Pittsburgh area alone had been laid off, and by the sixteenth day of the fall, 1946, strike over 13,000 employees of the Chesapeake & Ohio were idle.

The loss in revenue suffered by the coal-hauling railroads is of course substantial. It was estimated that by the twenty-third day of the spring, 1939, bituminous strike—which was only a "partial" stoppage in comparison with the "big" strikes of the 1940's—the major coal haulers were losing $11,000,000 a week in revenues. By the sixth day of the fall, 1946, strike the daily losses were amounting to $3,500,000. If this rate of loss were maintained for the remaining twelve days of the strike (a conservative formula, since losses would certainly appear before the sixth day and continue for several days after the strike), the total losses in revenue would amount to more than $40,000,000. This figure does not, of course, represent the loss in net *income* to railroad companies, since variable costs would drop accordingly, but the decline in variable costs simply pushes the loss back from railroads to *their* suppliers of goods and services, including of course their employees.

Water transport also feels the effects of bituminous strikes. It was reported on the twenty-ninth day of the spring, 1939, stoppage that Atlantic coastwise colliers were "suffering" and on the thirty-second day of the spring, 1946, stoppage that "a number" of Hampton Roads colliers had been laid up. The shutdown of the mines does not immediately cause layups and layoffs in Great Lakes ore shipping; it was reported on the third day of the spring, 1949, strike that ships would continue to sail up through the Soo, empty of coal, in order to bring ore down. Nevertheless, on the thirty-eighth day of the spring, 1946, strike Great Lakes shipping was only 35 per cent of normal. Even tugboats may be affected; on the thirty-sixth day of the spring, 1939, strike twenty were idle in New York Harbor partly for lack of coal haulage.

Users of Bituminous Coal

How a bituminous strike affects coal users may best be understood by dividing direct users into six categories: (1) basic iron and steel industry, (2) coal-burning transport lines, (3) public utilities (electric power, city transit, gas), (4) chemical industries which use bituminous coal as a raw material, (5) manufacturing and processing industries which use bituminous coal for heat and power, (6) residential, institutional, and commercial buildings which use bituminous coal for heating purposes. Customers and suppliers of firms falling within the first five categories may be *indirectly* affected.

The extent to which users are affected by a strike is mainly a function of the length of the strike, the size of the stocks accumulated prior to the strike, the rate of consumption during the strike, and the percentage of total bituminous-producing facilities which are shut down. Each of these factors is significant only in relation to the others. Thus the industry-wide strike of 1949-1950 ran for almost five months and followed an eleven-week period during which the work week was limited to three days. But stocks were abnormally high at the beginning of the three-day week (on an over-all basis they amounted to a seventy-day supply at the prevailing rate of consumption) and still high (more than a fifty-day supply) at the beginning of the strike on September 19. Moreover, they were replenished throughout the strike as a result of the resumption of work in Western mines (October 3), a truce (November 9 to December 1), partial resumption of work in all Eastern mines in the form of a three-day week (which for technical reasons permitted only one or two days of actual coal extraction), and complete resumption of work in those mines which had signed contracts with the union (December 5-February 6). As may be the case in even the most nearly complete shutdowns, they were further increased by continued output from nonunion or "scabbing" mines and from mines under contract to the Progressive Mine Workers. While in the most nearly complete shutdowns only between 5 and 20 per cent of normal output continues to be mined, during the 1949-1950 strike output fell that low (19 per cent) only during October; in November it amounted to 90 per cent; in December 72 per cent; January 63 per cent, and February 26 per cent. The result of all this was that few users felt any pinch until the third month of the stoppage. In contrast, the strikes which occurred during 1946, characterized as they were by initial over-all stocks amounting to only a thirty to forty day supply and by elimination of all but 5 to 15 per cent of normal bituminous output, made themselves widely felt by the third and fourth weeks.

According to a statement from the Bureau of Mines, the danger point is reached when over-all stocks fall to a twenty-five-day supply. In how many of the fifteen industry-wide bituminous strikes have stock-consumption ratios fallen that low? Evidence tends to be unreliable: at the beginning of the spring, 1946, strike three different estimates were given by the Solid Fuels Administrator, the Secretary of Labor, and the National Coal Association, respectively, the highest differing from the lowest by 67 per cent. For some strikes it is lacking altogether. But it is fairly certain that this danger point was reached during the fifty-nine-day strike of spring, 1946 (perhaps by the twenty-ninth day), during the forty-day strike of spring, 1948 (perhaps by the twelfth day), and during the 146-day 1949-1950 strike (perhaps by the 119th day).

The promptness and strictness with which a rationing program is instituted will also determine the extent to which bituminous users are affected by a strike. Federal government orders such as those issued at the beginning of the May, June 1, and June 20, 1943, strikes, prohibiting delivery of railroad-borne bituminous to any consumer with more than a ten day supply, prevent the gobbling up of the available supply by consumers with relatively less urgent needs. An order like that issued five days before the beginning of the fall, 1946, strike, prohibiting all deliveries except those necessary to bring the supplies of public utilities, shipping lines, domestic users, and establishments concerned with health and safety up to a ten-day level and those necessary to allow manufacturers to complete processes started or to prevent damage to equipment (with government agencies, schools, and "others" permitted to submit petitions for emergency needs), insures that coal supplies will be conserved for the most vital social needs, but it forces non-stock-piling, nonessential industrial and commercial firms to curtail operations abruptly.

In only six of the fifteen bituminous strikes under study did the federal government issue rationing orders. Its action in four of the six has been indicated above. At the beginning of the November, 1943, strike it prohibited all deliveries except those of one ton to householders and those of sufficient size to bring the stocks of nonindustrial users (for example, hospitals and office buildings) up to a ten-day supply level, and industrial users' stocks up to the same level if the coal was needed to prevent irreparable damage to materials or equipment. At the beginning of the spring, 1946, strike the federal government restricted deliveries to those made to gas companies, hospitals, and householders with less than a five-day supply; all other users could secure deliveries only by an emergency petition to the Solid Fuels Administration. After the thirty-seventh day deliveries to householders were limited to those with less than a five-day supply, and after the forty-second day, to "hardship" cases.

No rationing program was instituted by the federal government in the 146-day 1949-1950 strike; this function was performed by state and local governments or even by local retail coal dealers. Dealers were "rationing" bituminous coal—allowing only a small amount to each customer—in Chicago and northern Indiana by the sixty-fourth day, in Cleveland, Detroit, and Pittsburgh by the 103rd day, in Massachusetts by the 133rd day, and in New Jersey by the 135th day. The more effective and equitable rationing programs of public authorities were instituted in New York State on the 133rd day and in Muncie, Indiana, by the 141st day.

Whatever the level of the over-all stock-consumption ratio, and in spite of nation-wide rationing programs, the fate of users in any particular industry or area depends largely on the size of each industry's or area's own stock piles. (There is always much unevenness in the distribution of coal stocks, and reallocation during a strike is limited by administrative difficulties, costs of transport, and by the less than perfect substitutability of the several types of bituminous coal.) Thus local stocks were low enough to necessitate the establishment of municipal rationing in Pueblo, Colorado, during the fall, 1946, strike and dealer rationing in Chicago, Cleveland, Detroit, and Pittsburgh during the 1949-1950 strike at times when over-all stocks were still above the danger point.

What is the likelihood that users can substitute other fuels during the course of a strike? New York City's electric utility, Consolidated Edison, enjoys a relatively secure position during bituminous strikes, partly because of its large stock-piling facilities but also because much of its remaining coal-burning equipment can quickly be converted to the use of oil. New York City in general has an alternative not readily available to Middle Western cities—anthracite. Anthracite can be substituted for or used to supplement bituminous in most heating and power plants with little or no adjustment. In the spring, 1939, and fall, 1946, strikes a number of New York City buildings, institutions, ferries, and fireboats fell back on this alternative.

With these general comments applying to all users, let us now consider in greater detail the impact of a stoppage on specific groups among coal's publics.

1. Iron and Steel Industry

Bituminous is an essential ingredient in the manufacture of iron and steel; anthracite, oil, or natural gas cannot be satisfactorily substituted. The stoppage of coal production halts the production of coke; a shortage of coke requires the banking of blast furnaces; the resulting fall in the output of pig iron requires curtailment of steelmaking operations; curtailed output of steel ingots means less rolled-steel output.

There are two peculiarities about the way a bituminous strike affects steel output. In the first place, curtailment of production of finished steel products may not occur until after the strike is over, since it takes some time for the effects of a coal shortage to pass down the stages of production, but the end of the strike does not mean that all steel operations can be promptly resumed, since it takes a long time for the pipe lines to be refilled. It was reported that steel output would not return to normal until thirteen days after the settlement of the April, 1941, strike. At the end of the spring, 1946, strike it was announced that it would be forty-two days before Carnegie-Illinois was again making full shipments.

As a second condition peculiar to steel, the technical processes of pig iron and steel making are such that total shutdown has a permanently damaging effect on facilities. Since total shutdown must be avoided at all costs, steel companies seek to stretch their stocks of coal by reducing iron and steel production fairly promptly. Stocks are usually large enough to permit several weeks of full operation, and if it could be known with certainty that the strike would last no longer, little curtailment of steel output would be necessary. But since the length of the strike is an unknown factor, a stoppage which actually lasts only two weeks will nevertheless usually cause perceptible curtailment of operations. Part of the prompt curtailment, however, is due to the industry's dependence on coke from beehive ovens. Because these ovens, located near mines, do not maintain stock piles, stoppage of mining necessitates their immediate shutdown.

There is a rough correlation between the size of the industry's stock-consumption ratio and the severity of effects. This correlation is understandably higher than that between simple duration of the strike and severity of effects. Thus the November, 1943, strike lasted only two days but it was the fourth bituminous strike of that year, and these recurring interruptions to coal production plus the industry's sustained high level of operations had rendered stocks very low. By the seventh day following the onset of the strike (and five days after its end) steel output as measured by percentage of steelmaking capacity utilized had fallen by around 7 per cent. (Recovery to previous levels of production was very rapid, however.) In the fifty-nine-day spring, 1946, strike, when stocks again were low, steel output had fallen by about 30 per cent by the thirty-sixth day and by around 40 per cent by the forty-fourth day. Greatly in contrast is the 146-day 1949-1950 strike. The outstanding characteristics of that strike as it affected the steel industry—abnormally large initial stocks of bituminous, partial maintenance of bituminous production during the strike, and a 32-day (and for some companies longer) strike in the steel industry itself—so softened the impact of the bituminous stoppage that no cuts in any processes were reported until the ninety-third day, and not until the 134th day was steel output reported to have fallen by as much as 10 per cent.

Some cuts in pig-iron production generally occur within the first week of the strike—sometimes on the first day (as in fall, 1946, and spring, 1947). Cuts in steel production inevitably follow from these, sometimes within the first week also, but usually not amounting to more than 5 per cent. Even if the strike ends then, steel output may continue to fall. (In the seven-day June 1, 1943, strike output had fallen 2 per cent by the end of the strike, but 4 per cent by the end of the following week.) If a strike lasts three weeks the fall in output may range from 2 per cent, as in spring, 1939, to 20 per cent, as in spring, 1948. At the end of a month the fall in output may reach only 5 per cent, as in spring, 1941, but may run as high as 23 per cent, as in spring, 1948. The severest effects were felt in the spring, 1946, strike, when steel output had fallen 30 per cent by the thirty-sixth day, 40 per cent by the forty-fourth day, and 52 per cent by the fifty-ninth (last) day. For the fifteen bituminous strikes as a group, the approximate maximum percentage decline in steel output occurring during or immediately following a strike has been 7 per cent or less for ten of the strikes, 20 to 25 per cent for three strikes, 33 per cent for one, and around 50 per cent for another.

Cuts in production, of course, necessitate layoffs of employees. The roll of steelworkers unemployed owing to a bituminous strike mounted fastest during the fall, 1946, strike. By the second day at least 5000 workers had been laid off; by the fourth day 10,000; by the sixth day 30,000; and by the seventeenth (last) day 70,000. In the fall, 1941, strike not until the eighth day were 5000 layoffs reported. In the severe spring, 1946, strike layoffs came late but then cumulated rapidly: not until the twenty-ninth day were as many as 30,000 steelworkers reported laid off, but this number rose to 96,000 on the forty-third day and 100,000 on the fifty-ninth (last) day.

Total loss of steel due to the thirty-day spring, 1941, strike was estimated at one million tons; the same figure was given for the first thirty days of the spring, 1946, strike, and a much larger figure for the entire fifty-nine days.

How much of this loss and the loss in employee pay rolls is permanent depends on the current level of operations. When the industry is operating at full capacity, as during the war, lost production cannot easily be recovered. Even in this case, however, the entire loss may not be a net loss, since companies may use the period to make needed repairs which increase subsequent production, as reported during the spring, 1941, strike.

Layoffs and curtailment in production frequently are not spread evenly among the various steel companies. At the beginning of the spring, 1946, strike, Carnegie-Illinois Steel Corporation's stocks at its Pittsburgh area plants were so much lower than those of other steel companies (twelve-day supply as compared to thirty-five-day supply for Jones and Laughlin) that its Pittsburgh steelmaking operations had fallen to 45 per cent of capacity by the fourth day of the strike and to 26 per cent by the nineteenth day whereas the other major steel producers ran full tilt until the twenty-fifth day. Most of the 32,000 idle by the twenty-ninth day were Carnegie-Illinois employees. In the 1949-1950 strike, however, Carnegie-Illinois maintained production for more than five weeks after cuts had been made in the output of other steel companies.

The effects of a bituminous strike may extend back to the steel industry's suppliers. It was reported that by the fortieth day of the spring, 1946, strike "several thousand" iron ore miners and Great Lakes shipping personnel were idle as a result of curtailment of iron and steel output.

Likewise the effects extend forward to the steel industry's customers (and these customers' customers), who should be considered *indirect* users of coal. It was reported that by the fortieth day of the spring, 1946, strike fabricators of steel products in the Pittsburgh area were operating at about 50 per cent of capacity and had laid off some 45,000 employees. The head of the Civilian Production Administration announced on the seventeenth day that "scores" of plants were "going down because of a lack of parts, which in turn is a result of other plants going down because of a lack of steel." Later reports of the Civilian Production Administration asserted that the 32,000-ton loss of merchant pig iron had seriously set back the veterans' housing program, while the steel loss had delayed production of consumers' durable goods and agricultural and textile machinery and repair equipment. The intricate ramifications of a bituminous stoppage are illustrated by the CPA's statement that curtailment of steel output had caused a shortage of "tin" cans, which shortage, in turn, was responsible for a loss of part of the food crop. During the wartime strikes newspaper editorials and government officials often announced the lost steel tonnage in terms of the number of ships, tanks, or guns which could have been constructed from it.

Foundries are also affected by bituminous strikes. Shortage of coke caused a Portland, Oregon, pipe plant to shut down on the fourteenth day of the spring, 1946, strike and a Chattanooga foundry to close down on the seventh day of the fall, 1946, strike.

2. Coal-Burning Transport Lines

The effect of a coal strike on railroads as users is more widespread than its effect on railroads as suppliers of services to the bituminous industry, since coal-burning mileage is greater than coal-hauling mileage.

Like the steel industry, railroad lines maintain stocks which act as a buffer against the effects of a bituminous stoppage. But also like the steel industry, railroads cannot run at full tilt until the stocks are exhausted. To insure that essential movements of freight and passengers are maintained as long as possible, federal authorities have, in four of the fifteen post-1939 bituminous strikes, ordered curtailment of less essential traffic.

At the beginning of the spring, 1946, strike over-all coal stocks held by railroads amounted to a forty-day supply. Not until the thirty-second day when stocks had fallen to a twenty-seven-day supply and four lines had been forced to petition for 17,000 tons from the government's "frozen stock," did the Office of Defense Transportation order a 25 per cent cut in passenger service on trains using coal-burning locomotives and an embargo on all nonessential freight and express, both to be effective as of the fortieth day. By the fortieth day over-all railroad stocks had fallen to a twenty-day supply with some lines having only an eight-day supply. A further cut of 25 per cent in passenger service was ordered for the forty-fifth day. (The freight embargo and second cut in passenger service were rescinded on the forty-first day when a truce in the strike was announced.)

At the beginning of the fall, 1946, strike, however, railroads had only a thirty-day supply of coal. Three days before the strike began, the Office of Defense Transportation ordered a 25 per cent cut in passenger service, effective as of the third day of the strike; on the thirteenth and fourteenth days a freight embargo and a further 25 per cent cut in passenger service were imposed, effective as of the sixteenth and seventeenth day.

Again in the spring, 1948, strike railroad stocks fell to a twenty-five-day supply by the twelfth day; on the seventh a 25 per cent cut in passenger traffic was ordered, and on the sixteenth, a 25 per cent cut in freight traffic. When on the thirtieth day the strike was officially ended these restrictions were lifted, though the strike continued on a partial basis for eleven more days.

In the 1949-1950 strike the timing of the initial government orders was much the same as those in the spring, 1946, strike, but a more selective approach was employed. The Interstate Commerce Commission directed each railroad to institute as of the thirty-eighth day a 25 per cent cut in passenger service utilizing coal-burning locomotives as soon as its stocks fell below a twenty-five-day supply, provided it had no "dependable source of coal." This order was rescinded at the beginning of the second week of the truce but then restored in more drastic form —a $33\frac{1}{3}$ per cent cut, to be effective on the ninety-first day of the strike. At this point railroad stocks had fallen to an average of a twenty-four-day supply. When on the 122nd day stocks had fallen to a fifteen-day supply, the ICC increased the passenger cut to 50 per cent and ordered a 25 per cent cut in freight service. On the 144th day the passenger cut was increased to 65 per cent and the freight cut to 40 per cent, to become effective on the 147th day. Before the date set, however, the parties to the bituminous dispute reached agreement, whereupon the ICC lifted all restrictions except a 25 per cent cut in passenger service for lines having less than a ten-day supply of coal.

Curtailment of service often occurs prior to government action. Freight traffic had already been reduced by the major Eastern railroads prior to the issuance of government orders in both 1946 strikes. On the first day of the fall strike the American Association of Railroads had embargoed freight shipments for export.

Who is affected by curtailment of railroad service? The companies lose revenue, customers lose transportation services, and sizable numbers of employees lose employment. The day before the first ODT orders of the spring, 1946, strike, 51,000 railroad employees were reported idle owing to the strike, but much of this idleness was due to the drop in railroads' coal-hauling traffic rather than to curtailment of coal-burning service. The 25 per cent cut in passenger service on the third day of the fall, 1946, strike had caused 10,000 layoffs by the seventh day; by the sixteenth day a total of 50,000 railroad employees were idle.

Likewise in the 1949-1950 strike within thirteen days after the first ODT order some 50,000 railroad employees were idle; recalling of these began with the onset of the fourteen-day coal truce. Following strike resumption, by the day before the 33⅓ per cent passenger and 25 per cent freight cuts were to take effect, 30,000 were idle again. Curtailment of services affects maintenance as well as operating employees: by the twenty-eighth day of the spring, 1948, strike 12,500 employees in the Pennsylvania Railroad's Altoona shop were out of work. On the day of the second cuts in the 1949-1950 strike the Chesapeake & Ohio laid off more than 1000 employees in its mechanical department.

Most obviously, users of railroad passenger and freight services—an important category of indirect coal users—are affected, but how drastically it is hard to say. The cuts in service apply only to traffic hauled by coal-burning locomotives, with the result that the 25 per cent reduction in service during the spring, 1948, strike meant an elimination of only about 10 per cent of the *total* passenger mileage, and owing to increased dieselization the 50 per cent cut during the 1949-1950 strike really meant only a 13 per cent total cut. It has been the area east of the Mississippi which in the past has borne the brunt of the curtailment since a smaller proportion of its traffic has been oil-powered. The 25 per cent passenger cuts in fall, 1946, caused an immediate discontinuation of 500 trains by the eight major railroads serving the New York City area; the 1949-1950 strike's 33⅓ per cent cut led to dropping more than 650 trains nationally within three weeks. A week after the 25 per cent cut of spring, 1946, 2,000 out of a total of 17,500 passenger trains had been canceled; a week after a cut of the same magnitude in the 1949-1950 strike, only about a thousand trains had been canceled. The New York Central alone dropped 233 trains, the Pennsylvania 130, the Jersey Central 124.

Among passengers to whom the continuance of railroad service is important are commuters. The 25 per cent cut in the 1949-1950 strike did not much affect the 400,000 to 500,000 commuters in New Jersey, Long Island, Westchester, and Connecticut, however, since most of their trains were powered by electricity. Most of the reduction from 33⅓ per cent to 50 per cent was achieved by cuts on other suburban and branch lines, but outside of commutation hours. Probably few commuters were kept from reaching their destinations by these curtailments, but some inconvenience in the way of alteration of schedules and crowding resulted.

Among the long-distance traffic the first casualties are "specials"— "snow" trains and those to sporting events. Since they are, for the most part, powered by oil, the "crack" expresses keep on running, even in the East. During any of the curtailments a determined long-distance traveler could get to his destination, but what he had to contend with was set forth in a railroad company advertisement during the spring, 1946, strike: a smaller number of alternative trains (and times) from which to choose, extra stops along the route, disappearance of diners and "luxury" accommodations, sold-out sleeping cars, and standing room only in coaches. According to a War Department announcement during the spring, 1946, strike, the curtailments were expected to slow down the demobilization of troops situated in the United States.

Freight curtailments likewise apply only to cargo hauled by coal-burning locomotives; it was estimated during the 1949-1950 strike that the 25 per cent reduction would amount to only an 11 per cent cut in total railroad service. (The actual reduction might be greater than this, however, since oil-burning lines might lose that part of their traffic which originated from or terminated upon coal-burning lines.) Although certain categories (such as livestock and poultry, food, fuels, and printing and medical supplies) are exempted in the case of outright embargoes or given preference in the case of percentage reductions, there may be delays in their shipment.

The repercussions of freight curtailments may occur quickly. Five days after the spring, 1946, freight embargo was announced but three days before it went into effect it was estimated by the Civilian Production Administration and the Association of American Railroads that 250,000 to 400,000 employees of industries served by railroads had been laid off. The automotive industry is particularly vulnerable to freight curtailment. Lack of supplies and access to markets prevents operation for more than a few days following an embargo, according to a Ford Motor Company spokesman. By the end of the spring, 1946, strike 106,000 Ford employees were idle, but part of this idleness was the result of other aspects of the bituminous strike—a need to conserve coal and steel supplies, delays in shipment of parts from suppliers handicapped by the coal-saving "dimout" in Chicago—and of strikes in the plants of parts suppliers. Chrysler, General Motors, and Briggs announced that layoffs amounting to over 300,000 would be completed within ten days after the embargo, but the embargo's short duration reduced actual unemployment to around 20,000. The fall, 1946, freight curtailments caused layoffs of some 40,000 auto workers. Agricultural implement manufacturers also seemed vulnerable to freight embargo; it was announced that six Oliver plants had closed down the day the spring, 1946, embargo became effective and that International Harvester would shut down all of its plants when the fall, 1946, embargo became effective. Other closings were probably unreported.

Two other types of transport lines which feel the user effects of a bituminous strike are tugboat and trucking lines. It was reported during the spring, 1939, strike that shortages and inferior quality of bituminous coal were causing New York Harbor tugboats to work at far less than normal efficiency and that twenty had been laid up altogether, partly as a result of high prices of coal.

3. Public Utilities

Public utilities, like steel and railroad companies, cannot afford to operate until their stocks of coal are exhausted and then shut down. When stocks are believed to have reached dangerously low levels, electric power companies or, more generally, public authorities seek to conserve the dwindling prospective supply of power for the most essential uses. Depending on how serious the shortage of power has or is expected to become, conservation efforts may take the form of (a) appeals to industrial, commercial, and domestic customers to cut their consumption of power, sometimes with a percentage reduction specified; (b) voluntary or compulsory "dimouts" or "brownouts," under which display, decorative, informational, and street lighting and use of electricity for air conditioning are prohibited or restricted and in some cases certain reductions in all nonresidential lighting are ordered; (c) actual curtailment of power to industrial, commercial, or even residential users, or some combination of all three methods. There seems to be no clear agreement on the level at which stocks may be considered dangerously low. The Civilian Production Administration ordered dimouts for twenty-one states, effective on the fifth day of the fall, 1946, strike, at the beginning of which electric power companies possessed over-all stocks amounting to a sixty-day supply. Not until the thirty-eighth day of the spring, 1946, strike (which the power companies had entered with only a twenty-one-day supply of bituminous) did the CPA act, and then merely by ordering Eastern utilities to substitute other fuels, interchange power, and establish curtailment programs. Similarly, during the spring, 1946, strike, when confronted with a less than twenty-eight-day supply of coal for power companies, public authorities ordered a compulsory dimout for sixty-four Virginia counties but only a voluntary dimout for Philadelphia. New York City was subjected to a voluntary dimout when its stocks were still at a thirty-six-day level.

The fall, 1946, strike probably affected users of electric power over a wider area than did any of the other bituminous strikes. As noted, dimouts were promptly imposed by the CPA on all communities getting electric power from coal-burning generators or from systems interconnected with the latter in twenty-one states (mostly east of the Mississippi) and the District of Columbia. The dimout directive included an order for a 25 per cent reduction in all nonresidential lighting, to be increased to 50 per cent for any area whose electric utility's stocks had fallen to a fifteen-day supply, and to 70 per cent when a ten-day supply was reached. At the fifteen-day and ten-day supply levels, industrial and commercial consumption of electric power was to be reduced to 15 per cent and 7 per cent of normal, respectively. Thus for some thirteen days over half the population of the country lived under mild dimout conditions. The inhabitants of Hamilton, Ohio, in addition, were put under a stage 3 dimout—nonresidential lighting cut by 70 per cent and industrial and commercial consumption by 93 per cent—on the fourteenth day; the inhabitants of Logansport, Ohio, under a stage 2 dimout on the sixteenth day.

Dimouts were supplemented by urgent appeals for the conservation of power, accompanied in Connecticut and Virginia by gubernatorial declarations of a state of emergency.

In the spring, 1946, and 1949-1950 strikes the effects on the public of prospective power shortages were more selective but perhaps more intense. In the former strike, voluntary dimouts were imposed as of the thirty-third day on Philadelphia and on twenty-two Indiana counties (in Indiana, industrial consumers were asked to cut to one-seventh of the preceding month's consumption), and on New York City as of the fortieth day. Compulsory dimouts were imposed on northern Illinois (thirty-third day), Washington, D.C. (thirty-fifth day), Detroit (thirty-ninth day), and sixty-four Virginia counties (fortieth day). In addition, in the northern Illinois area industrial firms were given power for only twenty-four hours each week, and none at all on Saturdays and Sundays; commercial firms were permitted to consume electricity only between 2 and 6 P.M., six days a week. In Virginia amusement places were denied electricity entirely, and all other users, except hospitals, transit lines, food handlers, and domestic consumers, were limited to twenty-four hours a week.

In the 1949-1950 strike a voluntary dimout was imposed on Chicago on the 135th day; compulsory dimouts on Lansing and Peoria (123rd day), New York State (133rd day), and Illinois (140th day). The Jamestown, New York, and Pittsburgh power companies were rationing electricity by the 126th and 130th days, respectively; by the 142nd day only 50 per cent of the normal supply of power for industrial and home use was being furnished in the Pittsburgh area. Industrial users were being forced to cut their consumption of power in Illinois by the 140th day.

Current newspaper stories supply some information on the ways in which persons were affected by electric power conservations. Three days after the imposition of the twenty-four-hours-a-week limitation in northern Illinois in the spring, 1946, strike, the Illinois Manufacturers Association estimated that nearly half of the state's industrial workers had been laid off. There were four times as many applicants as normal at the United States Employment Service offices in Chicago. Republic Steel had begun shutting down its Chicago plant, laying off 3500 employees. Office workers at Inland Steel were working by candlelight. Shortened hours in commercial establishments were hindering pickup and delivery of freight and express. All but a few movie houses were shut down. Six days after imposition of the curtailment orders for northern Illinois, it was estimated, over a million workers had been laid off, pay rolls had been cut by 33 per cent, and $100,000,000 in production was being lost weekly. At the same time an estimated 100,000 workers had been laid off as a result of Indiana's (twenty-two counties) voluntary conservation program.

During the 1949-1950 strike Illinois industry was again affected. Republic Steel was forced to shut down three of its seven electric furnaces. But Pittsburgh was in the spotlight this time. When on the 130th day Duquesne Light and Power, principal source of electricity for a million and a half persons, cut daytime power supplies to industrial and commercial users by 20 per cent, electric furnace production of steel dropped 50 per cent and a large fabricator was forced to shift 25 per cent of its force to night work, thereby "unbalancing production." It was reported that the power cut, by lessening output of a Pittsburgh lead plant, would indirectly affect operations at a large Akron rubber factory. A subsequent (142nd day) 50 per cent cut by Duquesne was applied to residential as well as industrial and commercial current.

In New York City the dimouts mainly affected the operators and customers of retail and amusement establishments. During the fall, 1946, strike it was reported that restaurants had suffered a cut in sales of up to 50 per cent, and that business in movie houses was very bad "due partly to the psychological effects of the dimout." The head of a large department store complained that merchants were hardest hit by the dimout, which started on November 25, because "each day between Thanksgiving and Christmas is worth three times the sales volume of any other day." It was estimated that the patronage of bars, theaters, restaurants, and stores had fallen off 25 per cent or more during the February, 1950, dimout.

Outside of the March, 1950, cut for Pittsburgh domestic users, no specific mention of an outright curtailment of power to households was discovered. But appeals for home conservation usually accompanied dimouts and curtailments to business establishments, and it is safe to assume that after reading statements like the following (made by the head of the CPA on the third day of the fall, 1946, strike), some domestic users felt themselves "affected" by the bituminous strike: "I urge every member of a household which burns gas and electricity to exercise the greatest economy in their use, for only with such cooperation will disastrous discontinuance of service in many areas be avoided. . . . Discontinuance of utility services would have an immediate and drastic effect on the daily life of every individual. Housewives would have no electricity or gas with which to cook, and water could not be pumped to their faucets. Electric and gas refrigerators would be useless, perishable food could not be preserved by stores or distributors."

One important category of electricity users is city transit systems. Since many operate their own power systems and since they render a special type of service, their fate during a bituminous strike may differ from that of enterprises receiving power from "general" systems. During the spring, 1939, strike, although there was no dimout or general curtailment of power in New York City, services on the two subway lines which maintained their own power plants were cut by 20 to 25 per cent. The main effects were inconvenience and crowding during weekdays and only part-time work for some subway employees. The fall, 1946, strike caused a scheduled return to normal peacetime services on New York subways (amounting to a 16⅔ to 50 per cent increase during non-rush hours) to be postponed; as an additional conservation measure, heat was supplied for trains only in very cold weather and only when trains were above ground. Limitations on heating of transit vehicles were part of the northern Illinois electricity curtailment program in the spring, 1946, strike.

Several of the bituminous strikes have affected users of manufactured gas. On the fourteenth day of the spring, 1946, strike a steel company shut off gas supplies to 1200 houses in three Utah communities; on the thirty-ninth day, the Massachusetts Public Utilities Commission warned householders to cut consumption to a minimum. In the fall, 1946, strike the CPA ordered all manufactured-gas producers in twenty-one states to institute uniform prorata cuts in gas supplies to all "nonessential" customers. The Connecticut Public Utilities Commission ordered residential and industrial customers to reduce use of gas to a minimum, with temperatures in gas-heated houses limited to 68° and commercial customers instructed to use gas to maintain only essential services. A company in the Albany-Schenectady area on the ninth day cut off gas to all but essential users. On the 145th day of the

1949-1950 strike a gas company in New York State shut down completely.

4. Chemical Industries Using Coal as a Raw Material

During the June 1-7, 1943, bituminous strike the head of the War Production Board stated that even a short strike would cause the shutting down of by-product coke ovens and a consequent drop in the output of coal tar, a basic ingredient in aviation gas, synthetic rubber, explosives, plastics, and sulfa drugs. Any stoppage or even retardation of operations in coal-tar-using plants would destroy the "delicate balance" necessary for full production, which could not be reachieved for weeks.

The only report discovered of definite effects on plants in this category was a statement by the CPA that by the thirty-fourth day of the spring, 1946, strike a Du Pont plant in West Virginia had shut down, virtually stopping the production of nylon hose and causing a shortage of antifreeze, a loss of 50 per cent in plastic raw materials, and a serious setback to the fertilizer program.

5. Manufacturing and Processing Companies Using Bituminous Coal for Heat and Power

Companies not affected by steel shortages, freight embargoes, or electricity and gas cuts may nevertheless be forced to curtail operations because they cannot get coal to furnish heat or power for their plants. Small companies, which cannot or do not maintain sizable stocks of coal, are likely to be first and worst hit, but large firms may suffer, too.

The effects of such curtailment of operations may be far-reaching. By the forty-first day of the spring, 1946, strike some paper plants had reduced output because of low coal reserves; this reduction (plus delays in shipment due to the freight embargo) had so lowered the newsprint stocks of the *Pittsburgh Press* that it was deemed necessary to omit all advertisements from the issues of the forty-first and forty-second days—with a resultant loss of revenue to the newspaper and loss of sales to advertisers, especially retailers.

The effects of curtailment of operations may also extend backwards to suppliers of the firms involved. It was reported that much of the curtailment of steel output which occurred during the spring, 1939, strike was prompted by a falling off of orders for steel from companies which had curtailed or expected to curtail operations owing to a lack of coal for heating and power purposes.

Following is a résumé of information gathered regarding the ways in which manufacturing and processing operations have been affected by inability to secure bituminous coal for their heat and power requirements.

Spring, 1939, strike
 19th day: Some North Carolina industries, especially the textile industry, on verge of shutdown.
Spring, 1946, strike
 17th day: CPA head says "scores" of plants closed down for lack of coal.
 31st day: Wheeling, West Virginia, tobacco plants shut down. Minnesota creameries and milk-processing plants about to shut down.
 33rd day: Pullman Car Manufacturing Company's operations curtailed.
 34th day: Two Wisconsin cheese plants shut down. Rubber companies' operations curtailed. Two zinc-lead companies shut down; one partly shut down. Two building materials firms shut down, with 430 employees laid off; seven more firms about to shut down and lay off 2850 employees. One pipe-covering plant shut down. Three cotton mills shut down, with 1275 employees laid off; industry scheduled to cut operations by 25 per cent in a few days.
 38th day: Western cement plants' operations curtailed.
 39th day: Six building materials firms shut down, with 1500 laid off; thirteen more firms about to shut down and lay off 11,000. Some sawmills shut down. Four paper mills shut down, with 11,500 laid off.
 59th day: Many New England plants, particularly small ones, shut down over a four-day week end.
Fall, 1946, strike
 4th day: Seventy-five small plants in New York metropolitan area, including garment, dyeing, and brick plants, shut down, with 3000 employees laid off.
 5th day: Some milk and cheese plants shut down. In Chicago, Stewart-Warner Corporation and Oliver Corporation's operations curtailed, with 11,000 laid off. At General Electric's Schenectady plant, 3000 laid off.
 6th day: Link Aviation Devices Company shut down, with most of its 450 employees laid off.
 7th day: Twenty-five thousand Toledo workers laid off, including some at Owens-Illinois Glass Company.
 9th day: One hundred small, "nonessential" plants in northern New Jersey shut down or on verge of shutdown. In Chicago area several

small manufacturing plants' operations curtailed with "hundreds" laid off.

13th day: Eighty small firms in New York metropolitan area shut down with 5000 laid off.

17th day: Estimated that it would take thirty to sixty days for New York City's garment, furniture, leather goods, and electrical supplies industries to "get back to normal."

1949-1950 strike

121st day: Knitting mill shut down, with 100 laid off.

122nd day: "Scores of small establishments" laying off workers. At General Motors' plants all Saturday and overtime work canceled.

126th day: Canning plant shut down.

133rd day: Felt plant shut down with 450 laid off.

135th day: At Ford plants all Saturday and overtime work canceled.

137th day: "Long" week ends scheduled for 40,000 at Ford plants and 5000 at Chevrolet plants.

139th day: In many large concerns, including General Electric and International Harvester, work week shortened and overtime canceled.

143rd day: Five-million-dollar crop of hothouse tomatoes threatened with ruin "in a day or two."

Such a catalogue, gleaned only from the files of the *New York Times,* must obviously be incomplete.

6. Residential, Institutional, and Commercial Buildings Using Bituminous Coal for Heating Purposes

Newspaper accounts suggest the extent to which users in this category have been affected by a given bituminous strike. References are found to "critical situation in Buffalo hospitals," "shortages in Delaware public institutions" (spring, 1939, strike); "emergency needs just being met in Pittsburgh," "establishment of community eating and sleeping places suggested by governor of Colorado" (fall, 1946, strike); "Pittsburgh hospitals on truck-to-furnace basis" (1949-1950 strike); and to declarations that the situation is critical, desperate, tragic, or one of emergency by public authorities in Virginia, Indiana, Illinois, Maine, West Virginia, Massachusetts, New York, Rhode Island, and Michigan, and in Cleveland and Detroit (1949-1950 strike). These references alone do not give much in the way of clues to the extent to which persons involved in the situations were inconvenienced or left chilly or cold by a lack of coal for heating purposes, but presumably public authorities were worried.

It can be established, however, that bituminous strikes have on occasion impeded educational programs. On the sixth day of the fall, 1946, strike all Denver schools were closed with lessons thereafter broadcast over the radio, and a few universities and colleges extended Thanksgiving holidays to conserve fuel. Between the 121st and 123rd days of the 1949-1950 strike four state teachers' colleges in Illinois closed down, their stocks being given to prisons and welfare institutions; Buffalo schools dropped night courses and extracurricular activities, and heat was cut in Chicago schools. Between the 133rd and 144th days, St. Louis schools instituted a five-day week end, all but a few of the Buffalo and Chicago schools and all the schools in two Illinois towns and in Indianapolis were closed, and some night classes were dropped in New York City. It was estimated that by the 145th day some 250,000 students across the nation were out of classes as a result of the strike.

Occupants of other institutional and of commercial buildings have been affected by bituminous strikes. During the spring, 1946, strike consumption of coal in Ohio state welfare institutions was reduced. During the 1949-1950 strike heat was reduced in Indianapolis office buildings and temperature limits were set for all New York public and private buildings except those getting heat from steam produced as a by-product of electricity. (Since the New York electric power company also produced some steam directly from coal and the occupants of buildings served by the power company had no means of telling which kind of steam they were getting, the 1949-1950 bituminous strike must have produced some agonies of indecision as to whether to turn down the thermostat.) In the 1949-1950 strike Army, Navy, and Air Force installations were required to cut temperatures and concentrate troops, with the coal thus saved being turned over to civilian hospitals and food-processing plants.

It is impossible to determine how many persons have had to live in unheated residences during bituminous strikes. During a severe period of the 1949-1950 strike, when over-all bituminous stocks had reached a thirty-year low, "an intense cold snap" carried the mercury to 6° in the East, but it was reported that "few householders were without heat." A good many may have been very chilly, of course. In similar acute situations—Chicago during the spring, 1946, strike and Denver during the fall, 1946, strike—there were complaints of cold apartments.

At the same time that it helped prevent real hardships for coal users, a strict rationing program like that adopted in New York City near the end of the 1949-1950 strike would certainly cause inconvenience to many individuals. Nobody, without exception, could get delivery of bituminous coal without a certificate of necessity which was procurable only from police headquarters and only after policemen had inspected the petitioner's bin. Hospitals, food processors, and municipal health and safety services were not exempted, though their applications were given priority. Out of 365 applications submitted on the first day of this program, only 125 were granted. Apparently the rationing plan adopted in Muncie, Indiana, was similar to this one.

Likewise, the nature of some of the substitutes for bituminous coal employed near the end of the 1949-1950 strike indicates that considerable inconvenience (and perhaps hardship) was being experienced by persons dependent on bituminous coal for heating purposes. In Detroit and Des Moines homeowners with empty bins were supplied with wood obtained from dead trees chopped down in city parks or pulled out of city dumps. Furnace fires in an Iowa high school were fed with corncobs. The offices of an Ohio steel company were warmed by placing in them firebrick casings containing molten metal.

Effects on National Security Programs

During the wartime bituminous strikes there were many statements by public officials to the effect that the war effort required immediate resumption of mining, but little information as to the extent to which output of war material was being or would be hindered. Most appraisals ran along the lines of the *New York Times* editorial of June 4, 1943, which stated that as a result of the seven days of strikes between May 1 and June 3 there had been a loss of 11,000,000 tons of bituminous or enough to make 6,000,000 tons of steel, which in turn was enough steel to build 170 battleships, 6000 cruisers, or 120,000 tanks. How many servicemen, relatives of servicemen, or other members of the public felt themselves affected through belief that the seven days of strikes had cost the armed forces military equipment cannot be estimated.

Most of the government's concern was directed toward the effects of bituminous strikes on the output of steel. This was a realistic attitude since of all the industries vital to the war effort whose continued operations depend on use of bituminous coal, steel is normally the first to suffer curtailed operations for lack of it. This is particularly true when a long-sustained high rate of operations has prevented the accumulation of large stocks of coal and a severe shortage of scrap has increased the demand for pig iron (for whose manufacture coal is principally needed) in the steelmaking processes. Altogether, there were only about thirteen days of nearly industry-wide stoppages during the war, though there were additional days lost owing to scattered stoppages. These thirteen days, which occurred between May 1 and June 30, 1943, resulted, according to government estimates, in the loss of 18,000,000 tons of bituminous coal and from 75,000 to 100,000 tons of steel.

No accounts of any immediate perceptible effects on war-important users in the other five categories were discovered. One would not expect transport lines or utilities to be much affected by strikes of as short a duration as the wartime "industry-wide" bituminous strikes (the longest lasted only five working days). Some manufacturing and processing plants using coal for heat and power may have been affected, since many war-born plants had been operating on a hand-to-mouth basis with respect to coal. Because the bituminous industry was operating at close to full capacity during the war, the 18,000,000-ton loss was a permanent loss which could not be made up subsequently.

Whether the strike in the spring of 1941 was hurting the defense program was a matter of some controversy. The President and the Secretary of Labor asserted that the strike had not seriously affected the defense program; the War Department said that the situation had become "alarming" and pointed to cuts in ammonia production and to the loss of a million tons of steel—enough, it said, to build 100 freighters.

In the postwar period, many persons linked American national security to European recovery and rehabilitation. The spring, 1946, strike forced a lowering of coal exports for foreign relief below what had been promised and, through its effects on railroad services, delayed food shipments. The fall, 1946, strike resulted in low food supplies and a reduction in railroad services in Italy. The *New York Times* on December 1 stated that a prominent Cleveland industrialist, with interests in coal, steel, and shipping, was supporting negotiations to end the strike partly because he feared a prolonged bituminous strike would cause "a throwing of France, Italy, and other European nations into Communist hands."

What can be said, in a general way, about the effects of an industry-wide bituminous strike on the American public?

Estimates of the total number of workers outside the bituminous industry who have been made idle as a result of a bituminous strike give some idea of how members of the public, in their role as producers, have been affected. The following estimates are of course only approximate.

Spring, 1946:
   15th day: over 30,000 ⎫
   22nd day: over 60,000 ⎬ mainly steel and railroad employees
   32nd day: over 70,000 ⎭
   39th day: over 1,000,000 (Civilian Production Administration estimate)

Fall, 1946:
   4th day: 200,000
   6th day: 250,000
   18th day: 300,000

Spring, 1948
   21st day: 70,000
   23rd day: 100,000

1949-1950
   52nd day: 39,000 ⎫
   123rd day: 35,000 ⎬ mainly steel and railroad employees
   135th day: 60,000
   145th day: 230,000, plus 200,000 on two- to three-day week

The wide variation in these figures makes generalization hazardous. The CPA's figure of 1,000,000 idle in the spring, 1946, strike is more than three times greater than any other figure cited and may be skeptically regarded in the absence of more detailed information. The next largest number is 300,000, reported on the eighteenth day of the fall, 1946, strike. If we take this as an outside figure, and assume that each of these idled workers had two dependents, and then include the estimated 680,000 dependents of bituminous employees, we might chance the opinion that an industry-wide coal strike may directly affect *up to* 1,580,000 members of the public in their roles as producers or producers' dependents, within the experience of the last twelve years. A much smaller number may be affected in any given strike, while a strike of greater severity than any yet experienced since 1939 could substantially expand this number.

According to CPA estimates, the spring, 1946, strike cost members of the public in their role as current or ultimate consumers $2,000,-000,000 worth of consumers' and producers' goods and services. This loss amounted to about 1 per cent of gross national product for 1946. The CPA also claimed that output of durable consumers' goods was set back at least three months, largely owing to the bituminous strike. Part of such losses in the production of goods may, however, be recovered if a subsequent drop in the level of economic activity makes available otherwise underutilized resources.

All areas of the country and all industries do not suffer equally from a bituminous strike. Taking all bituminous strikes as a whole, it is the region east of the Mississippi and north of Tennessee and North Carolina which, because its industries, commerce, and residents depend most heavily on bituminous coal, bears the brunt of a bituminous strike. Likewise, it is the basic steel industry and the coal-hauling railroad lines which, in more strikes than not, are the first and worst affected.

It is for these reasons that in most bituminous strikes the Pittsburgh area is more strongly affected than any other. It contains many basic steel and steel-fabricating plants; it is a terminus for coal-hauling railroads; its industries and homes are powered and heated by bituminous coal; it contains many suppliers of persons employed in the bituminous coal industry. By the twenty-fifth day of the spring, 1949, strike, business activity in the Pittsburgh area had fallen 23 per cent; by the 4th day of the June 20, 1943, strike, 16 per cent. Certainly at least a sizable proportion of these declines can be attributed to the strikes. Of the 300,000 workers idled by the end of the fall, 1946, strike, 120,000—40 per cent—were located in Pittsburgh.

CHAPTER 5

The Relative Impact of Eleven Coal Strikes: I. Spring, 1946

WHICH of the eleven peacetime coal strikes occurring between 1939 and 1952 most affected the public, and why? We turn now from considering the consequences of coal strikes generally for each of several categories of the public, a view which cuts across strikes, to examine the total impact on all publics of each of the strikes, considered by itself. Following the procedure described in Chapters 2 and 3, we shall rate each of the stoppages so that we may compare the total effects of any one with the effects of all others.

To facilitate analysis, we shall rate one of the major strikes first, rather than that strike which merely occurred first in point of time during the period studied. The important strike of spring, 1946, had its influence on most of the public categories identified in the preceding chapter, and we shall examine that strike in considerable detail in this chapter. The effects of the ten remaining bituminous stoppages can then be more simply presented by reference to this key strike.

The data on which we have had to rely have often been inadequate, and "best guesses" have often had to be substituted for actual information. The results should therefore be viewed as tentative, approximations requiring refinement before they may be accepted as reliable. Nevertheless, they *are* approximations, and the result of considerable and careful calculation.[1]

---

[1] We are only too well aware that the values which have been assigned to each of the numerous components of any strike rating are subject to criticism. Any single figure might be attacked. It should be noted, however, that our ratings are all relative to each other, so that an error of judgment with respect to any component (say, the possibility of recovering strike losses) is reflected in that component in all ratings. And since the ratings have no absolute but only relative significance, the effect of such a *systematic* error is materially reduced. In any event, we should like to stress that it is the rating system *as a whole* which is important. If a more precise understanding of the impact of strikes is to be gained, it

The fifty-nine-day bituminous strike of spring, 1946, broken briefly by a fourteen-day truce shortly before its end, came at a time when the country was in the throes of conversion from war to peacetime production. The coal industry had been operating at peak levels, and there was no immediate prospect of any lessening of activity. While government agencies could not agree on the size of coal stocks at the beginning of the stoppage, concern over the effects of the closing of the mines was sufficient to prompt federal restrictions on coal deliveries on the first day of the walkout. Railroad services were subsequently curtailed on the fortieth day of the strike to conserve stocks, with the orders bearing most severely on freight haulage. Coal-using power companies were also directed to conserve fuel, and voluntary or compulsory rationing was initiated by a number of states and municipalities.

The rating of effects has been made for the fortieth day (Friday, May 10), since this was the last weekday before the truce went into effect.

The total strike rating is 338. This figure in itself has no signifi-

---

must be by quantitative analysis. It is this need to which we have addressed ourselves. The advantage of the rating device is that it forces the assessment, in relatively precise terms, of all the numerous variables which together determine the impact of a strike on the public.

In this chapter, as well as Chapters 6, 8, and 10, the following sources have been used: U.S. Department of Commerce, *Survey of Current Business, 1951 National Income Supplement*; U.S. Bureau of the Census, 1948 *Census of Business*, 1940 *Census of Housing*, 1939 and 1947 *Census of Manufacturing, Statistical Abstract of the United States* (annual); U.S. Bureau of Labor Statistics, 1947 and 1950 *Handbook of Labor Statistics, Monthly Labor Review*; U.S. Interstate Commerce Commission, *Fuel and Power Statistics, Freight Train Performance, Passenger Train Performance, Revenue Traffic Statistics, Tons of Revenue Freight Originated and Tons Terminated, Wage Statistics* (all the foregoing are monthly series), *Statistics of Railways in the United States* (annual); U.S. Federal Power Commission, *Industrial Electric Power, 1939-1946*; U.S. Bureau of Mines, *Minerals Yearbook* (annual); U.S. Post Office Department, *Cost Ascertainment Report* (annual); U.S. Weather Bureau, *Normal Weather for the United States* (1943); *New York Times*; Bituminous Coal Institute, *Bituminous Coal Annual*; Association of American Railroads, *A Review of Railway Operations* (annual); *Railway Age*; *Steel*; *Iron Age*; annual reports of various companies; National Association of Manufacturers, *The Economic Impact of an Industry-Wide Strike* (1950); Rand-McNally Commercial Atlas and Marketing Guide (1952); American Iron and Steel Institute, *Annual Statistical Report, Steel Facts* (monthly).

In these and the ratings for railroads and steel we have used an absolute rather than proportionate basis for the numbers affected. (For a discussion of these two procedures the reader is referred to Chapter 3.) There is some objection to this choice, since in the case of coal the strikes rated cover a ten-year period, and in the case of railroads two of the three strikes—while national in effect—were geographically concentrated. It is believed, however, that the data are sufficiently homogeneous with respect to time and place to warrant use of the simpler procedure. The result, however, is to understate the relative importance of the earlier coal strikes and the partial railroad strikes of 1950 and 1951.

cance. It is a relative measure, and acquires meaning only in comparison with the other strike ratings, which will be presented in the following chapter. How this score is derived is described below. In the case of each category of the public, we first estimate the urgency rating by the method described in Chapter 2, multiplying this by the number affected computed according to the methods set forth in Chapter 3. For convenience, the three scales (continua) on which the urgency rating is based are here reproduced:

Cultural Necessity
(the importance of the product, or substitutes for it, to its users)

0	1	2	3	4	5	6	7	8	9	10

Unnecessary	Necessary for pleasures and conveniences of varying degrees of importance	Necessary if hardship (physical, mental, pecuniary), in varying degree, is to be avoided	Necessary in varying degree, for health and safety, ranging up to "absolutely necessary"

(It will be recalled that, for producer-users, cultural necessity is replaced by production necessity, and for suppliers its counterpart is market necessity.)

Stock Effect
(the extent to which consumption declines owing to diminishing stocks)

0	1	2	3	4	5	6	7	8	9	10
0%	10%	20%	30%	40%	50%	60%	70%	80%	90%	100%

Substitutability Effect
(the extent to which substitutes for the product are inadequate)

0	1	2	3	4	5	6	7	8	9	10

Completely acceptable substitutes		No acceptable substitutes

Let us turn now to consider, quantitatively, the impact of the spring 1946, soft-coal strike on each of the publics affected.

I. Direct Consumers. Score: 34.4

    A. Residences. Score: 28.8

       Urgency rating: .063

1. Cultural necessity: 5. Except for the South Atlantic States, average temperatures for May in the principal bituminous-using regions range from 53.5° in Michigan to 64.5° in Missouri. According to the Bituminous Coal Institute, days with mean temperatures below 65° are considered to require heat. Actually the weather was quite chilly on May 10, 1946. Minimum temperatures were 48° for New York City, 43° for Boston, 35° for Buffalo, 39° for Cleveland, 35° for Duluth, 43° for Pittsburgh, 55° for Chicago, 43° for Denver. For the great majority of users, the indispensability of heat on May 10 was moderately high, and its deferrability almost zero.

2. Stock effect: .25. Stock-consumption ratio for retail stocks in yards on the first day was twelve days; on the thirty-first day it was eighteen days. Since only about 5 per cent of the industry operated between the first and fortieth days of the strike, the increase is almost entirely attributable to declining use of coal by consumers—largely due to warmer weather but to some, probably slight, extent to self-rationing. Since actual stocks on hand were declining, on the thirty-seventh day government order restricted deliveries to householders having less than five days' supply, and local rationing orders in some places supplemented this general order. It is estimated that on an over-all basis consumption declined about 2.5 per cent.

3. Substitutability: 5. Residences cannot commonly switch to gas or oil heat. Anthracite is not readily available in many bituminous-using areas. However, at this time of year many can get sufficient heat from little electric or gas heaters or wood-burning fireplaces.

Number affected: 457

Total occupied dwelling units in U.S. using bituminous coal numbered 13,222,000 in 1940. From this we subtract 958,635, the number of bituminous-using residences in seven Southern states whose average temperatures for the entire month of May are over 68° (this is presumed to include all states whose mean temperature on May 10 was over 65°, the point at which heat is said to be "necessary"). The 1940 *Census of Housing* gives 3.78 occupants per dwelling. This figure is slightly high for our purpose, because of the higher averages of the southern states (omitted in our calculation of coal users). We therefore use 3.7 occupants per dwelling, giving 45,374,450 people relying on bituminous for needed heat on May 10. (There were more households in 1946 than in 1940 but use of bituminous has been declining proportionately; we trust the two effects to offset each other.) In 1940 the welfare-institution population numbered about 1,000,000. We assume that the proportion of these people relying on bituminous is the same as the proportion of private householders, or about 35 per cent. This adds 350,000 people for a total of 45,724,450. In our unit of 100,000, this gives a score of 457.[2]

B. Nonprofit places of assembly. Score: 5.6

Urgency rating: .08

1. Cultural necessity: 4. The considerations applying to residences apply here, except that most assemblies can close down completely in a way that residences cannot.
2. Stock effect: .25. Approximately the same as for residences.
3. Substitutability: 8. Assemblies more frequently have facilities for switching and access to alternative fuels but cannot use small space heaters, as homes can.

Number affected: 70

May 10 fell on Friday, affecting perhaps 6,000,000 of a total 26,000,000 school children, 5-20 years. Add 1,000,000 for libraries, lodges, church activities, etc. Total: 7,000,000 people, for a score of 70.

II. Indirect Consumers. Score: 1

A freight embargo on nonessential items became effective on the fortieth day. No doubt some freight began piling up by the thirty-seventh or thirty-eighth day, but with little effect on consumers.

---

[2] It may be helpful to explain in detail how the score of 28.8 for residences was computed, as a guide to readers who wish to make their independent computations.

The urgency rating is obtained, it will be recalled, by taking the substitutability effect times the stock effect, and multiplying the resulting figure by the cultural necessity effect. The ratings here are expressed on a scale of 10, but the reader may find it convenient to work with percentages. Thus, with respect to residences, scored above, we would take 50 per cent (substitutability rating) of 2.5 per cent (stock rating), or 1.25 per cent, and this times 50 per cent (cultural necessity), for an urgency rating of .63 or, on our scale of 10, .063. The urgency rating is then multiplied against the number affected (457, when computed in units of 100,000), to give a total score for residences of 28.8.

There were no electricity cuts or dimouts required directly of consumers. By the fortieth day consumers were affected, however, by (1) dimouts of commercial places in Philadelphia, New York City, Washington, Detroit, Indiana, Northern Illinois, Virginia, and (2) closing until 2 P.M. of commercial places in Illinois and Virginia and complete closing of amusement places in Virginia. These effects are difficult to rate and of questionable importance. A passenger cut of 25 per cent in coal-burning locomotive mileage, effective on the fortieth day, amounted to a 13½ per cent cut in total passenger service. This had little or no effect on commuters but it did affect long-distance passenger service, which we rate.

A. Long-distance passenger service. Score: 1

Urgency rating: .08

1. Cultural necessity: 4. Travel, while not generally a matter of health or safety, is an important convenience. Its deferrability and dispensability vary enormously, of course, among individuals. For some it must be performed on the day in question or not at all, and among these the importance ranges from canceling attendance at a friend's wedding to missing an urgent business conference. For others the trip can be postponed indefinitely. The over-all estimate of cultural necessity must necessarily be a matter of judgment, and judgments will differ. However, we conclude that for long-distance travelers denied the opportunity to travel on the day in question, cultural necessity should be viewed as involving moderate hardship—a rating of, say, 4.

2. Stock effect:[3] .5. Effective May 10 railroads were forbidden to operate a total daily coal-burning passenger service in excess of 75 per cent of mileage operated on April 1. Coal-burning mileage in April was only 54 per cent of total passenger mileage, making the reduction equal to 13½ per cent of total mileage. However, there was some substitution of oil-burning for coal-burning equipment, so that total mileage did not shrink as much as 13½ per cent, but per-

[3] It is possible to take account of the fact that only coal-burning transport was affected by either of two methods. Stock effect may be calculated to show the continuing percentage of non-coal-burning traffic, or alternatively the number affected may be reduced proportionately. Both procedures yield the same result. The first method is illustrated with respect to long-distance passengers, the second with respect to freight traffic where it facilitates taking account of the industries exempted from the government embargo.

haps by about 10 per cent. Certainly consumption did not shrink as much as mileage since people utilized remaining trains more intensively. We estimate a 5 per cent decline.

3. Substitutability: 4. Long-distance bus service can expand up to 50 per cent. Air lines and private cars were also available.

Number affected: 12.8

In April, 1946, 38,566,961 noncommutation passengers were carried, for a daily average of 1,285,566, which converts to a score of 12.8. We take this as an estimate of the number of persons wishing to travel long distance by rail on the first day of the curtailment.

III. Direct-User Producers. Score: 65.7

A. Basic steel industry. Score: 35.2

Urgency rating: 2.2

1. Production necessity: 6. The struck mines provided virtually all of the bituminous used by the basic steel industry. Coal stocks were such that steel output began falling off on the fifth day and continued to fall gradually, declining by 40 per cent on the forty-fourth day. In view of this, on the fortieth day employment (output) to the extent of perhaps 80 per cent depended on coal. That is to say, had there been no stocks of coal or substitutes for coal on the fortieth day about 80 per cent of the labor force would have been idle, the 20 per cent still employed being mainly supervisory, maintenance, and clerical workers whose services would still have been needed on the fortieth day plus those who could have obtained temporary jobs with other firms.

How much of a user industry's loss is recoverable (in the special sense of mitigating strike effects) depends on such factors, among others, as the percentage of plant capacity at which the industry would otherwise (had there been no strike) have been operating during the succeeding period, the length of the scheduled work week, the tightness of the labor market—and on these factors as they apply to both the struck industry and the user industry, and possibly to suppliers and users of the struck industry and user industry. Even if the struck industry (coal) can expand output to the user industry (steel), how much steel can recover depends in part on its own possibility of expansion. In this case we assume that bituminous operations could be expanded so as to recover in the succeeding six months about 50 per cent of the losses of the strike (the amount recoverable being determined not so much by limits to production of coal as by the inadequacy of facilities for transporting coal) but that owing to the relatively high level of operations in the steel industry and particularly to the non-interchangeability of steel-finishing equipment, only about 25 per cent of the losses of steel output (and employment) could be recovered. The pertinent measure of recoverability is thus 25 per cent, and we reduce the 80 per cent dependency figure by this amount to indicate the net effect on the user industry of dependency on coal supplies on the fortieth day.

2. Stock effect: 3.8. We have estimated that 80 per cent of employees would have been idle on the fortieth day had there been no stocks of coal or substitutes available on that day, so that consumption of coal would have fallen to zero. Actually, however, by the fortieth day consumption of coal had declined only an estimated 38 per cent. (Utilization of steel capacity had fallen 30 per cent by the thirty-sixth day and 40 per cent by the forty-fourth day. By interpolation we might expect a fall of 35 per cent by the fortieth day. We assume that the decline in the consumption of coal *and substitutes for coal* was equal to the decline in output as represented by utilization of capacity. Since substitutes for an estimated 5 per cent of consumption of coal existed [see substitutability rating, below], a decline of 35 per cent in the consumption of coal *and coal substitutes* is equivalent to a 38 per cent decline in coal consumption.) [4]

---

[4] In this and certain other estimates we work backward from the very figure we seek! The estimate of the extent to which steel production declines during the coal strike would itself give us the combined stock and substitution effects and could itself be applied to the production necessity rating. Nevertheless, we have here gone on to estimate the stock and substitution effects (which then provide us with the same answer we would have obtained from the figure of the decline of steel output with which we started). We do so to emphasize that we regard the strike-rating technique here used as something which, with experience, can be used to calculate strike effects *before* the strike occurs, on the basis of data known at the time. This would require, for example, in connection with the stock effect rating above, sufficient knowledge of past steel practice to be able to convert stock-consumption ratios of the struck product to *expected* declines in the consumption of the struck good.

Therefore, the effects of the deprivation of coal are not represented by the net production necessity of 6 (or 60 per cent) but only by 38 per cent of 60 per cent or 22.8 per cent.

3. Substitutability: 9.5. Similarly, the effects of deprivation of coal are mitigated by the existence of substitutes for bituminous (which in this case, however, are highly inadequate: scrap can replace coal-made pig iron, but only to a limited extent). Thus the above figure of 22.8 per cent must further be reduced by the extent to which satisfactory substitutes are available (95 per cent × 22.8 per cent).

Number affected: 16

Production employees in basic steel numbered 467,000 in March, 1946. For 1947, average total employees in basic steel were 113.8 per cent of production employees, so the total number of employees in the industry for March, 1946, is estimated at 531,787. Allowing two additional members per family, this gives 1,595,361 people, which converts to 16.

B. Coal-burning railroads. Score: 12.8

Urgency rating: .52

1. Production necessity: 2.25. The struck mines provided virtually all of the bituminous used by coal-burning railroads. Coal stocks and substitutes were such that coal-burning railroads maintained their output (and employment) virtually unaffected up until the date of the freight embargo and cut in passenger service (fortieth day). Thus on the fortieth day, had no stocks of coal or substitutes been available, we estimate that only about 30 per cent of the work force would have been dependent on bituminous, the remaining 70 per cent being clerical, maintenance, or other nonoperating employees who would still have been retained on the first day without coal. As noted above we estimate that 50 per cent of the losses of bituminous output (and employment) could be recovered in the succeeding six months, but because of the high level of activity in the railroad industry only about 25 per cent of the losses of railroad services could be recovered during that period.

2. Stock effect: 3.3. The 25 per cent cut in passenger-service locomotive mileage initiated on the fortieth day resulted in a 25 per cent cut in coal consumption. In addition, by

government order no freight could be loaded which at any point traveled on coal-burning trains, except in certain specified categories. The categories barred were responsible for some 55 per cent of total freight shipments originating in April, 1946. About 67 per cent of all freight traffic was carried in April, 1946, by coal-burning locomotives, but also barred were all nonexempted shipments which at any point had to travel by coal locomotion. A conservative estimate of the total amount of freight traveling at some point by coal-burning locomotive would be 75 per cent. Applying this percentage to the 55 per cent of *all* freight in the barred categories gives 41 per cent of freight shipments embargoed. The cut here is not in locomotive mileage, however, but in tons shipped; the former dropped less than the latter presumably because of the use of short trains. We assume the reduction in freight-engine coal consumption to be less than proportionate to the decline in tons shipped, perhaps 35 per cent. Then:

Total Coal Consumed by Rail- roads in April, 1946		Per Cent Reduction		Tons Reduced
Freight service	6,158,000 $\times$	.35	=	2,155,300
Passenger service	1,858,000 $\times$	.25	=	464,500
Total	8,016,000			2,619,800

Total consumption of coal by coal-burning railroads was thus reduced by 33 per cent.

3. Substitutability: 7. Oil-burning or electric locomotives can be substituted for coal-burners to some extent, and a more intensive use can be made of these.

Number affected: 24.6

Total employees on Class I railroads numbered 1,367,000 in March, 1946. Not all of these are dependent on coal-burning operations, however. About 60 per cent of total train miles depended on coal. (Since freight shipments originating on non-coal-burning railroads but terminating on coal-burning lines were also affected, this figure is conservative for our purposes.) Most of this coal-burning traffic depended for coal on the struck mines. We take 60 per cent of the base figure to obtain the 820,200 employees on coal-burning railroads affected by the coal strike. With two dependents each, the total is 2,460,600 or, when converted to our unit of account, 24.6.

C. Electric power. Score: .08

Urgency rating: .025

1. Production necessity: 4.2. The struck mines provided virtually all of the bituminous coal used by electric power companies. Beginning on about the thirtieth day electric companies in affected areas had begun to curtail output of power. We estimate that by the fortieth day about 60 per cent of employees were dependent on bituminous coal, the remaining 40 per cent being clerical, maintenance or other nonoperating employees who would have been retained on the first day after all coal supplies were exhausted plus those who could have secured temporary work elsewhere.

   We assume that electric plants would be able to expand output during the succeeding six months to fill whatever deferred demand exists. Nondeferrable demand (for such uses as illumination) we estimate to be 25 per cent of total demand. That portion of demand which has some *potential* element of deferrability (such as for industrial use) was thus 75 per cent, but we judge that actual recoverability was limited to 40 per cent of this amount. Thus, of the 60 per cent of electric output dependent on coal on the fortieth day of the strike, 70 per cent was nonrecoverable in the six months following termination of the strike, giving a production necessity rating of 42 per cent or 4.2 on our scales.

2. Stock effect: .1. Though the stock-consumption ratio was seventy days on the thirty-first day of the strike, compulsory and voluntary dimouts may have reduced coal consumption of power companies by as much as 1 per cent by the fortieth day.

3. Substitutability: 6. Some plants (Consolidated Edison of New York, for example) can shift to oil. Plants are sometimes able to secure power from other plants using oil or water.

Number affected: 3.2

   Light and power company employment numbered 236,000 in March, 1946. About 45 per cent of all energy produced in

1946 came from bituminous coal, so we estimate about 106,200 employees affected. With two dependents each, the total is 318,600 or, converted, 3.2.

D. Manufacturing and processing plants using bituminous coal for heat and power. Score: 17.6

Urgency rating: .168

1. Production necessity: 4.8. We estimate that after several weeks of dwindling stocks the fortieth day would find about 80 per cent of employees dependent on supplies of coal in the sense that absence of such supplies (or substitutes) would cause that much unemployment. The level of activity in manufacturing industries would suggest that perhaps 40 per cent of losses were recoverable in the succeeding six months.

2. Stock effect: .5. The stock-consumption ratio for "industry" declined only from forty-eight to forty-four days during the first month of the strike. This slight decline is probably partially attributable to conservation of coal. While there was considerable variation in conservation practices, an overall cut of 5 per cent in coal consumption is probably not too high an estimate.

3. Substitutability: 7. Some plants, even on short notice, can switch to alternative fuels or purchased power, though power companies themselves at this time were also affected.

Number affected: 104.5

There were 12,014,000 employees in all manufacturing in March, 1946. Of total fuel and energy purchased by manufacturers for heat and power in 1947, approximately 29 per cent was bituminous. The simplest assumption is that the same percentage of employees worked in plants dependent on bituminous. This gives about 3,484,000 employees or, with two dependents each, a total of 10,452,000 persons affected. This converts to a figure of 104.5.

IV. Indirect-User Producers. Score: 165

There is inescapably some measure of duplication between the last category of direct users (manufacturing plants using bituminous for heat and power) and the first two categories of indirect users which follow (manufacturing customers of the basic steel industry and of coal-burning railroads), and between all categories of indirect users. The *same* plant which is directly affected by lack of coal for heat and power *may* also be indirectly affected by lack of steel or lack of railroad transportation or lack of power; to include it in each of these ratings obviously overstates the strike's impact with respect to these categories. We have no way of knowing how much of such duplication is present. In this and in most other cases where the possibility of duplication exists we have sought to minimize overstatement by adopting a conservative urgency rating. (The chief exception is in the category of customers of coal-burning railroads, a category in which, as will there be explained, we have sought to eliminate the duplication between customers relying on railroads for materials supply and those relying on railroads for finished-goods shipments, with a resulting understatement of strike effects.) Any overstatement from duplication in particular categories is, however, almost certainly compensated for by the fact that not all categories of strike effects have been included.

A. Customers of the basic steel industry. Score: 72.6

    I. Steel fabricators. (This group, which includes all principal types of steel-using manufacturers except makers of machinery, consumed 44 per cent of all steel tonnage.) Score: 38.6

Urgency rating: 1.35

1. Production necessity: 6. We estimate dependence on steel for all fabricator employment at 80 per cent by the fortieth day and likely recovery of losses at 25 per cent (as in the basic steel industry).

2. Stock effect: 2.5. By the fortieth day, Pittsburgh fabricators had cut operations by 50 per cent. We assume the consumption of steel was reduced in similar proportion. Because of their proximity to basic steel mills, Pittsburgh manufacturers might normally carry smaller stocks of steel. We estimate a 25 per cent reduction in steel consumption by fabricators due to reduced steel output.

3. Substitutability: 9. In the short run, the possibilities of substitution of other metals are very poor.

Number affected: 28.6

Production of employees in the various subdivisions of the classification "iron and steel and their products," minus those in "blast furnaces, steel works, and rolling mills" for March,

1946, numbered 800,700. In 1947 average total employees in "fabricated metal products" were 118.9 per cent of production employees, so we estimate total employees in steel fabricating for 1946 at 952,032. With two dependents each we then have 2,856,096, or 28.6.

II. Machinery makers. (The categories here considered consumed approximately 41 per cent of all steel tonnage.) Score: 33.3

Urgency rating: .41

1. Production necessity: 4.5. Steel is not so large a component of total value of product in this category. Other materials are important, and some operations can continue longer without steel. Moreover, up to the day of rating several large users of steel—Allis-Chalmers and Westinghouse, for example—had themselves been closed by strike, and numerous smaller plants were involved in the unusual wave of postwar stoppages just coming to a close at this time. Some of these belong in the fabrication classification, above, but it seems most reasonable to take account of them here. In view of this concurrence of strikes, we estimate dependence on steel at only 60 per cent on the fortieth day. Recovery is set at 25 per cent.

2. Stock effect: 1. Part of the Ford curtailment was due to a shortage of steel. It was reported as of the seventeenth day that "scores" of plants were closing for lack of parts due to lack of steel. On an over-all basis, a cut in the consumption of steel of 10 per cent is estimated.

3. Substitutability: 9. In the short run, substitutability is very low.

Number affected: 81.1

Production employees in machinery and transportation equipment groups numbered 2,153,000 in March, 1946. For 1947 average total employees in these groups were 125.5 per cent of production employees, so we estimate total employees for March, 1946, at 2,702,015—with two dependents each, 8,106,045 or 81.1.

B. Manufacturing customers of coal-burning railroads. Score: 34.2

Transportation services provide a special problem with respect to producer-users, since such services perform two functions: (1)

They make inputs available; (2) they make outputs market-able. How can we measure the impact of loss of these two services on the producer's operations? The procedure followed is to make a separate urgency rating for each of these two types of transportation services, and to use the higher of the two ratings, since it is the one with the greater impact which governs the producer's operations. If difficulties in physically disposing of his product curtail his operations before or to a greater extent than difficulties in securing his materials, it is this that gives us the measure of the strike's critical effect on the pro-ducer. This procedure admittedly understates the strike effect, since the manufacturers affected by materials shortages *may* be an entirely separate group from those who are affected by in-ability to move their product. Each of the two effects may thus occur in different plants and so be additive, though here we treat them as concurrent in the same plants.

Urgency rating: .31

Transportation of inputs (urgency rating .31)

1. Production necessity: 4.5. For most manufacturers using rail services or some substitute, the need for such transport to secure inputs is inescapable, whether these services are cur-rently performed or have been performed in the past. There had been almost no curtailment of freight services up to the fortieth day, and therefore the cessation of them then, with no stocks of "incorporated" services available, would have caused a dependency of only about 60 per cent (the remain-ing 40 per cent being clerical or maintenance workers, production workers employed on non-affected operations, and those temporarily working elsewhere). As for recover-ability, manufacturers' own operations were perhaps ex-pansible enough to permit 40 per cent of the losses to be recovered in the succeeding six months, but this result was limited by the pressure on railroad services. We therefore put recoverability equal to that of railroads, or 25 per cent.

2. Stock effect: 1. As of the fortieth day, use of coal-burning railroad services by nonessential manufacturers was reduced to zero. However, most manufacturers had stocks of mate-rials on hand, into which railroad services had already been incorporated. Nevertheless, two factors were important in

creating a stock effect. The period of postwar materials shortages meant that some operations were on a hand-to-mouth basis, at times literally dependent on the day's receipt of materials to continue production. And a number of manufacturers reduced their consumption of already stocked materials in anticipation of the freight embargo, in a self-rationing program. Estimates of layoffs of from 250,000 to 400,000 workers were made even on the thirty-eighth day. A 10 per cent reduction due to lack of current performance of railroad services and to self-rationing of goods already transported is estimated.

3. Substitutability: 7. Truck transport could be substituted, but at higher cost. Water transport was available to some.

Transportation of outputs (urgency rating 0)

1. Production necessity: 0. There having been almost no curtailment of freight service during the previous period, on the first day of the freight embargo so few manufacturers would be forced to suspend operations owing to inability to stock their finished product (which is to say, so little employment would depend on transport of output) that we set the rating at the minimum.

2. Stock effect: 9. There was no coal-burning railway transport for goods in the nonexempt categories and obviously no means of stock-piling the services of coal-burning railroads in transporting finished goods. However, perhaps 10 per cent of the embargoed shipments could be moved with oil-burning or electric equipment. Consumption of rail services thus declined 90 per cent.

3. Substitutability: 8. The alternatives were the same as under inputs, but with perhaps less economic urgency to substitute more expensive forms of transport, since with product shortages customers at this time would wait, while with input shortages a labor force would be idled, at cost of money and morale.

The urgency rating for transportation of inputs is thus .31, while that for transporting outputs is 0. The higher governs, so we adopt the rating of .31.

Number affected: 110.3

In March, 1946, there was a total of 12,014,000 employees

in manufacturing, with about 1,181,700 production employees in the "essential" categories exempted from the embargo. In 1947 on the average nonproduction employees in these categories were 27.7 per cent of production employees, so we estimate all employees in these categories at 1,509,031. Total employees in manufacturing minus total employees in exempted categories leaves 10,504,969 manufacturing employees in non-exempted categories. We assume that one-half of all manufacturers rely on railroad freight services (the number of employees being proportionate), of which about 70 per cent rely on coal-burning freight transport, giving 3,676,739 employees—with two dependents each, 11,030,217 or, converted, 110.3.

C. Customers of electric power suppliers (Illinois producers). Score: 58.9

Urgency rating: 1.44

1. Production necessity: 4.5. By the fortieth day the curtailments had been in effect for one week. We estimate that on that day some 75 per cent of employment depended on power. Recoverability is assumed to have been 40 per cent.
2. Stock effect: 4. On the fortieth day, all industrial and commercial users of electric utilities were being allowed only twenty-four hours of power per week. Assuming a forty-hour week as normal, this is a 40 per cent cut in the consumption of power.
3. Substitutability: 8. Some user firms have their own stand-by facilities, but not many.

Number affected: 40.9

Those affected were in northern Illinois (the Chicago area). Total 1947 employment in Illinois manufacturing, trade, finance, and service was 2,377,300. The Chicago metropolitan area contains approximately 63 per cent of the state's population but a larger percentage of workers in the above-mentioned categories. Thus in 1947 it contained 71 per cent of the state's employees engaged in manufacturing and in 1948, 70 per cent of the state's employees engaged in retail trade. We assume that 70 per cent of all employees in the listed occupations in Illinois were in the Chicago metropolitan area, or 1,664,110. Of electric power produced in April,

1946, 82 per cent was supplied by public utilities. We assume the same ratio holds for Illinois workers dependent on purchased power, giving 1,364,570 employees, with two dependents each, or, converted, 40.9.

V. Direct Suppliers. Score: 15.8

  A. Railroads hauling bituminous coal. Score: 13.5

    Urgency rating: 3.0

     1. Market necessity: 3.75. Properly here we should show the proportion which coal-hauling services constitute of the total services supplied by railroads primarily engaged in hauling bituminous coal, and this proportion would be applied to the total number of persons employed by such railroads. But data showing total revenues, coal-hauling revenues, and employment for coal-hauling railroads are not available. We are forced then to approximate the correct figures by using for number affected an estimate of the number of employees of all (Class I) railroads who are engaged in coal-hauling operations and for market necessity a ratio representing the extent to which these employees are dependent on the bituminous industry for their employment.

       As of a given day of the strike the extent of such dependency is a function of the extent to which purchases of the suppliers' goods or services have been continued prior to the given day and of the extent to which the supplier has been able to avoid curtailment of operations by stocking his finished product. In this case, where stocking of the suppliers' services is impossible but where the coal industry's purchase of services (for hauling coal already stocked at the mine head) has continued up to the fortieth day, though in dwindling amounts, we estimate that complete cessation of coal hauling on the fortieth day would idle only 50 per cent of employees (the others being those engaged in supervisory, clerical, maintenance, and nonoperating jobs plus those who could have obtained fill-in employment elsewhere). We further assume that (as noted before) about 50 per cent of the losses of bituminous output (and employment) could be recovered in the next six months, but that (particularly in view of the shortage of coal cars) only about 25 per cent of the losses of coal-hauling services were recoverable. Thus 75 per cent of 50 per cent represents the *net* effect on the supplier of dependency on bituminous markets on the fortieth day.

2. Stock effect: 9. On the fortieth day, however, purchases of coal-hauling services had not declined to zero, but rather, we estimate, to about 10 per cent of pre-strike levels, with the result that output of such services had declined by 90 per cent owing to inability to accumulate stocks of them. Thus the net dependency effect is reduced from 37.5 per cent to 33.75 per cent (90 per cent of 37.5 per cent) because of the continuation of some purchases.

3. Substitutability: 9. In the short run opportunities for substituting other customers are virtually nonexistent. We assume that new markets can be substituted for at best 10 per cent of the market provided by hauling bituminous, with the result that only 90 per cent of the reduced net dependency effect of 33.75 per cent represents an actual loss to the coal-hauling railroads.

Number affected: 4.5

In 1946 railroad revenue from bituminous haulage was $850,935,015. (This figure understates since it does not include the imputed value of non-revenue coal carried.) As a rough means of estimating the total number of employees engaged in railroad coal-hauling operations, we divide this expenditure figure by the ratio of the number of total employees in all (Class I) railroad operations in 1946 to a figure representing total sales of all (Class I) railroads (in this case "total operating revenue").[5] This ratio, which amounts to $5612, has been termed the "1946 railroad employment divisor." The result indicates that the equivalent of 151,627 full-time employees are devoted to railroad coal-hauling operations. When this figure is multiplied by 3 (on the assumption of an average of two dependents for each employee), we procure an estimate of 454,881 persons affected

[5] In the ratings for all the strikes (bituminous, railroad, steel) the absence of comparable data on total sales of supplier industries has forced us to use those available statistics which were as nearly comparable as possible. Thus here we have used total operating revenue; in some cases we have used total sales, in other instances, value added, in still other instances, total sales of corporations (in the supplier industry).

by virtue of their relation to railroad coal-hauling operations, or 4.5.

B. Suppliers of electric power. Score: .2

Urgency rating: .98

1. Market necessity: 2.0. Here as with coal-hauling railroads we are forced to make our calculations on the basis of an estimate of the (equivalent) number of persons engaged solely in producing electric power for the bituminous industry. Again, in this case, where stocking of the suppliers' services is impossible but where the coal industry's purchases of services (for pumping and illumination, for example) have continued up to the fortieth day, we estimate that complete cessation of such purchases on the fortieth day would idle only 40 per cent of employees. We further estimate recoverability of power output losses at 100 per cent, but since recoverability of bituminous output losses has been estimated at only 50 per cent, this lower figure must control.

2. Stock effect: 7. Since electric power cannot be stocked, the decline in output would be at the maximum of 10 were it not for some continued use of electric power during the strike, for such purposes as pumping and lighting. We estimate that 30 per cent of normal power purchases were continuing on the fortieth day and that output therefore had declined 70 per cent owing to inability to stock output.

3. Substitutability: 7. The possibility of substituting other markets for electric power is somewhat better than in the case of coal-hauling railroads, but still not very great in the short run.

Number affected: .166

The latest available figure for purchases by the bituminous coal industry of electric power comes from the 1939 Census of Mineral Industries—$24,711,000. To get a more up-to-date figure, we adjust as follows: In 1939 total value of output of the bituminous industry was $754,173,000; purchases of electric power amounted to 3.28 per cent of this total value. In 1946 total value of output of the bituminous industry was $1,835,539,000, 3.28 per cent of which amounts to $60,205,679. This is taken as the value of purchases of electric power for 1946. Dividing this figure by the "electric and gas employment divisor" for 1946 ($10,888) we get a figure of 5529 as the equivalent full-time employees devoted to producing electric power for the bituminous coal industry. Assuming two dependents per employee, we get a final figure of 16,587 or .166.

C. Suppliers of machinery and equipment. Score: .05
   Urgency rating: .224
   1. Market necessity: 3.2. Some purchases of machinery and equipment would probably continue after the beginning of a strike. Moreover, this is a kind of output which can be stocked, up to a point. In view of these factors a complete cessation of bituminous industry purchases of machinery on the fortieth day would not bring a complete shutdown of operation. We estimate that some 20 per cent of employees would be retained or carried in alternative employments, making dependency on coal markets only 80 per cent, and that about 60 per cent of these suppliers' losses could be recovered in the succeeding six months, since purchases of equipment represent "overhead" expenditures (except for capital expenditures on current account). This percentage would not be much reduced by the fact that the bituminous industry could not recover more than 50 per cent of its losses (a fact pertinent only to suppliers of goods and services which depend primarily on rate of output).
   2. Stock effect: 1. By the fortieth day, despite continued purchases of machinery and equipment and (to a lesser extent) the accumulation of inventories, there would have been perhaps a 10 per cent decline in the output of such goods.
   3. Substitutability: 7. In the short run other procurable markets would be inadequate substitutes.
   Number affected: .225
      Using the 1939 figure for expenditures on machinery and equipment and adjusting by the same method that was used for electric power expenditures (above), we get an estimate of machinery and equipment expenditures for 1946 of $61,-490,556. Dividing by the 1946 "iron and steel products employment divisor" of $8213 gives us an estimated 7487 equivalent full-time employees devoted to machinery and

equipment for the bituminous industry, and with dependents, 22,461, or .225.

D. Suppliers of other materials. Score: .4

Urgency rating: .576

1. Market necessity: 4.8. Dependency is set at 80 per cent by the fortieth day, and recoverability at 40 per cent.

2. Stock effect: 3. The items in this category (explosives, timber for framing, etc.) are more dependent on the rate of operation than are machinery and equipment, and thus continued purchases and inclination to accumulate stocks would be less than in the case of machinery.

3. Substitutability: 4. For many of the items here, suppliers would not be so specialized to the bituminous industry, and therefore, in view of the generally higher demand prevailing during the reconversion period, the inadequacy of substitute markets would be less.

Number affected: .68

Expenditures for other materials for 1946 are estimated at $214,390,955. Dividing by the "general manufacturing divisor" for 1946 of $9446 gives an estimated 22,696 equivalent full-time employees devoted to providing other materials to the bituminous industry, and with dependents, 68,088, for a rating of .68.

E. Suppliers of goods and services to employees of the struck unit. Score: 1.6

Urgency rating: .8

1. Market necessity: 2.5. During the first thirty-nine days of the strike output of services of retail employees would have been sustained by continuing expenditures by miners for "essential" items (such expenditures being financed by credit, savings, gifts, and relief payments). Thus a complete falling off of purchases on the fortieth day would bring, we estimate, idleness to only 50 per cent of the labor force of suppliers of goods and services to miners. Recoverability of losses is judged to be the same as for the bituminous industry (50 per cent).

2. Stock effect: 4. It seems probable that on the fortieth day output of retail services, in spite of continued miners' purchases, had declined by 40 per cent.

3. Substitutability: 8. For local suppliers there would be few alternative customers.

Number affected: 1.98

Total payroll of the bituminous industry in 1946 was $1,099,879,000. We estimate that approximately two-thirds of this amount, or $733,619,293, went for the purchase of goods and services. (The principal excluded items are taxes, rent—involving virtually no supplier employees—and savings. While the proportion of income which these individual items represent varies over the years, we trust the variation to be roughly compensating—taxes rising as a percentage of income, rent falling, for example.) Since the 1946 divisor for retail trade is $11,101, our figure for the equivalent of full-time employees devoted to furnishing goods and services to employees of the struck unit is 66,086, and with dependents, 198,258, or 1.98.

VI. Indirect Suppliers. Score: 49.2

According to our procedure we take one-fifth the total scores for direct and indirect users and direct suppliers.

VII. Nonparty Members of the Struck Unit. Score: 6.4

As explained in Chapter 3, two of our three continua are not well suited to the measurement of the impact of a strike on nonparty members of the unit. Stock effect and substitutability are meaningless concepts where the hardship on a firm's employees stems not from temporary lack of markets for the firm's output but from temporary inability of the firm to produce any output. Nevertheless, the impact of a strike on nonparty members of the struck unit can be measured in terms which take account of the same sort of factors which underlie the continua, and which make the results entirely comparable to those obtained for other supplier categories.

A. Nonstriking employees. Score: 3.3

Urgency rating: 3.5

When the mines first shut down, maintenance, supervisory, and clerical employees must be retained to perform such tasks as storing away equipment and making out the last payroll. Perhaps about 50 per cent of all nonstrikers would have been employed during the first week. As these tasks are completed, the number of layoffs grows. Even after thirty-nine days of shutdown, however, some nonstrikers would have been retained for custodial duties, manning the pumps, answering correspondence, etc., but probably not more than 25 to 30 per cent. Of the employees who were idle, very few could have found jobs in other industries—because much bituminous mining is carried on in small and isolated communities, opportunities for alternative employment are limited. Thus about 70 per cent of nonstrikers were completely without employment on the fortieth day. Some of the losses—perhaps 50 per cent—which this idleness entailed could have been recovered during the next six months, however, through make-up operations in the bituminous industry. Our urgency rating is thus 3.5.

Number affected: .94

In 1946 there were 391,000 employees in the bituminous industry. About 95 per cent of the industry was shut down, involving about 371,450 workers. If 340,000 of these were strikers, nonstrikers must have numbered about 31,450; with two dependents each, 94,350.

B. Families of strikers. Score: 3.1

Urgency rating: .45

Strikers' only opportunity for employment was in other industries, and again probably not more than 10 per cent were so employed on the fortieth day. But as for nonstrikers perhaps 50 per cent of the losses could have been recovered through subsequent expanded employment in the bituminous industry. Moreover, to take account of the fact that the intimate involvement of strikers' families with the strike is in one sense an offset to strike losses, we further reduce our estimate of the losses permanently sustained by 90 per cent. The urgency rating is therefore .45.

Number affected: 6.8

Two dependents each for 340,000 strikers.

Because so much discussion of strike effects is in terms of the hardship caused to ultimate consumers, perhaps the most significant point revealed by the foregoing quantitative analysis of the effects of this one major bituminous strike is this: Members of the public in their function of consumers were much less affected than were members of the public in their function as producers.

As Table 1 shows, about 90 per cent of the total measurable effects of the strike fell on producer members of the public in the form of curtailed employment, revenues, and income. Only about 10 per cent of the total measurable effects fell on consumer members by depriving them of the use of coal or products requiring coal for their production.

It is true, of course, as Table 1 indicates, that almost four-fifths of the strike's effects fell on persons who *used* coal—either in households or industry. Nevertheless, about one-fifth of total effects bore on individuals—suppliers—not because they themselves needed coal but because the coal and other affected industries constituted normal markets for the sale of their goods or services.

TABLE 1. EFFECTS OF THE BITUMINOUS COAL STRIKE OF SPRING, 1946

	Rating	Per Cent of Total Effects
Total effects (rounded)	338.0	100.0
Effects on direct consumers	34.4	10.2
Effects on indirect consumers	1.0	.3
Total effects on consumers	35.4	10.5
Effects on direct producer-users	65.7	19.5
Effects on indirect producer-users	165.0	48.9
Total effects on producer-users	230.7	68.4
Total consumer and user effects	266.1	78.8
Effects on direct suppliers	15.8	4.6
Effects on indirect suppliers	49.2	14.6
Effects on nonparty suppliers within the struck industry	6.4	2.0
Total effects on suppliers	71.4	21.2
Total effects on producers (users and suppliers)	302.1	89.5
Total indirect effects	215.9	63.7

The quantitative analysis further suggests that any evaluation of the repercussions of a soft-coal strike which does not take into account indirect as well as direct effects is likely to understate seriously the strike's significance. Table 1 shows that almost two-thirds of the measurable impact of the spring, 1946, strike fell not on household consumers or industrial users of coal itself, or on suppliers of the coal industry, but on household and industrial users of products and services requiring coal in their production and on suppliers of goods and services to industries using coal, sometimes several degrees removed. The fact that we found it infeasible to include all such secondary ramifications within our system of measurement means that the contribution of indirect effects to the total effects of the strike is not likely to be exaggerated in our ratings.

We shall have to postpone further observations concerning strikes in the bituminous industry until after we have similarly rated the remaining ten peacetime strikes which occurred during the period under study.

CHAPTER 6

The Relative Impact of Eleven Coal Strikes: II. Spring of 1939 to Winter of 1950

ONLY four other major bituminous strikes of the period from January, 1939, to January, 1952, will be examined in any detail. These are the strikes of January, 1939, fall, 1946, spring, 1948, and winter, 1949-1950. The remaining six strikes are all minor, and their effects will simply be summarized without explanation.

Spring, 1939

This strike lasted for forty-five days and came at a time when industrial production was falling off. In the bituminous industry itself the level of activity was slowly rising, but it was still well below the level of the immediate past (1937) and the levels it was to gain in the immediate future. Coal stocks at the start of the strike were substantial, and these were augmented during the first thirty days of the strike by the output of a portion of the industry which had not been shut down. No governmental rationing was invoked. We rate the strike as of its forty-first day (Monday, May 11) to facilitate comparison of effects with those of the strike of spring, 1946, which was analyzed in the preceding chapter.

The total rating is 62. The impact on the publics affected is as follows:

I. Direct Consumers. Score: 27.5

In spring, 1939, as in spring, 1946 (our reference strike), the forty-first day of the stoppage fell in the same period in May. Thus the need for heat in the various regions, the sufficiency of auxiliary heating devices, and the numbers affected would have been approximately the same as in the 1946 strike. The available data indicate, however, that the larger stock-consumption ratios prevailing throughout the 1939 strike enabled households to maintain coal consumption at better levels than in 1946. It seems probable that the impact on direct consumers in this strike amounted to no more than 80 per cent of the impact of the 1946 strike (34.4), giving a score of 27.5.

II. Indirect Consumers. Score: 0

By the forty-first day, use of steel capacity had declined only 6 per cent, with no perceptible effect on consumers. As of April 19, all the major Eastern railroads had adequate coal supplies (from forty-two days on the New Haven to 120 days on the Pennsylvania) except the B & O, but even here bituminous was available from the Illinois fields until the thirty-sixth day. There were no reported cuts in use of electricity except that service on two New York City subways was reduced by from 20 to 25 per cent. We consider indirect-consumer effects insufficient to rate.

III. Direct-User Producers. Score: 17.4

There were no appreciable effects on the railroad and electric power industries.

A. Basic steel. Score: 3.3

   Urgency rating: .25

   1. Production necessity: 4.2. Declines in steel output came late and were small in amount. Probably no more than 70 per cent of basic steel employees would have been idled on the fortieth day of the strike had there been no stocks of or substitutes for coal. Activity in both the bituminous and steel industries was sluggish, improving the opportunity by both for the recovery of losses. In the former it was perhaps as high as 80 per cent, in the latter (which is pertinent here) about half of that.

   2. Stock effect: .63. Utilization of steel capacity had dropped by 6 per cent on the forty-first day. Assuming that this decline measures the decline in consumption of coal and substitutes for coal, and that substitutes for coal amount to 5 per cent, the cut in bituminous consumption was 6.3 per cent.

   3. Substitutability: 9.5[1]

---

[1] Throughout this chapter, a value which is not followed by any explanation, as here, is the same value as that given in our "key" spring, 1946, strike, rated in the preceding chapter, and the underlying reasons are the same as were set forth there.

Number affected: 13.3

Total employees in basic steel in March, 1939, are fixed at 442,046. Allowing two dependents per employee, this gives 1,326,138 persons, or 13.3.

B. Manufacturing and processing companies using bituminous coal for heat and power. Score: 14.1

Because for the first four weeks stocks were augmented by continued output from a portion of the industry, the forty-first-day effects on producer-users were reduced from those of spring, 1946, rated as 17.6. As for consumers, 80 per cent of this score is considered appropriate.

IV. Indirect-User Producers. Score: 0

A 6 per cent decline in steel capacity utilization did not affect steel users perceptibly. No effects on customers of railroads or electric power suppliers were reported.

V. Direct Suppliers. Score: 9.3

A. Railroads hauling bituminous coal. Score: 8.6

Urgency rating: 2

1. Market necessity: 2.5. As in 1946, for the forty-first day of the strike dependency of coal-hauling railroad employees on bituminous markets is set at 50 per cent. Because of lower utilization of capacity, recoverability of losses for the bituminous industry was higher than for the railroad industry, which we set at 50 per cent.

2. Stock effect: 9. Again, as in spring, 1946, continuing purchases of hauling services are calculated as 10 per cent, meaning that output of such services declined 90 per cent owing to inability to stock such services.

3. Substitutability: 9

Number affected: 4.3

In 1939 railroad revenue from bituminous haulage was $580,249,411. Dividing this figure by the 1939 railroad employment divisor of $4045 gives the equivalent of 143,449 full-time employees devoted to railroad coal-hauling operations; with dependents, 430,347, or 4.3.

B. Suppliers of electric power. Score: .0

Urgency rating: .39

1. Market necessity: .8. Corresponding to the early 1946 stoppage, dependency on the forty-first day is set at 40 per cent.

Recoverability (in our sense of offsets to strike losses) is chiefly determined by the possibility of make-up operations in coal. As in coal, it is put at 80 per cent.

2. Stock effect: 7
3. Substitutability: 7

Number affected: .1

The bituminous industry's expenditures for electric power in 1939 amounted to $24,711,000. Dividing by the 1939 electric and gas employment divisor of $7347 gives the equivalent of 3363 full-time employees engaged in providing electric power to the bituminous industry; with dependents, 10,089, or .1.

C. Suppliers of machinery and equipment. Score: .0

Urgency rating: .056

1. Market necessity: .8. As for the fortieth day of the spring, 1946, strike we estimate dependency at 80 per cent. Because of the capital-goods nature of the supplying industries, recoverability was probably about 90 per cent.
2. Stock effect: 1
3. Substitutability: 7

Number affected: .145

In 1939 bituminous expenditures for machinery and equipment were $25,258,000, which divided by the 1939 iron and steel employment divisor of $5172 and adjusted for dependents gives 14,508 persons or .145.

D. Suppliers of other materials. Score: .2

Urgency rating: .432

1. Market necessity: 2.4. Dependency is like that for spring, 1946 (80 per cent), but recoverability, because of generally lower level of activity, is estimated at 70 per cent.
2. Stock effect: 3
3. Substitutability: 6. Since a lower level of general economic activity would make for a weaker demand, alternative markets would be less available than in the spring, 1946, strike.

Number affected: .46

In 1939 bituminous expenditures for other materials were $88,064,000, which divided by the 1939 general manufacturing divisor of $5735 and adjusted for dependents gives 46,-068 persons or .46.

E. Suppliers of goods and services to employees of the struck unit.
Score: .5
Urgency rating: .32
1. Market necessity: 1. Dependency is the same as in spring, 1946 (50 per cent), and recoverability like that for the bituminous industry (80 per cent).
2. Stock effect: 4
3. Substitutability: 8
Number affected: 1.45
Total pay roll of the bituminous industry in 1939 was $446,-186,000. We take two-thirds of this (the portion estimated as going for purchase of goods and services, $297,606,000), divide by the 1939 retail trade employment divisor of $6178, and adjust for dependents to obtain a figure of 144,516 persons, or 1.45.

VI. Indirect Suppliers. Score: 5.3
One-fifth the total scores for categories III and V, in line with our decision to use this proportion of total direct and indirect producer-user and direct supplier ratings as an arbitrary allowance for indirect supplier effects.

VII. Nonparty Members of the Struck Unit. Score: 2.3
A. Nonstriking employees. Score: 1.17
Urgency rating; 1.3
About 65 per cent of the bituminous industry had been shut down throughout the preceding forty days, a period almost exactly the same length as that preceding the day of rating in the spring, 1946, strike. We would expect, then, that on the forty-first day about 30 per cent (as in the spring, 1946, strike) of all nonstrikers working for companies included in this segment of the industry would still have been employed or would have found jobs elsewhere. On the thirty-fifth day mines representing an additional 25 per cent of the industry were struck. Because for these mines the strike had been going on for only a week on the day of rating, so that many tasks incidental to the closing down of operations were still being performed, perhaps as many as 50 per cent of their nonstriking employees were still employed. The average employment (after weighting each employment estimate by the number of nonstrikers in each group) on the day of

rating was 35 per cent. The lower level of activity in the bituminous industry in 1939 operated in the direction of increasing the amount of strike losses which could be recovered during the following six months. Thus we estimate recoverability at 80 per cent instead of the 50 per cent estimated for the spring, 1946, strike.

Number affected: .9

Assuming that the number of nonstrikers bears the same relationship to the number of strikers as in the spring, 1946, strike, 29,925 were involved; with two dependents each, 89,775.

B. Families of strikers. Score: 1.15

Urgency rating: .18

The relevant considerations here are the opportunities for the temporary alternative employment of the striking head of the household and the recoverability of strike losses.

Number affected: 6.4

Two dependents each for 320,000 strikers.

Recapitulation of Spring, 1939, Strike Effects

Direct consumers	27.5
Indirect consumers	0.0
Direct-user producers	17.4
Indirect-user producers	0.0
Direct suppliers	9.3
Indirect suppliers	5.3
Nonparty members of struck unit	2.3
	61.8 (or 62 when rounded)

Strike of Fall, 1946

The economy was still undergoing reconversion from wartime to peacetime operations and the general level of activity in the bituminous industry was still high when this seventeen-day strike occurred. A shortage of railroad coal cars had forced curtailment of output in some areas, however. Coal stocks were somewhat below normal in consequence of the fifty-nine-day strike that spring. In this more than in any of the other bituminous strikes government action directed toward the preservation of coal stocks was prompt and drastic. By the fifth day of the strike coal deliveries had been severely restricted, railroad passenger service reduced, and use of electricity curtailed in twenty-one states.

Effects have been rated as of the sixteenth day of the strike (Friday, December 6), the last weekday of the strike. The total rating is 306.

I. Direct Consumers. Score: 118.4

    A. Residences. Score: 100.8

       Urgency rating: .20

          1. Cultural necessity: 8. In December every state has an average temperature under 60°, all but a few southernmost states have temperatures under 50°, and the largest bituminous-using regions have temperatures under 33°. Normal December weather is colder in *every* state except Florida than in any state in May, the date of our key strike, which may be used for comparison. We judge that the indispensability of heat on December 6 was higher than on May 10, the day of the spring, 1946, rating.

          2. Stock effect: .5. The stock-consumption ratio for retail yards was only about eleven days at the start of the strike. Despite additions to stock from the 15 to 20 per cent of the industry which continued to operate, by the tenth day the stock-consumption ratio had fallen to nine. Some government restrictions on coal deliveries were imposed, as in the spring, 1946, strike, and self-rationing by householders was specifically reported from Pittsburgh and Denver. In view of the prospects of colder weather, self-rationing was probably instituted earlier than in the spring strike. A 5 per cent decline in household consumption appears to be a conservative estimate.

          3. Substitutability: 8. Except for some apartment houses, residences did not have "switchable" equipment. The small supplies of anthracite available did not provide an alternative fuel for many. Small space heaters and fireplaces are not very satisfactory for December weather.

       Number affected: 504

       The number of residences using bituminous was 13,222,000. Census of Housing estimates 3.78 occupants per dwelling, for a total of 49,979,160. Assuming the proportion of the institutional population relying on bituminous is the same as for private dwellings, this adds 380,000 more.

B. Nonprofit places of assembly. Score: 17.4
   Urgency rating: .24
   1. Cultural necessity: 6. The considerations applying to residences are also pertinent here, except that assemblies can suspend, as Denver schools did, giving a somewhat lower rating.
   2. Stock effect: .5. Curtailments of coal consumption presumably were similar to those made in residences.
   3. Substitutability: 8. The greater use of "switchable" equipment is offset by inability to rely on small space heaters.
   Number affected: 72.5
      This is the same figure as for the key strike of spring, 1946, raised to include the Southern states, which required heat in December (as they did not in May).

II. Indirect Consumers (long-distance passengers). Score: 1.5
   For considerations similar to those mentioned in the spring, 1946, strike, the only measurable indirect-consumer effect was long-distance passenger travel. A 25 per cent cut in passenger service, instituted on the third day, was still operative on the sixteenth day. On the first day of a period in which travelers are deprived of rail services, as in the spring, 1946, strike, only those persons are affected who had scheduled trips for that day. By the thirteenth day of the period, as in this strike, lack of services affects not only those persons who have scheduled trips for that day but also persons who have wanted to make trips on each of the preceding days and still want to make them at the first opportunity. The importance of transport on the thirteenth day for those who for the first time want to travel on the thirteenth day is no greater than the importance of transport on the first day was for those who had wanted to travel on the first day. But the need for transport on the thirteenth day is perceptibly greater for at least some of those who want to undertake at the first opportunity their strike-interrupted journeys. Our procedure below takes account of these differences.
   A. Long-distance passengers wanting to travel for the first time on the day of rating. Score: .756
      Urgency rating: .07
      1. Cultural necessity: 4. As explained above, importance of travel for this group would be the same as for all long-dis-

tance travelers on the first day of the spring, 1946, rail curtailments.

2. Stock effect: .5. Because of similar circumstances with respect to size of reduction in coal-burning passenger service, percentage of total passenger service furnished by coal-burning trains, substitution of oil-burning for coal-burning equipment, and more intensive utilization of remaining facilities, the decline in consumption of long-distance passenger rail service is the same as that in the spring, 1946, strike.

3. Substitutability: 3.5. Air and private car transportation are less reliable substitutes in December than in May. On the other hand, the longer period of curtailment would have provided more opportunity to organize alternative means of transport. The second factor probably more than offsets the first, so that substitutability was slightly better than in the spring, 1946, strike.

Number affected: 10.8

During October, 1946, the last month unaffected by the strike, 33,485,431 noncommutation passengers were carried, giving an average daily figure of 1,080,175. We take this figure as an estimate of the number of persons who, for the first time, wished to travel on the thirteenth day of the curtailment period.

B. Long-distance passengers who because of inability to travel on previous days of the curtailment wanted to travel on the day of rating. Score: .715

Urgency rating: .11

Necessity of travel for persons in this group *as a whole* would be somewhat greater than for those who were wanting, for the first time during the curtailment, to make a journey (even though for some *individuals* in the latter group the need would be greater). We estimate it to be 6. Stock effect and substitutability would be the same, however, or .5 and 3.5 respectively.

Number affected: 6.5

As noted above, average daily noncommutation passengers amounted to about 1,080,175 at the time of the strike. We assume that this figure represents the number of persons who had wanted to travel on each of the preceding days of the curtailment period. However, on each day some of those who could not travel because of the curtailment would have permanently canceled their trips and would thus no longer require travel. As each succeeding day passed without re-opening of rail facilities, more of the travelers who had planned trips for the early days of the curtailment period would have canceled or indefinitely postponed them. Still another group would have made use of substitute transportation facilities and consequently would no longer be among those affected on the thirteenth day by a shortage of rail transport. Thus by the thirteenth day perhaps only 2 per cent of travelers who had originally planned rail trips on the first day were wanting to undertake their deferred trips at the first opportunity—that is, on the thirteenth day if transport had been available on that day—but perhaps 3 per cent of the fourth-day travelers, 7 per cent of the eighth-day travelers, and so on. We take 5 per cent as the *average* proportion òf travelers who, having wanted to travel on each preceding day, now wanted to travel on the thirteenth day. Since twelve days had passed, the total number of previously affected travelers was 12,962,100, and the number still wanting transport on the thirteenth day, 648,105. In our unit of account this is 6.5.

III. Direct-User Producers. Score: 71.7

A. Basic Steel. Score: 27.2

Urgency rating: 1.68

1. Production necessity: 5.6. Coal stocks were such that steel output began falling off on the first day of the strike and fell sharply, declining 30 per cent by the sixteenth day. Such a sharp fall means a relatively longer period during which output is reduced and tends to make dependency greater as of a given date. Thus we estimate that the sharp fall of 30 per cent by the sixteenth day caused about as much dependency on coal (80 per cent) on that day as the more gradual fall of 40 per cent by the fortieth day caused *on* the fortieth day of the spring, 1946, strike. We judge that, since the reconversion period was nearer to its end, recoverability

was somewhat higher than for the spring strike—30 per cent as against 25 per cent.

2. Stock effect: 3.16. On the basis of a 30 per cent decline in the utilization of capacity and allowing substitutes for 5 per cent of coal consumption, the decline in the consumption of coal by the sixteenth day is estimated to have been 31.6 per cent.

3. Substitutability: 9.5.

Number affected: 16.2

The estimated total number of steel employees for October, 1946, is 538,843; with dependents, 1,616,529, which converts to 16.2.

B. Coal-burning railroads. Score: 26

Urgency rating: 1.05

1. Production necessity: 4.55. As in the spring strike, a freight embargo had been instituted on the day preceding the day of rating, which would make dependency of freight employees similar to that estimated for the spring strike. But a 25 per cent cut in coal consumption for passenger service had been in effect for fourteen days prior to the day of rating. On the day of rating, therefore, the jobs of more maintenance, clerical, and nonoperating employees in the passenger service depended on the remaining supplies of coal or substitutes. We estimate the over-all dependency of employees on coal-burning railroads on the sixteenth day at 65 per cent, with recoverability at about 30 per cent.

2. Stock effect: 3.3. The reduction in passenger service and the freight embargo similar to that of the spring strike permit the following calculations:

Total Coal Consumed by Railroads in October, 1946		*Per Cent Reduction*		*Tons Reduced*
Freight	6,089,425	× .35	=	2,131,299
Passenger	1,510,356	× .25	=	377,589
Total	7,599,781			2,508,888

This gives a total reduction in coal consumption by railroads of 33 per cent.

3. Substitutability: 7.

Number affected: 24.8

Total employees on Class I railroads numbered 1,376,000 in October, 1946. Of these about 60 per cent were dependent on coal-burning operations, or 825,600. With two dependents each, 2,476,800 persons were affected, or 24.8.

C. Electric power. Score: .5

Urgency rating: .142

1. Production necessity: 4.73. In this strike widespread curtailment of power output began on the third day, and thus by the day of rating had been in effect for two weeks. This means that by the day of rating more employees than in the spring strike would have been dependent on coal or substitutes for coal. We estimate dependency on the sixteenth day at 75 per cent. Again we assume that electric plants will be able to expand output to fill that portion of the demand for current which is potentially deferrable, amounting to 75 per cent of the total demand, but that actual recoverability is limited to 50 per cent of this amount.

2. Stock effect: .5. As of the fifth day, nonresidential lighting was ordered reduced by 25 per cent in eighteen states east of the Mississippi plus Minnesota, Iowa, and Missouri. More drastic cuts were required where coal stocks were especially low. A 5 per cent reduction in coal consumption by electric utilities is estimated.

3. Substitutability: 6.

Number affected: 3.3

As of October, 1946, there were 249,000 employees in electric utilities, with about 45 per cent of this number dependent on bituminous. With two dependents each, a total of 336,000 persons were affected.

D. Manufacturing and processing plants using bituminous coal for heat and power. Score: 18

Urgency rating: .14

1. Production necessity: 4. Here, too, the fall in output and employment was sharper, making dependency as of the earlier day of rating the same (80 per cent) as for the later day of rating in the spring strike. Recoverability was about 50 per cent.

2. Stock effect: .5. Three weeks before the strike the average

stock-consumption ratio for "other industrials" was fifty-five days. On the tenth day, despite only minor additions to stock, the ratio was fifty-two days. The slight decline is attributable to voluntary rationing, since general stocks were frozen by government order. On an over-all basis, there was perhaps a 5 per cent decline in the consumption of coal.

3. Substitutability: 7

Number affected: 128.4

In October, 1946, there were 14,763,000 workers in all manufacturing. We assume, as before, that 29 per cent of this number were dependent on bituminous coal for heat and power, the same proportion as manufacturers' purchases of coal bear to other fuels. With two dependents each, a total of 12,843,510 was affected.

IV. Indirect-User Producers. Score: 71.6

A. Customers of the basic steel industry. Score: 19.3

I. Steel fabricators. Score: 7.6

Urgency rating: .22

1. Production necessity: 4.9. The dependence on steel supplies of all fabricating operations is put at 70 per cent on the sixteenth day, and recovery of losses at 30 per cent (as in the basic steel industry).

2. Stock effect: .5. The cut in steel output was not as drastic as in spring, 1946. Moreover, in the earlier coal strike fabricators' steel stocks had been limited by the steel strike of January-February, 1946. Since then, they had been able to rebuild stocks, so that cuts in the consumption of steel now were kept low, perhaps about 5 per cent.

3. Substitutability: 9.

Number affected: 34.5.

Total number of employees in the affected categories in October, 1946, is estimated at 1,151,547. With two dependents each, a total of 3,454,641 persons was subject to strike effects.

II. Machinery makers. Score: 11.7

Urgency rating: .11

1. Production necessity: 4.9. Dependence on steel is estimated at 70 per cent on the sixteenth day and recoverability at 30 per cent.

2. Stock effect: .25. The stock effect was lower than in the spring strike, probably no more than 25 per cent.

3. Substitutability: 9

Number affected: 106.6

Total number of employees in the affected categories in October, 1946, is calculated at 3,554,150. With two dependents each, 10,662,450, or 106.6.

B. Manufacturing customers of coal-burning railroads. Score: 52.3

Urgency rating: .382

Transportation of inputs (urgency rating: .382)

1. Production necessity: 4.55. Since in this strike the freight embargo occurred on the day preceding rather than on the day of rating, as in the spring strike, dependency would be slightly higher. We put it at 65 per cent. Recoverability is 30 per cent.

2. Stock effect: 1.2. This too would be slightly higher than for the spring strike—say, 12 per cent.

3. Substitutability: 7. As in the spring, 1946, strike, truck, water, or air transport could be substituted but only at higher cost or with slower delivery.

Transportation of outputs (urgency rating: .22).

1. Production necessity: .35. One day without rail transport would have created relatively slight problems in stocking output. By the second day of the freight embargo perhaps at most 5 per cent of employment depended on transport of outputs. Recoverability is estimated at 30 per cent.

2. Stock effect: 9. Transport services for the movement of current output cannot, of course, be stock-piled. This inability to fall back on accumulated stocks of rail services means that the potential dependency of 5 per cent, calculated above, would have been realized in the form of unemployment, except insofar as the railroads were able to continue some portion of their services or other carriers could fill in the gap. Coal-burning railway transport for the affected categories was completely eliminated, but substitution of oil-burning or electric equipment probably prevented more than a 90 per cent decline in use of rail services.

3. Substitutability: 7. As in spring, 1946, substitutes were similar to those for carrying inputs, but with less economic

urgency to use them. The urgency rating for transportation of inputs is .382 while that for transporting outputs is .22. The higher governs, so we adopt the rating of .382.

Number affected: 136.9

For October, 1946, the total number of employees in manufacturing was 14,763,000. Total employees in the exempted categories numbered about 1,721,140, leaving 13,041,860 employees in the non-exempted categories. Of these we judge at least one-half to be in businesses relying on freight services, and 70 per cent of these to rely on coal-burning freight, and each employee to have two dependents, making a total of 13,693,953, or 136.9.

V. Direct Suppliers. Score: 7.5

In all cases, numbers affected were as in the spring, 1946, strike.

A. Railroads hauling bituminous coal. Score: 6.9

Urgency rating: 1.54

   1. Market necessity: 2.45. On the sixteenth day dependency would be less than on the fortieth day of the 1946 strike, perhaps about 35 per cent. Recoverability for railroads we set at 30 per cent.

   2. Stock effect: 7. The lower level of stocks suggests that mine-head stocks had fallen to the point where only 30 per cent of normal hauling services were still being purchased by the sixteenth day.

   3. Substitutability: 9

Number affected: 4.5

B. Suppliers of electric power. Score: .1

Urgency rating: .49

   1. Market necessity: 1. The shorter duration makes dependency as of the day of rating only 25 per cent. Recoverability, limited by make-up operations in the bituminous industry, is put at 60 per cent.

   2. Stock effect: 7. We assume that purchases of a continuing nature (as for pumping and illumination) would be no greater on the sixteenth than on the fortieth day, so the rating is the same as for the forty-day strike.

   3. Substitutability: 7

Number affected: .166

    C. Suppliers of machinery and equipment. Score: .o
       Urgency rating: .08
        1. Market necessity: 2.275. For the sixteenth day we estimate dependency at 65 per cent, recoverability at 65 per cent.
        2. Stock effect: .5. As of the sixteenth day continuing purchases and accumulation of inventories, it is judged, had prevented a decline of more than 5 per cent of output of these goods.
        3. Substitutability: 7
       Number affected: .225

    D. Suppliers of other materials. Score: .1
       Urgency rating: .195
        1. Market necessity: 3.25. Dependency is 65 per cent, recoverability 50 per cent.
        2. Stock effect: 1.5. A smaller accumulation of inventories by the sixteenth day should have lessened the pressure to curtail output.
        3. Substitutability: 4
       Number affected: .67

    E. Suppliers of goods and services to employees of the struck unit. Score: .4
       Urgency rating: .224
        1. Market necessity: 1.41. On the sixteenth day dependency was perhaps 35 per cent, recoverability (like that for the bituminous industry) 60 per cent.
        2. Stock effect: 2. Purchases were probably somewhat greater in volume on the sixteenth day than they were on the fortieth day of the spring, 1939 and 1946, strikes; therefore, we estimate the decline in output of suppliers' services to have been about 20 per cent.
        3. Substitutability: 8
       Number affected: 1.98

VI. Indirect Suppliers. Score: 30.2
    One-fifth of the total scores for Categories III, IV, and V.

VII. Nonparty Members of the Struck Unit. Score: 5
    A. Nonstriking employees. Score: 2.6
       Urgency rating: 2.8
        With mining of coal suspended, nonstriker idleness on the sixteenth day of the strike was probably close to 70 per cent. Recoverability is set at 60 per cent.

Number affected: .93

Our best estimate is that 31,000 nonstrikers were involved in this stoppage; with two dependents each, this gives 93,000.

B. Families of strikers. Score: 2.4

Urgency rating: .36

No more than 10 per cent of striking miners could have found temporary work, to ease the burden on their families. An allowance of 60 per cent is made for recoverability, as for nonstrikers, but an additional 90 per cent of strike losses is considered to have been offset by the close concern of strikers' families with the outcome of the dispute, an involvement peculiar to this category.

Number affected: 6.7

Two dependents for each of the 335,000 strikers gives 670,000.

Recapitulation of the Fall, 1946, Strike Effects

Direct consumers	118.4
Indirect consumers	1.5
Direct-user producers	71.7
Indirect-user producers	71.6
Direct suppliers	7.5
Indirect suppliers	30.2
Nonparty members of struck unit	5.0
	305.9 (or 306 when rounded)

Strike of Spring, 1948

This strike had an "official" duration of only thirty days, although varying amounts of the bituminous industry's facilities remained shut down for an additional ten days. The stoppage occurred during a period of relatively high activity in the bituminous industry but of mild recession in the economy in general. Bituminous stocks were apparently rather low at the start of the strike. The federal government took no action with respect to coal deliveries or consumption of electric power but did order reductions in railroad passenger service on the seventh day and in freight service on the sixteenth day.

Effects are rated as of the twenty-ninth day (April 12) since that was the last day before the official end of the strike, which terminated the restrictions on rail services.

The total rating is 101.

I. Direct Consumers.

There is no evidence of any direct consumer effect. The only measurable indirect consumer effect is long-distance railroad passenger service.

II. Indirect Consumers (long-distance railroad passenger service). Score: 1

Urgency rating: .064

1. Cultural necessity: 5.33. By the twenty-ninth day of the strike a 25 per cent reduction in coal-burning passenger service had been operative for twenty-one days. The importance of transport to those prevented for the first time from traveling on that day was no greater than to persons wanting for the first time to travel on the day of rating in the spring and fall, 1946, strikes. We therefore assign the same rating for cultural necessity, or 4. For persons who because of inability to travel on previous days of the curtailment now wanted to travel on the day of rating we assign a cultural necessity—7—which is higher than that in the fall, 1946, strike, since their trips had been delayed for a longer time. With the rating for each group weighted by the number affected in each group, the average cultural necessity rating is 5.33.

2. Stock effect: .4. For February, 1948, coal-burning passenger train miles were only 38 per cent of total passenger car miles, owing to increasing dieselization. The 25 per cent cut thus amounted to only 9.5 per cent of total passenger traffic. As in the other rail curtailments, passengers used the remaining services more intensively, but unlike the situation in the other curtailments, substitution of oil-burning locomotives for eliminated coal-burning equipment was not permitted. The actual reduction in passenger travel is estimated to have been about 4 per cent.

3. Substitutability: 3. On the assumption that April weather permits as full a use of air and motor transport as does May weather and that the longer period of curtailment would have enabled a more efficient use of alternative forms of transport, substitutability would have been better than in either spring or fall, 1946.

Number affected: 15.6

In February, 1948, 25,140,736 noncommutation passengers were carried, or a daily average of 866,922. We take this figure as an estimate of the number of persons who on the twenty-first day of the curtailment wanted, for the first time during the curtailment, to make a journey. We also take it as an estimate of the number of persons who had wanted to make trips on each of the twenty preceding days, giving a total of 17,338,440 for the period. The longer the restriction is in effect, however, the greater is the proportion of each day's quota of disappointed travelers who cancel or indefinitely postpone their journeys. By the twenty-first day of the curtailment, perhaps only 4 per cent of the total of previously disappointed travelers still wanted to travel on that day, or 693,538. Adding the two groups, we get a total of 1,560,460 persons affected on the twenty-first day by reduction of rail passenger services.

III. Direct-User Producers. Score: 37.5

A. Basic steel. Score: 16.8

Urgency rating: .966

1. Production necessity: 4.2. By the twenty-third day utilization of capacity had declined by about 23 per cent and remained at that level until the twenty-ninth day. Employment was about 60 per cent dependent on coal (or some substitute), with recoverability 30 per cent.

2. Stock effect: 2.42. The decline in consumption of coal by the twenty-ninth day is estimated to have been 24.2 per cent.

3. Substitutability: 9.5

Number affected: 17.4

Total number of employees in basic steel in February, 1948, is computed as 578,673; with dependents, 1,736,019, or 17.4.

B. Coal-burning railroads. Score: 20.7

Urgency rating: 1.05

1. Production necessity: 5.25. By the twenty-ninth day a 25 per cent cut in passenger traffic had been in effect for three weeks, a 25 per cent cut in freight traffic for two weeks. Thus dependency on the day of rating would be higher than in the case of the fall, 1946, strike—say, 75 per cent, with recoverability 30 per cent.

2. Stock effect: 2.5. By the twenty-ninth day, both passenger and freight locomotive mileage had been cut by 25 per cent, producing an equal cut in coal consumption.

3. Substitutability: 8. The order reducing coal-burning passenger traffic prohibited the substitution of non-coal-burning locomotives. The rating here is therefore higher than for spring, 1946.

Number affected: 19.7

Total employees in Class I railroads numbered 1,312,000 in February, 1948. In that month coal-burning train miles amounted to approximately 50 per cent of total train miles. We therefore take 50 per cent of the total number of employees, crediting each with two dependents, for a total of 1,968,000 persons affected.

IV. Indirect-User Producers. Score: 30.2

A. Customers of the basic steel industry (steel fabricators—there is no evidence of any effect on machinery makers). Score: 4.6

Urgency rating: .118

Dependency on steel by all fabricating operations is set at 75 per cent on the thirtieth day, recoverability at 30 per cent, with stock effect rated .25 and substitutability 9.

Number affected: 38.7

Total employees in the relevant categories were 1,290,660 in February, 1948; with two dependents each, 3,871,980 or 38.7.

B. Manufacturing customers of coal-burning railroads. Score: 25.6

Urgency rating: .22

Transportation of inputs (urgency rating: .084)

1. Production necessity: 5.6. The curtailment in coal-using freight services had been in effect for two weeks prior to the day of rating, but it was only a partial curtailment (25 per cent) rather than a complete embargo as in the 1946 strikes. We estimate that by the twenty-ninth day it must have caused about 80 per cent dependency. That is, if all rail services and substitute forms of transport (including stocks of goods into which transportation services had previously been incorporated) had been withdrawn on this day, the services of only 20 per cent of employees in manufacturing companies relying on transportation could have been utilized,

either within the user firm or by some other (temporary) employer. Recoverability is assumed to have been about 30 per cent.

2. Stock effect: .25. The 25 per cent reduction in coal-burning freight service for thirteen days, rather than an embargo of all nonessential freight categories as in the two 1946 strikes, probably led to self-rationing which reduced the volume of manufacturers' inputs by an estimated 2.5 per cent, both in anticipation and in actual consequence of nondelivery.

3. Substitutability: 6. This was somewhat improved over spring, 1946, as the passage of thirteen days permitted a more effective organization of such alternative forms of transport as were available, and the lesser extent of the curtailment eased the burden on shippers of arranging for their use.

Transportation of outputs (urgency rating: .22)

1. Production necessity: 1.4. After two weeks of partial restriction on the use of railroads for transporting outputs, dependency would probably be about 20 per cent. Recoverability is estimated at 30 per cent.

2. Stock effect: 2.2. The 25 per cent reduction in freight mileage is here figured to have resulted in a 22 per cent reduction in the consumption of coal-burning rail freight services. Such services cannot be stock-piled. While a more intensive use was made of the service remaining, this was offset by the fact that shipments originating or terminating on dieselized or electrified lines were affected if at some point they connected with coal-burning lines. On the other hand, some substitution of oil-burning and electric equipment for coal-burning equipment could be made, so that the 25 per cent reduction in coal-burning freight mileage did not lead to quite the same proportionate reduction in use of rail transport.

3. Substitutability: 7. As with the movement of manufacturers' inputs, the fact that almost two weeks had passed during which rail service had been curtailed permitted a more effective use of substitute methods of transporting finished products than in the key strike of spring, 1946.

The urgency rating for manufacturers' use of freight services for outputs is higher than that for inputs; therefore, we adopt it as the rating for the category as a whole.

Number affected: 116.5

Total employees in manufacturing numbered 15,531,000 as of February, 1948. Estimating that 50 per cent of these work in firms relying on railroad freight services, and that 50 per cent of this figure depend on coal-burning freight (a figure reduced from 1946 because of increasing dieselization), we obtain 3,882,750 employees affected. With two dependents each, this gives 11,648,250 persons.

V. Direct Suppliers. Score: 11.7

The use of the twenty-ninth day for rating purposes makes dependency (without respect to recoverability) and stock effects for the following categories lower than in the forty-day spring, 1939, and spring, 1946, strikes but higher than in the sixteen-day fall, 1946, strike. Tighter demand and supply conditions in the economy make recoverability lower than in the spring, 1939, strike and roughly comparable to recoverability in the fall, 1946, strike.

A. Coal-hauling railroads. Score: 10.5

Urgency rating: 2.14

Market necessity 2.8 (dependency 40 per cent, recoverability 30 per cent), stock effect 8.5, substitutability 9

Number affected: 4.9

In 1948 expenditures were $1,179,833,757, which, divided by the 1950 railroad employment divisor of $7197 and adjusted for dependents, gives 491,802 persons affected, or 4.9.

B. Suppliers of electric power. Score: .1

Urgency rating: .588

Market necessity 1.2 (dependency 30 per cent, recoverability 60 per cent), stock effect 7, substitutability 7

Number affected: .22

Estimated 1948 expenditures were $98,817,545, which, divided by the 1950 electric and gas divisor of $13,367 and adjusted for dependents, gives 22,179, or .22.

C. Suppliers of machinery and equipment. Score: .o

Urgency rating: .098

Market necessity 1.75 (dependency 70 per cent, recoverability 75 per cent), stock effect .8, substitutability 7

Number affected: .23

Estimated 1948 expenditures are $100,270,659, which divided by the 1950 iron and steel employment divisor of $12,956 and adjusted for dependents, gives 23,217, or .23.

D. Suppliers of other materials. Score: .2

Urgency rating: .315

Market necessity 3.15 (dependency 70 per cent, recover-ability 55 per cent), stock effect 2.5, substitutability 4

Number affected: .73

Estimated 1948 expenditures are $349,600,387, which, divided by the 1950 general manufacturing divisor of $14,404 and adjusted for dependents, gives 72,813, or .73.

E. Suppliers of goods and services to employees. Score: .9

Urgency rating: .384

Market necessity 1.6 (dependency 40 per cent, recoverability 60 per cent), stock effect 3, substitutability 8

Number affected: 2.25

Wages spent on goods and services in 1948 (estimated as two-thirds of pay roll) were $1,063,673,906, which, divided by the 1950 retail trade divisor of $14,181 and adjusted for dependents, gives 225,021, or 2.25.

VI. Indirect Suppliers. Score: 15.9

One-fifth of the total scores for categories III, IV, and V.

VII. Nonparty Members of the Struck Unit. Score: 4.4

A. Nonstriking employees. Score: 2.3

Urgency rating: 2.5

After twenty-eight days without production of coal only an estimated 30 per cent of nonstriking employees would have been retained or would have found other jobs. A slight tapering off of the demand for coal made post-strike expansion of output by the bituminous industry easier, and to some extent, therefore, improved the chances for recovery of nonstrikers' losses (65 per cent, in contrast to 60 per cent for the strike of the preceding fall).

Number affected: .9

About 30,000 nonstriking employees were involved in this strike; with dependents, 90,000.

B. Families of strikers. Score: 2.1

Urgency rating: .32

This estimates the loss of income to members of strikers' households, after allowing for the chances of securing temporary work elsewhere and of recovering some portion of strike losses. It will be remembered that nonrecoverable losses are reduced by 90 per cent to take account of the intimate relationship of this group with the strikers themselves.

Number affected: 6.4

Two dependents for each of 320,000 strikers.

Recapitulation of Spring, 1948, Strike Effects

Direct consumers	0.0
Indirect consumers	1.0
Direct-user producers	37.5
Indirect-user producers	30.2
Direct suppliers	11.7
Indirect suppliers	15.9
Nonparty members of struck unit	4.4
	100.7 (or 101 when rounded)

Strike of Winter, 1949-1950

The strike of winter, 1949-1950, was really a sequence of stoppages with varying degrees of the bituminous industry's facilities involved. From September 19 to October 3 all sections of the country were involved, but after October 3 only the area east of the Mississippi. From November 9 through November 30 there was a nearly complete resumption of operations. From December 5 to February 6 the majority of mines were limited to one or two days of actual coal extraction, and during January many of these mines were shut down completely by "wildcat" strikes. From February 6 to March 5 the stoppage was again nearly industry-wide. We have combined the fifty-one days of the September 19-November 9 period and the ninety-five days of the December 1-March 5 period to form one 146-day "partial" strike.

This strike occurred during a period of high and expanding activity in the economy at large but of severely declining activity in the bituminous industry. The unusually large size of the over-all bituminous stocks at the beginning of the strike and the replenishment of them permitted by partial operation of the industry's facilities delayed for a long time the onset of many of the effects to be expected from bituminous strikes. The strike was characterized by relatively little rationing action by the federal government (only restrictions on use of railroad services were imposed) but by considerable drastic action on the part of state and local governments in the form of restrictions on coal deliveries and use of electric power.

Effects have been rated as of the 145th day (Friday, March 3), which was the last weekday of the strike.

The total rating is 492.

I. Direct Consumers. Score: 281.8

    A. Residences. Score: 247

        Urgency rating: .49

          1. Cultural necessity: 7. In March every state has a normal average temperature under 65° except Florida and requires heat. For all states in the major bituminous-using areas, average temperatures are below 44°, and for early March even lower. This compares with a cultural necessity of 8 for December in the fall, 1946, strike.

          2. Stock effect: 1. Shortages of residence coal were more widespread than in any other rated strike. Stringent rationing programs were instituted in New York City, Detroit, Des Moines, and Muncie, for example. Householders were given wood from city parks in a few locations. The situation was said to be "critical and desperate" in ten states. A 10 per cent cut in the consumption of coal appears conservative.

          3. Substitutability: 7. Auxiliary small heaters were useful primarily in the southern states, but these are not the principal bituminous users. Small space heaters are less effective to heat houses that have previously been chilled by conservation of fuel. Substitutability is higher than for spring, 1946, but lower than for fall, 1946.

        Number affected: 504.

        The number affected is the same as in the fall, 1946, strike since here, as there, normal temperatures were such that bituminous users in all regions would have required heat.

    B. Places of assembly. Score: 34.8

        Urgency rating: .48

          1. Cultural necessity: 6. The same considerations apply as for residences. Places of assembly can close altogether, but deferrability of school assemblies, for example, is low after several weeks of closing.

          2. Stock effect: 1. There were many more reports of school

closings than in any other rated strike. State colleges in Illinois, public schools in Buffalo, Chicago, Indianapolis, and St. Louis suspended. It was estimated that 250,000 students were out of school on this day. An Iowa school was using corncobs for fuel. A cut of 10 per cent in coal consumption seems probable.

3. Substitutability: 8. As in fall, 1946, the advantage over residences of greater use of "switchable" equipment is offset by inability to make use of small space heaters.

Number affected: 72.5.

Approximately the same number of bituminous users would have required heat as in fall, 1946.

II. Indirect Consumers. Score: 68.2

A 25 per cent reduction in railroad freight locomotive mileage had been effective for twenty-three days, but essentials were given priority, stocks of goods acted as a buffer, and there is no evidence of a consumer effect. By the 145th day, a 33⅓ per cent cut in passenger service had been operative for fifty-five days, except that for the last twenty-three days the reduction was 50 per cent. In this instance commuters were affected; most of the additional decrease in locomotive mileage was achieved in suburban and branch lines. Thus total, not only long-distance, passenger traffic is rated here.

Domestic electricity consumption was reduced by 50 per cent in the Pittsburgh area. Other areas may have been affected of which we have no knowledge.

A. Passenger railroad traffic. Score: 1.6

Urgency rating: .073

1. Cultural necessity: 7.3. Importance of travel for persons wishing, for the first time during the curtailment, to make long-distance trips on the day of rating is the same as for first-time travelers in the other strikes, namely, 4. Importance of travel to long-distance passengers whose desire to travel on the day of rating is a carry-over of thwarted attempts on previous days is assumed to have risen to 8 by the fifty-fifth day.

Because of its regular and periodic nature, a commuter's need for travel on a particular day is generally not carried over to a following day—the need rises anew each day and, satisfied or not, disappears at the end of the day. But the need on any one day is greater the longer has been the period during which transport services have been lacking. For those who commuted in order to get to places of work, the daily need for transport in order to acquire income would probably have reached a maximum after six weeks of no transport and no income, and would have remained at this level through the fifty-fifth day. Need for transport for shopping, social, or recreational purposes would on the fifty-fifth day still have been less. For commuters as a group, the cultural necessity of transport on the fifty-fifth day would probably average 9.

With the rating for each group weighted by the number affected in each group, the average cultural necessity rating is 7.3.

2. Stock effect: .5. In December, 1949, 26 per cent of total passenger car miles was attributable to coal-burning locomotion. A 50 per cent cut in coal-burning traffic therefore produced only a 13 per cent reduction in total passenger car mileage, a reduction very similar to that of the spring and fall, 1946, strikes. The same 5 per cent reduction in passenger travel is therefore assumed.

3. Substitutability: 2. Because circumstances of weather and opportunity for organization of alternative forms of transport are similar to those prevailing in the spring, 1948, strike, but the inclusion of commuters in our "number affected" base brings in a category of travelers for whom private transportation (car pools) is particularly feasible, substitutability becomes 2 (in comparison with 3 for spring, 1948).

Number affected: 21.6

The seasonal difference between December, the last "normal" month, and March is so great that it seems best to use passenger traffic figures for March, 1949. Total noncommutation passenger traffic during that month amounted to 18,814,891 or a daily average of 606,932, which we take as an estimate of the number of persons who had originally scheduled long-distance trips for the fifty-fifth day of the curtailment and the number who had wanted to travel for each of the preceding days. The total number of long-distance travelers affected throughout the previous fifty-four days was thus 32,774,328. We estimate that by the fifty-fifth day about 2 per cent of these "carry-overs," or 655,487, still desired to travel at the first opportunity and must thus be classed as "affected" on the day of rating. Total commuter traffic during the month amounted to 27,966,577 or a daily average of 902,148, which we take as an estimate of the number of rail commuters requiring transport on the fifty-fifth day. The total for all three groups is 2,164,567.

B. Residential users of electricity in the Pittsburgh area. Score: 66.6

  Urgency rating: 4.5

  1. Cultural necessity: 9.5. For most household uses electricity is neither dispensable nor deferrable.
  2. Stock effect: 5. On this day electricity furnished to residences had been cut by 50 per cent.
  3. Substitutability: 9.5. Battery-run torches and candles are not generally satisfactory for lighting; there are no adequate substitutes for powering appliances.

  Number affected: 14.8

  At the end of 1949, the Duquesne Light Company reported 332,063 residential customers with one family per meter; the Census of Housing figure of 3.78 occupants per dwelling would give 1,256,198 persons on one-family meters. In addition, there were 22,514 multiple-dwelling customers, with more than one family per meter; a conservative estimate would be ten persons per meter in such units, or 225,140, for a total of 1,481,338.

III. Direct-User Producers. Score: 53.0

  A. Basic steel industry. Score: 18.2

    Urgency rating: 1.04

    1. Market necessity: 5.2. Cuts in steel output did not occur until around the 120th day. By the 134th day output had fallen by 12.5 per cent, on the day of rating (145th) by 20 per cent. Thus there was a fairly gradual fall of 20 per cent over a period of twenty-five days. We estimate that as of the 145th day probably about 65 per cent of basic steel employment was dependent on coal or substitutes for it. The high level of operations in the steel industry made recoverability

(within the ensuing six months) low—perhaps about 20 per cent.

2. Stock effect: 2.1. Coal consumption had declined by an estimated 21 per cent.

3. Substitutability: 9.5.

Number affected: 17.5

In January, 1950, there was a total of 584,800 employees in basic steel; with two dependents each, 1,754,400 or 17.5.

B. Coal-burning railroads. Score: 18.3

Urgency rating: 1.34

1. Production necessity: 6.4. By the day of rating passenger cuts of 33⅓ per cent had been in effect for fifty-five days, passenger cuts of 50 per cent and freight cuts of 25 per cent for twenty-three days. Thus dependency would be higher than for any of the other strikes, probably as high as 80 per cent. Twenty per cent recoverability is allowed.

2. Stock effect: 3. The 50 per cent cut in passenger locomotive mileage and the 25 per cent cut in freight locomotive mileage involve equivalent reductions in coal consumption. In December, 1949 (December figures are used because continuing dieselization requires use of the latest figures) 828,-736 tons of coal, almost entirely bituminous, were used in road passenger service and 3,521,392 tons in road freight service. A reduction of 50 per cent in the former and 25 per cent in the latter amounts to a total decrease in consumption of 1,284,716 tons, or 30 per cent below normal use.

3. Substitutability: 7

Number affected: 13.68

In December, 1949, coal-burning mileage was about 38 per cent of all railroad train miles. We assume the same ratio for employees, and allow two dependents for each, for a total of 1,368,000.

C. Electric power. Score: .165

Urgency rating: .05

1. Production necessity: 5. In the spring, 1946, strike, power curtailments had been occurring for ten days prior to the day of rating, and for about thirteen days prior to the day of rating in the fall, 1946, strike. In this strike, reductions in the output of power had been made for about three weeks

prior to the day of rating. Thus we assume that as of the 145th day dependency was greater than in any of the other bituminous strikes—perhaps 80 per cent. Again we assume that electric plants will be able to expand output to fill all the potentially deferrable demand, consisting of about 75 per cent of total demand, permitting actual recovery of perhaps 50 per cent of this amount.

2. Stock effect: .2. Although there were no federal curtailment programs, compulsory and voluntary dimouts in Chicago, Lansing, Peoria, New York State, Illinois, and outright cuts to industrial and commercial users in Illinois, Jamestown, Pittsburgh, and to residences in Pittsburgh meant a decline in the consumption of coal by the electricity-supplying companies of at least 2 per cent.

3. Substitutability: 5. Greater than in 1946 because of increased use of convertible generating equipment.

Number affected: 3.3

Approximately the same number as in fall, 1946.

D. Manufacturers and processing plants using bituminous coal for heat and power. Score: 16.3

Urgency rating: .134

1. Production necessity: 4.8. Dependency on coal supplies is estimated to have been 80 per cent and recoverability 40 per cent, as in the spring, 1946, strike.

2. Stock effect: .4. Cuts in coal consumption were somewhat less than in spring, 1946.

3. Substitutability: 7

Number affected: 121.7

In January, 1950, there were 13,997,000 workers in all manufacturing. Of these approximately 29 per cent were dependent on bituminous coal for heat and power. With two dependents each, a total of 12,177,390 was affected.

IV. Indirect-User Producers. Score: 54

The curtailment of steel output came late in the strike; until February the industry had been running at 95 per cent of capacity. Hence, even on the 145th day of the strike there is no evidence that users of steel were measurably affected by the 20 per cent decline in steel that had occurred by that date, and we do not rate them.

A. Manufacturers using freight services of coal-burning railroads.

Score: 31.8

Urgency rating: .336

Transportation of inputs (urgency rating: .204)

1. Production necessity: 6.8. Here a 25 per cent cut in coal-burning freight traffic had been in effect for three weeks instead of two weeks, as in the spring, 1948, strike. We estimate that this fact raises dependency to 85 per cent. Recoverability is about 20 per cent.
2. Stock effect: .5. The reduction in coal-burning freight traffic probably led to self-rationing, reducing the volume of manfacturers' inputs by about 5 per cent.
3. Substitutability: 6. As in spring, 1948, somewhat improved over spring, 1946, as the passage of twenty-three days permitted a more effective use of such alternative forms of transport as were available.

Transportation of outputs (urgency rating: .336)

1. Production necessity: 2.4. The three-week 25 per cent curtailment in coal-burning freight service had probably created something like a 30 per cent dependency. Recoverability is 20 per cent.
2. Stock effect: 2. As in spring, 1948, the reduction in coal-burning freight mileage was 25 per cent, and the more intensive use of remaining coal-burning service was offset by restrictions on shipments over dieselized and electrified lines interconnecting with coal-burning systems. But substitution of non-coal-burning equipment would have been easier in 1950 than in 1948 because of greater use of such equipment. Thus the decline in consumption of rail services would have been slightly less.
3. Substitutability: 7. Again, improved over spring, 1946, because of the greater time to organize alternative means of transport.

    Since the urgency rating for transport of outputs is greater than that for inputs we adopt it as the rating for the category as a whole.

Number affected: 94.7

    In December, 1949, there were 14,031,000 employees in all manufacturing operations. Assuming one-half to be dependent on railroad freight services, and as of December,

1949, 45 per cent of these to depend on coal-burning transport, 3,156,975 employees were affected, with two dependents each.

B. Pittsburgh users of electric power. Score: 22.2

Urgency rating: 2.04

1. Production necessity: 5.1. By the day of rating these cuts had been in effect for two weeks, twice as long as the Illinois cuts in the spring, 1946, strike. We estimate dependency after two weeks at 85 per cent, recoverability at 40 per cent.
2. Stock effect: 5. By the 145th day industrial and commercial consumption of electricity in the Pittsburgh area had been reduced by 50 per cent.
3. Substitutability: 8. In respect to availability of substitutes, Pittsburgh users would have been in approximately the same position as were Illinois users in spring, 1946.

Number affected: 10.9

Allegheny and Beaver counties were affected, with 427,354 employees in manufacturing, retail, wholesale trade, and service establishments, who were employed in companies purchasing an estimated 85 per cent of their power from utilities. The same proportion of employees is assumed to have been affected (363,251), with two dependents each.

V. Direct Suppliers. Score: 9.3

This was not a "total" strike, with all or almost all of the bituminous industry shut down for 145 days. Varying amounts of capacity had been operating for various periods of time throughout the 145 days. Hence market necessity and curtailment of output are not higher than in much shorter strikes. Numbers affected are approximately as in the three immediately preceding strikes.

A. Railroads hauling bituminous coal. Score: 9.2

Urgency rating: 1.87

1. Market necessity: 2.6. As suggested above, there had been .up to the day of rating some continuation of purchases of railroad services for hauling of currently mined coal as well as for hauling mine-head stocks. Hence dependency on the day of rating would be relatively low, perhaps as low as 35 per cent. Despite the opportunity for expanding bituminous output in make-up operations, recoverability was relatively low for railroads (25 per cent), particularly because of a shortage of coal cars.

    2. Stock effect: 8. On the 145th day, continuing purchases of hauling services are estimated at 20 per cent.

    3. Substitutability: 9

    Number affected: 4.9

B. Suppliers of electric power. Score: .0

    Urgency rating: .14

        Market necessity .4 (dependency 20 per cent, recoverability 80 per cent), stock effect 5, substitutability 7

    Number affected: .22

C. Suppliers of machinery and equipment. Score: .0

    Urgency rating: .028

        Market necessity .4 (dependency 40 per cent, recoverability 90 per cent), stock effect .1, substitutability 7

    Number affected: .23

D. Suppliers of other materials. Score: .0

    Urgency rating: .06

        Market necessity 3 (dependency 50 per cent, recoverability 40 per cent), stock effect .5, substitutability 4

    Number affected: .73

E. Suppliers of goods and services to employees. Score: .1

    Urgency rating: .048

        Market necessity .6 (dependency 30 per cent, recoverability 80 per cent), stock effect 1, substitutability 8

    Number affected: 2.25

VI. Indirect Suppliers. Score: 23.3

One-fifth of the total for III, IV, and V.

VII. Nonparty Members of the Struck Unit. Score: 2.5

A. Nonstriking employees. Score: 1.3

    Urgency rating: 1.4

        Over the preceding 144 days the output of the mines shut down on the day of rating had fluctuated greatly. During the immediately preceding four weeks, however, no output at all had been forthcoming. Therefore, probably about 70 per cent of their nonstriking employees were idle on the day of rating, having no employment in either the bituminous or other industries. Because activity in the coal industry at this time was extremely sluggish, perhaps as much as 80 per cent of the strike losses could have been recaptured in the next six months.

Number affected: 9.4

An estimated 31,450 nonstrikers were involved; with two dependents each, 94,350.

B. Families of strikers. Score: 1.2

Urgency rating: .18

After deductions for alternative employment and recoverability (including the allowance for the closeness of the tie between nonparty and party, in this category), the urgency rating is .18.

Number affected: 6.8

On the day of rating about 340,000 were on strike. If each had two dependents, the number involved in the families of strikers was 680,000.

Recapitulation of Winter, 1949-1950, Strike Effects

Direct consumers	281.8
Indirect consumers	68.2
Direct-user producers	53.0
Indirect-user producers	54.0
Direct suppliers	9.3
Indirect suppliers	23.3
Nonparty members of struck unit	2.5
	492.1 (or 492 when rounded)

The remaining six peacetime bituminous strikes during the 1939-1952 period have several characteristics in common. In none of them was there any evidence of hardship on consumers, direct or indirect, or on indirect producer-users. Persons employed in the basic steel industry were affected as direct producers, except in the spring, 1949, strike. Thus except for basic steel employees, the only members of the public significantly affected by the six minor strikes were suppliers—direct, indirect, and nonparty members of the coal industry itself.

The methods and data used for rating the minor strikes are identical with those used for the major strike ratings. The resulting component scores and total rating for each of the minor strikes are summarized in Table 2.

What conclusions can be drawn from the ratings of the eleven bituminous strikes? The most obvious one is that the strikes differed greatly in the degree to which they affected members of the public. The most affecting strike (winter, 1949-1950, rating of 492) had al-

TABLE 2. RELATIVE EFFECTS OF SIX MINOR BITUMINOUS STRIKES

Strike	Day of Rating	Total Rating (rounded)	Component Scores						
			Direct Consumers	Indirect Consumers	Direct Producer-Users	Indirect Producer-Users	Direct Suppliers	Indirect Suppliers	Nonparty Suppliers in Coal
Spring, 1941	30th	26	—	—	6.7	—	11.2	3.6	4.2
Fall, 1941	7th	10	—	—	.2	—	6.0	1.2	2.8
Spring, 1947	13th	23	—	—	6.9	—	9.0	3.2	4.2
Summer, 1947	19th	34	—	—	14.8	—	10.1	5.0	4.4
Spring, 1949	13th	10	—	—	—	—	5.8	1.2	2.5
Summer, 1949	7th	12	—	—	3.7	—	4.6	1.7	2.3

most fifty times the impact of the least affecting strikes (spring, 1949, fall, 1941, ratings of 10).

As Table 3 indicates, there is no very close correlation between the severity of effects and the duration of a bituminous strike. It is true that the most public-affecting strike was the longest; one of the least public-affecting was as short as any rated; the four least public-affecting were the four shortest strikes. But of the two "forty-day" strikes, those of spring, 1946, and spring, 1939, the impact of the former was more

TABLE 3. SEVERITY AND DURATION OF ELEVEN BITUMINOUS STRIKES

Strike	Total Rating	Duration (Day of Rating)
Winter, 1949-1950	492	145
Spring, 1946	338	40
Fall, 1946	306	16
Spring, 1948	101	29
Spring, 1939	62	41
Summer, 1947	34	19
Spring, 1941	26	30
Spring, 1947	23	13
Summer, 1949	12	7
Fall, 1941	10	7
Spring, 1949	10	13

than five times greater than that of the latter. Of the two "thirty-day" strikes, those of spring, 1948, and spring, 1941, the former was almost four times more injurious to the public than the latter. The two thirteen-day strikes show the same lack of correlation; the rating of one was twice that of the other. The sixteen-day strike of fall, 1946, though less than half as lengthy, was almost five times as affecting as the spring, 1939, strike. Thus beyond the fact that very long strikes are almost certain to produce severer effects than are very short strikes, duration does not appear to be a significant variable respecting the relative impact of bituminous strikes.[2]

This finding is not surprising since, as was pointed out in Chapter 2, duration has no determining influence of its own. Differences in

[2] A word of caution is advisable here. We have spoken of "the impact of a forty-day strike," and "the effects on the public of a sixteen-day strike," and so on. Such expressions, while almost necessary for exposition, are not, strictly speaking, accurate. For greater precision we should refer to the impact of the fortieth day of a strike, or the effects of the sixteenth day of a strike, since we have here rated only the "real costs" of a single day. The looser expression would be accurate only if we took into account all that had transpired on days of the strike previous to the day rated.

length of bituminous strikes are significant only because they have some influence on such actual determining factors as the dispensability and deferrability of the services of bituminous coal or things made from it, the size of bituminous stocks and of stocks of goods depending on coal, the availability of substitutes for coal and the products or services which rely on coal, the possibility of making up later for the loss of output. It is variations in these actual determining factors which cause variations in the impact of bituminous strikes.

The great difference in the repercussions of the fortieth day of the spring, 1939, and spring, 1946, strikes can be explained largely by two facts. First, though initial stock-consumption ratios were roughly the same in both strikes, a much larger portion of the bituminous industry remained operating during the 1939 strike, providing much greater subsequent additions to the original stocks. The widespread layoffs in user industries which characterized the later stoppage were thus avoided in the earlier one. Second, in 1939 the bituminous industry and its user and supplier industries were operating under conditions where demand for their products was insufficient to absorb, at current prices, all their capital equipment and work forces. This meant that much of the loss of employment and income was merely a concentration in time of unemployment and loss of income which would have occurred in any case. The 1946 strike, on the other hand, occurred during reconversion when the capital equipment and labor attached to the industries in question were hardly sufficient to meet the product demand existing at current prices. Thus not all the employment, income, and consumption lost during 1946 would have been lost in the absence of a strike, and because of the lack of excess capacity could not be fully recaptured by make-up operations following the strike.

Comparable circumstances explain most of the differences in impact between the thirteen-day spring, 1947, and spring, 1949, strikes. In neither were the effects on users severe, but steel stock-consumption ratios at the beginning of the 1947 strike were apparently low enough to force a small contraction in steel output, whereas the higher ratios prevailing during the 1949 strike permitted steel production to continue without perceptible decline. Much of the contrast in the total ratings, however, stems from the differential impact of these two strikes on suppliers. With user and supplier industries and especially the bituminous industry itself utilizing a greater percentage of its capacity in 1947 than in 1949 there was less opportunity for suppliers to recapture in the period following the strike the employment and income lost during the strike.

Differences between the two "thirty-day" strikes of spring, 1941, and spring, 1948, can be attributed solely to their differential influence on users, since the direct effects of both strikes on suppliers were almost identical. (Indirect supplier ratings differ, of course, since they reflect conditions in the user industries.) The underlying reason for the difference in effects on users is not readily apparent, since the available data suggest that initial stock-consumption ratios were not significantly dissimilar, but the immediate causes are clear. By the twenty-ninth day of the spring, 1948, strike utilization of basic steel capacity had fallen by about 23 per cent, and 25 per cent reductions in railroad passenger and freight service had been in effect for some time. On the same day of the spring, 1941, stoppage utilization of steel capacity had fallen only about 5 per cent and there had been no reported reductions in railroad service.

It will be recalled that analysis of the spring, 1946, strike in Chapter 5 revealed that the effects of that strike on producers had been proportionately much greater than on consumers, and proportionately greater on users than on suppliers, and that a higher proportion of the effects measured had been indirect rather than direct effects. Do the scores for the other ten coal strikes show the same relationships?

In all the strikes rated except one the influences on producers exceeded those on consumers. The exception is the top-ranking strike of winter, 1949-1950, in which the severe impact on household consumers dominated the rating. In general, the quantitative analyses demonstrate a rough direct correlation between relative size of consumer effects and total severity of effects. Consumer effects exceeded those on producers only in the highest rated strike, when they constituted a little more than 70 per cent of the total score. In the other major strikes (those with ratings of from 338 to 62) they contributed from 44 per cent to less than 1 per cent to the total rating. In all of the minor strikes (those with ratings of from 34 to 10) measurable consumer effects were zero.

The proposition that effects on users (both household and industrial) proportionately outweigh influence on suppliers still holds for major strikes. Relative shares contributed by user effects ranged from 93 per cent in the most-affecting winter, 1949-1950, strike to 68 per cent and 73 per cent, respectively, for the spring, 1948, and spring, 1939, strikes, which were least affecting of the major strikes. But for all of the minor strikes supplier effects were dominant, and bore a rough inverse correlation to total severity of effects. The least affecting of all the strikes, those of spring, 1949, and fall, 1941, show a contribution of supplier effects amounting to 100 and 98 per cent, respectively. This result is attributable to two circumstances: First, in strikes of brief duration coal-hauling railroads—because so specialized to the industry's operations—are more immediately affected than any other group except nonparty members, and second, the latter group (nonstrikers, their families, and the families of strikers) feel the weight of a coal stoppage even when others outside the industry do not.

The spring, 1946, strike is revealed as unique in its preponderance of indirect effects. In all of the other strikes direct effects constitute a major share of total effects. But again one can discern something of a correlation between importance of indirect effects and over-all severity of effects. With the exception of the spring, 1939, stoppage, indirect effects were responsible for 30 per cent or more of the total effects of the major strikes. They supplied less than 15 per cent of the total effects of all the minor strikes.

In so far as the eleven bituminous strikes rated are representative of the bituminous strikes which may occur in the future and in so far as our rating procedures have validity, we may, then, expect the following conditions to prevail in future bituminous strikes: Except in unusual cases, the greater part of the burden on the public will be in the form of loss of employment and income by producers rather than in the form of consumer hardship. Indirect effects—the consequence of the close integration of American industry—will bulk larger as the strike takes hold. Primary concern with the fate of consumers would thus be misplaced. In minor strikes most of the burden will be concentrated on suppliers through loss of the markets provided by the bituminous industry; the deprivation of bituminous products and bituminous-using products will be less important.

These conclusions apply only to coal. The pattern disclosed may have no relevance to stoppages in other industries. To gain further insight into the impact of strikes on the public we must look for patterns in other sectors of the economy. We turn next to railroads.

NOTE

Results of another study of the effects of bituminous coal strikes have recently been published (Irving Bernstein and Hugh G. Lovell, "Are Coal Strikes National Emergencies?," *Industrial and Labor Relations Review*, Vol. 6 (1953), pp. 352-367). The authors studied ten bituminous strikes which occurred between 1937 and 1950, and undertook to discover whether any had created a "national emergency." They concluded that none did. "In fact, seven . . . strikes had no serious effect at all. Only the two 1946 strikes and the stoppage of 1949-1950 reached the threshold of emergency." Although our study has not attempted to rule on the question of what constitutes a national emergency strike, our findings seem to show that the impact of the major bituminous strikes has been greater than is suggested by the Bernstein-Lovell conclusions. There are several reasons for the differences in results.

The only effects which Bernstein and Lovell assess by systematic quantitative analysis are those on coal, steel, electrical power, general industrial output, freight rail traffic, and department stores sales. The data which they use for these sectors of the economy are *averages* for the whole nation, some taken over periods of time of as long as several months. Such averaging of effects over time conceals the maximum declines in outputs caused by coal strikes; our studies suggest that it is the depth and timing of these maximum declines which most significantly determine the amount of idleness that results from coal strikes. Confining the quantitative analysis to national series also obscures the very severe impact which bituminous strikes may have. The main effects of bituminous strikes tend to fall on consumers, user-producers, and suppliers in the eastern and northern parts of the nation; use of indices which reflect the fortunes of members of the public in little- or non-affected areas understates the strike effects when some minimum level of "hardship" is made the condition for considering any effects at all.

Moreover, no mention is made of the impact on manufacturing and processing plants using coal for heat and power, on steel-using firms (other than automobile manufacturers), on suppliers of goods and services to the bituminous industry (other than coal-hauling railroads), on indirect suppliers, or on nonstriking employees of bituminous firms and members of strikers' families, effects which account, for example, for almost 50 percent of the total effects in our rating of the Spring 1946 strike. In general, the authors seen to neglect supplier effects and indirect effects, and to some extent their attention is focussed on consumer effects at the expense of producer effects.

The most significant difference between the two studies, however, lies not in the use of statistics but in the basic concepts which are employed. As the title of their article suggests, Bernstein and Lovell are concerned only with strikes which create *national emergencies,* a designation which is reserved for those stoppages which actually impose "hardship rather than inconvenience" and whose impact is national rather than local.

No matter how many persons may be subjected to extreme inconvenience for extended periods of time, according to Bernstein and Lovell a strike does not create an *emergency* until suffering and elemental privation are actually experienced. All effects falling short of such an actual hardship level are dropped out of calculation. In this study we have treated the need for goods or income as a continuum; we conceive the urgency of such needs as varying continuously from a very low degree to a very high degree, and no effects are dropped out because they have not met some minimum (but uncertain) test of severity.

Bernstein and Lovell also set stringent conditions on what constitutes a *national* emergency. The number of localities in which hardship occurs must be "so numerous and so serious as to constitute together a national danger." One of the main characteristics of a bituminous strike, however, is, as we have emphasized, the unevenness of its effects on industries and localities. Half a dozen communities may be very badly off indeed, while the rest of the nation is relatively unaffected, yet even should these cities (hypothetically) be reduced to want and privation, according to Bernstein and Lovell these would constitute only scattered local incidences of the strike, despite the fact that only federal authorities can take such action as is necessary to mitigate their suffering. It would seem, then, that the authors construe "national emergency" to mean something like "general economic paralysis."

We wholly agree that none of the bituminous strikes here examined created a national emergency in this restricted sense. By a definition as limited as this, it would be possible to rule out of the classification virtually every strike on record. Perhaps no more than two or three, if that many, in all our national history, would qualify for the distinction—a distinction obviously without significance since neither public criticism nor legislative action concerning strikes has proceeded on so narrow a view.

In this study we have not been concerned with classifying strikes in terms of whether or not they created conditions loosely identified by some designation such as "national emergency." Indeed, we are inclined to believe that that term has no significance other than to provide a convenient label to justify public intervention in such strikes as the Administration—on whatever grounds—has decided that intervention is called for or to be invoked to satisfy the terms of federal legislation which itself provides no suitable administrative guides. In this investigation we have sought to identify and quantify *all* the major effects following from a strike in order to provide some indication of the relative impact of *any* strike.

CHAPTER 7

When Trains Don't Run: Rail's Publics

WHAT happens when railroad service is halted by a labor dispute? The answer is given by an examination of four stoppages in the period 1946-1951. Again we cut across strike lines to obtain a composite impression of the weight of a rail strike on the various groups which compose rail's publics.[1]

The May 23-25, 1946, strike of engineers and trainmen was nation-wide and probably achieved as nearly a complete cessation of railroad services as can be secured, but it lasted for only forty-eight hours. The firemen's five-lines strike of May 10-16, 1950, and the switchmen's "sickness" stoppage of January 30-February 8, 1951, halted only a portion of total railway traffic, but these partial stoppages lasted for seven and ten days respectively. Although the "mistaken" May 18, 1946, stoppage of engineers and trainmen occurred in a hit-and-miss manner and lasted only for several hours, the fact that it managed nevertheless to affect perceptibly a considerable number of persons makes a few items regarding its effects worth inclusion in this survey.

Character of the Strikes

The 1946 nation-wide strike became effective on Thursday, May 23, at 4:00 P.M. in each time zone. The striking unions barred their members from service on all trains departing after this hour, except those in exempted categories, and on all trains already under way at 4:00 P.M. after they had been driven into the first terminal point.

Nevertheless, a few trains moved throughout the strike. The unions permitted members to operate milk trains, military troop and hos-

---

[1] Unless otherwise noted, all factual material regarding these strikes has been taken from issues of the *New York Times*, supplemented by some materials from the *New York Herald-Tribune* and the *New Haven Register*. In most cases the issue is that of the day following the date to which the information pertains.

pital trains, and trains belonging to the Illinois Central (whose line at the time of the April strike call was already being operated by the federal government) and to twenty-seven feeder lines. Instances were reported of the post-deadline departure with union crews of trains bound for the home cities of the crews themselves and of three trains whose cancellation would have left 1000 shipyard workers stranded with no feasible alternative transportation. In general, however, the only trains in non-exempted categories which moved were those manned by "volunteer" engineers and trainmen, the volunteers being largely supervisory employees (but, it was reported, also including some "scabbing" members of the striking unions). In the East these crews' efforts were concentrated on keeping in service a few of the "name" express trains, a few commuter trains, and a few freight trains to move essential cargo. On the first day,[2] the Pennsylvania and the Baltimore and Ohio sent a total of at least five long-distance trains out of New York City terminals; at one Pennsylvania suburban station, the stationmaster reported operations "at perhaps 50% of normal, no better." On the second day, thirty long-distance passenger trains entered or left New York City. Lines serving Long Island and New Jersey commuters ran some trains—the much badgered Long Island Railroad astounded everyone by managing to transport (free of charge) 30,000 of its regular 300,000 customers to and from outlying subway stations—but the complete shutdown of the New York Central and New Haven railroads left commuters in Westchester, the Hudson Valley, and Connecticut without any railroad services. In a number of instances essential freight cargo was moved for short distances.

Volunteer efforts, while dramatic, had no appreciable effect. The Association of American Railroads estimated that by the evening of the second day freight traffic was about 1 per cent of normal (about 240 of a normal daily 24,000 trains were moving) and passenger traffic less than 1 per cent of normal (about fifty to seventy-five of a normal daily 17,500 trains were moving, and the majority of these were milk or commuter trains). By the third day the number of passenger trains had risen to 329, of which thirty-six were in exempted categories, but the number of freight trains had fallen to 112.

[2] Although the strike lasted for only forty-eight hours, it stretched across three calendar days. To facilitate use of newspaper material May 23 has been treated as the first day, May 24, the second day, and May 25, the third day.

After the strike ended at around 5:00 P.M. Saturday, May 25, resumption of full services was fairly rapid. The Association of American Railroads announced that normal passenger service had been restored by the close of the first day following the strike, and that restoration of normal freight services would require only two additional days.

On May 10, 1950, union firemen struck the entire systems of the Sante Fe and Southern railroads and the western portions of the New York Central and Pennsylvania systems. Subsequently firemen stopped work on certain portions of the Union Pacific lines. These lines were major carriers of passenger and freight throughout the southern half of the United States from the Atlantic to the Pacific and throughout that populous and industrialized region which is comprised of Illinois, Indiana, Michigan, Ohio, and Pennsylvania and New York west of Harrisburg and Buffalo. Altogether the struck lines (other than the Union Pacific) normally transported 39 per cent of the total passenger traffic and 24 per cent of the total freight traffic in the nation. On the first day of the strike, the Pennsylvania canceled all trains in its strike zone; the other systems operated only a few, the New York Central alone canceling 125 passenger and 300 freight trains. On the third day the Pennsylvania began running a few trains through its strike zone. By the sixth (next to last) day, all lines had increased their freight operations in the struck areas; the Pennsylvania was operating about 4 per cent of the normal number of freight trains.

The 1951 switchmen's stoppage began on January 31, with switchmen in Chicago, Detroit, and St. Louis yards which served sixteen railroads reporting "sick." By the third day forty-two lines in thirty cities were affected; by the fifth day fifty lines in more than a hundred cities. Only 10 per cent of normal freight traffic was moving through Chicago; the New York Central and Pennsylvania had canceled twenty-five express trains and had reduced service on some of their commuter lines by 50 to 100 per cent. By the seventh day the New York Central and New Haven had wholly suspended commuter service into New York City, and some other lines were furnishing only partial service. On the eighth day, switchmen in Eastern cities returned to work; by the ninth (next to last) day, the strike was largely confined to Chicago, St. Louis, and Peoria, which, however, are important junctions. Passenger service was nearly normal throughout the East and South, but freight traffic, according to railway officials, was still in a snarl the unraveling of which would require two to three weeks.

The May 18, 1946, stoppage, which wasn't meant to happen, lasted only three or four hours and because of the nature of the error included only some members of the striking unions, and for the most part only members working on lines operating in the Eastern time zone. (The nation-wide strike originally scheduled to begin at 4:00 P.M. in each time zone had been called off at 3:34 Eastern time, too late for notices to reach eastern district offices of the union.) Nevertheless, the very short, spotty stoppage was sufficient to halt the movement of most commuter and long-distance passenger trains in the regions east of Indiana (for a period of four hours no trains ran on the Long Island Railroad's lines), to leave thousands of travelers stranded, and to stall shipments of perishable freight in Toledo and Chicago. Acute disruption of Eastern traffic lasted for eight hours, and twenty-four hours after the beginning of the stoppage trains coming into New York City from the West were still running two to three hours late.

Persons Affected Through Relationship to Striking Employees

Probably the most authoritative estimate of the total number of railroad employees involved in the 1946 nation-wide strike is 350,000 as given by the Bureau of Labor Statistics.[3] Estimates of the number of striking employees range from 250,000 to 293,000, and since the *New York Times* in early February quoted the engineers' union as saying that there were "over 300,000" union engineers and trainmen, the higher figure is probably more nearly correct. If so, then some 57,000 nonstriking railroad employees were made idle by the walkout. This relatively low figure (in April, 1946, there were some 1,400,000 workers employed on railroads) can be explained by the fact that the strike ended before large-scale layoffs could materialize. If it is assumed that each idle employee (striking and nonstriking) had two dependents, then around 700,000 members of the public (in addition to the 57,000 nonstrikers) were affected through family ties by strike-caused idleness in the railroad industry.

The seven-day May, 1950, firemen's strike, although involving only five lines and only 18,000 striking employees, idled approximately

[3] *Work Stoppages Caused by Labor-Management Disputes in 1946*, Bulletin No. 918.

157,000 nonstriking railway employees[4]—substantially more than in the nation-wide 1946 strike. On the same assumptions made above, 500,000 members of the public were affected by virtue of their non-party relationships to the railway industry. This is only about two-thirds of the number thus affected by the nation-wide 1946 strike, but this smaller number was affected for more than three times as long a period.

The maximum of railroad idleness in the 1951 switchmen's strike came on the fifth day, when some 12,000 striking employees and about 58,000 nonstriking railway employees were involved.[5] No information could be found regarding the number of railway employees involved in the May 18 stoppage.

Although the extent to which loss of wages affects members of idle railway employees' families is undoubtedly influenced, as in bituminous strikes, by the employees' savings position and income expectations and by the continuance or noncontinuance of credit, the relatively short duration of the railway strikes under consideration made these factors less important than they customarily are in coal strikes.

Suppliers of Goods and Services to the Railway Industry

There is little information on the manner in which suppliers of the railway industry have been affected by its strikes. The forty-eight-hour nation-wide strike of 1946 had little effect on the revenues of local merchants or their suppliers, even those specialized to railway employees' markets. The effects on local and national sellers and on total national income of the up-to-seven-days' pay loss for the 175,000 railway employees involved in the May, 1950, firemen's strike or the up-to-ten-days' pay loss for the 70,000 railway employees affected by the 1951 switchmen's stoppage are less certain. During the 1950 strike Altoona's 16,000 idle railway employees represented about two-thirds of the city's total number of wage earners and earned a monthly pay roll of $1,850,000. There and in comparable communities local merchants' revenues might have been perceptibly affected.

Because coal-burning locomotives constitute one of bituminous coal's important markets, the bituminous industry must be affected as a supplier by any strike which is not confined to diesel-powered trains.

[4] U.S. Bureau of Labor Statistics, "Work Stoppages During 1950," *Monthly Labor Review*, May, 1951.

[5] U.S. Bureau of Labor Statistics, "Work Stoppages in 1951," *Monthly Labor Review*, May, 1952.

Since the impact of this temporary loss of markets is delayed through the buffer action of stock-piling, however, it is probable that most of the strike-caused idleness among miners reported *during* the 1950 and 1951 strikes was due to the effects of the strike on the bituminous industry as users of railroad services and that it was the inability of mines to secure transportation of their coal which forced most of the curtailment of coal-extracting operations.

Users of Railway Services and Their Suppliers

How railway strikes affect users of railway services may best be examined by dividing direct users into four categories: (1) commuting passengers; (2) long-distance passengers; (3) shippers of mail, and (4) shippers of express and freight cargo. It will be convenient to discuss along with them the customers and suppliers of these direct users who may be indirectly affected.

Because of the dissimilar characteristics of the product of the railway industry and that of the bituminous industry, some of the major considerations which determine the severity of a strike's effects likewise differ as between the two industries. The size of initial bituminous stocks, both overall and for particular users, has an important influence on the degree to which various members of the public are affected by a bituminous strike; recourse to substitute products is much less important, since the great majority of bituminous users are not able, for technical or economic reasons, to shift quickly to use of anthracite, oil, or gas. In contrast, stock-piling of railroad services is impossible. If forewarned, users may anticipate to some degree the effects of a railway strike by advancing the time of projected journeys, of out-shipments of processed goods, and in-shipments of goods and materials. The ability to make such adjustments is limited at best, however, and for some kinds of traffic—commuter, periodical mail, perishable food—impossible. On the other hand, there exist in the case of railway services alternative means of transportation which may be substituted for railroad services fairly quickly.

The ease with which the various types of railway users are able to shift to alternative forms of transportation has a vital influence on the extent to which they are affected by a given railway strike. Thus commuters living in Los Angeles were especially affected by the nation-wide 1946 strike because it occurred during a metropolitan-area-wide transit strike, halting the last remaining common carriers running into the city. The plight of long-distance travelers stranded in the Eastern zone by the May 18, 1946, strike was intensified by the cancellation due to weather conditions of all flights out of Cleveland and New York City. Since the major portion of Westchester and Connecticut commutation is regularly carried by trains, while the major portion of New Jersey commutation is carried by buses, commuters from the former regions fare worse during a railroad strike since the established facilities to which they may shift are not so plentiful.

Manufacturers and distributors were particularly handicapped during the 1946 nation-wide strike because of a government order requiring trucking and air lines to give priority to essential categories of cargo. The difference in the situations faced by strike-affected railroad users and bituminous users is reflected sharply in the responses of public authorities and of users themselves. In bituminous strikes, both governmental and private efforts are directed almost singly toward conserving bituminous stocks; in railroad strikes, toward securing alternative means of transportation.

Small variations in duration independently influence the degree of effect much more strongly in the case of railroad strikes. If the stock-consumption ratio is fairly high, the effects on users of a two-week industry-wide bituminous strike are not much more severe than the effects of a two-day or one-week strike. But for a given percentage of capacity involved, one would expect a considerable difference in breadth and intensity of user effects as between railroad strikes of two days, seven days, and two weeks. Perishable goods which can survive for a few days spoil if kept longer; stocks of perishable items require frequent replenishment; air, water, and trucking facilities sufficient to handle the emergency needs arising during the first few days of a strike become inadequate for the more general demands of subsequent days, and the differential cost of such transport mounts rapidly (use of trucks and barges to transport materials and goods from and to a San Francisco Ford plant during the 1950 firemen's strike was reported to have quadrupled the plant's transport costs). Statements of a number of manufacturers, distributors, and public authorities, published on the second day of the nation-wide 1946 strike, are indicative of the significance of small variations in duration, even after being discounted for alarmist tendencies. It was said that, though unaffected at present, manufacturing firms both large and small would have to shut down and city populations would face stringent food shortages if the strike lasted for a week, ten days, or two weeks.

The location of the strike is also important. Stoppage of operations in just a few important junctions like Chicago and St. Louis can disrupt traffic over large areas and affect distant users of railroad services, as the 1951 switchmen's strike clearly showed.

1. Commuting Passengers

According to reports of the Interstate Commerce Commission there were in May, 1946, approximately 1,000,000 railroad commuters in the United States. Some 400,000 to 500,000 of these, by *New York Times* and *Herald-Tribune* estimates, regularly commuted into New York City by train, and some 213,000 into Chicago.

In the Eastern time zone the 1946 nation-wide strike went into effect at the time when most commuters would normally be going home from work or shopping (5:00 P.M. daylight time). Having been forewarned, however, many commuters in New York, Boston, and Pittsburgh took earlier trains. This action was facilitated by employers' dismissing them at 3:00 P.M. and by railroads' running extra trains throughout the afternoon. The *Times* estimated that 80 to 85 per cent of New York City area commuters reached their homes before the strike began. The remainder arrived home from forty minutes to three hours late or spent the night in the city. On the second day, about 100,000 regular New York City area commuters stayed home. The remainder reached and left the city by the few trains still running and by buses, subways, taxis, private cars, and even airplanes.

The Long Island Railroad, by means of shuttle trains, managed to transport one-tenth of its regular customers to and from outlying subway stations. Lines serving New Jersey also ran a few commuter trains. Much of the New Jersey traffic, however, was forced to shift to buses. The major short-haul bus lines serving this area estimated that their loads increased by 50 to 80 per cent. One New Jersey line which normally transported a daily 14,000 passengers to and from New York carried an extra 11,000 passengers each way on the second day.

Traveling by bus involved many inconveniences. It was reported that some persons had been forced to rise at dawn to reach their places of work on time, and to leave their places of work several hours early in order to arrive home at a reasonable hour. Although most lines disregarded schedules, sending off buses as fast as they could be brought into service and loaded up, or cutting the usual ten-minute rush-hour headway to three minutes, long waiting periods faced many commuters. One reporter observed waiting lines of 200 to 300 persons during rush hours at a loading point in Jersey City. Once on the bus, as many as half the commuters could expect to stand, since most of the buses on lines to which railroad commuters had shifted left terminals loaded "double" (in violation even of the temporary regulation which had raised the number of permissible standees from 15 to 50 per cent of seated capacity).

Many commuters, sometimes singly but more often in car pools, reached New York on the second day by private automobile. Enough cars made the trip to swamp parking lots at outlying subway stations and seriously to congest main arteries, especially in the areas around the tunnels and bridges which are the only means of approach to Manhattan Island. One observer reported that for hours beyond the usual rush period both morning and evening traffic was so congested on the highways leading to the George Washington Bridge that "a man might have walked for miles from one car top to another." At the same time that cars were piled up around the bridge and around Lincoln Tunnel, little traffic was passing through the Holland Tunnel, owning to an official plea to commuter traffic to reserve the latter for trucks and long-distance buses. Although drivers were urged to leave their cars at the outskirts and take subways into Manhattan, enough drove into the midtown sections to increase traffic there by an estimated 20 per cent, an increment more serious than appears on its face because of the heavy normal traffic conditions.

Enough commuters took subways into New York City, after reaching the outskirts by other means, to increase traffic on them by 40 to 45 per cent, an increase which reportedly was "easily handled." There were a few reports of commuters traveling to Westchester and Connecticut by taxi and of persons patronizing flights to Easthampton, Long Island. At the other end of the luxury scale were the "several dozen'" employees of Wall Street firms who reached their New Jersey homes via extemporaneously solicited rides on trucks and the "considerable" number who hitchhiked to homes on Long Island.

Pressure on substitute forms of transport and inconvenience to the persons forced to use them were considerably less on the third day, since it fell on a Saturday.

How did the nation-wide 1946 strike affect customers and suppliers of railway commuters? The most important category of commuters' customers consists of the employers who hire their services. A survey (taken by a business association) of seventy New York financial institutions, department stores, and manufacturing firms revealed that although 23 per cent of their employees were commuters, absenteeism on the second day averaged only 4½ per cent, although for retail stores alone it averaged 10 per cent. The *Herald-Tribune* reported that absenteeism in advertising agencies, which have an especially large proportion of commuting employees, amounted to 25 to 30 per cent. Though absenteeism was surprisingly low, some firms lost hours of work from employees who arrived late or left early. Many financial firms closed down Thursday night for a long week end; an even larger number, including the New York Stock Exchange (and securities markets in all major cities except Baltimore) canceled Saturday operations.

Among suppliers of commuters, retail stores in New York City suffered "somewhat" during the 1946 strike, but sales of suburban stores increased. The business of New York theaters, restaurants, and night clubs was reported unaffected.

The strike also affected persons who supplied services to railway commuters in their new role of commuters by motorized transport. On the many bus lines which extended rush-hour schedules to midnight, drivers had to work overtime; maintenance men also worked overtime to keep regular and extra buses in running condition. Employees at tunnels and bridges were put on twelve-hour duty, with all leaves canceled. To secure an increase of 66 per cent in the daytime force, an increase considered necessary to handle the augmented traffic flow (and provide extra policing for railroad facilities), all New York City policemen were placed on twelve-hour duty. Midtown parking lots, filled to capacity in normal times, lost revenue because of the displacement of the more profitable short-term business by all-day parking. And the strike affected the other customers of these suppliers: regular bus riders and regular car drivers were inconvenienced by delays, crowding, or shortages of parking space.

In the New York City area the 1951 switchmen's strike was second only to the nation-wide 1946 strike in the extent to which it affected railway commuters. On the fourth day the closing of one line of the New York Central left 50,000 Hudson Valley commuters without rail transport; a cut in the Pennsylvania's New Jersey service of 50 per cent affected commuters in that region. On the sixth day the Pennsylvania restored its New Jersey service, but the New York Central canceled all, and the New Haven some, of its commuter trains, and the resulting shift to motorized transport, as in 1946, swamped the highways leading to Manhattan. When on the seventh day the New Haven, Jersey Central, and Erie commuter lines joined the ranks of the completely shut down, the *Times* estimated that 100,000 New York City area commuters had been deprived of their customary rail transport. On that day during the seventy minutes between 7:50 and 9:00 A.M., 6500 vehicles passed through the toll gates of just one entrance into New York City, and because officials, not foreseeing the increase in traffic, had failed to open extra gates, cars were backed up four miles.

No information was uncovered regarding the effects on commuters of the 1950 firemen's strike other than that on the first day "thousands" of commuters in Pittsburgh and Chicago were affected. Though the May 18, 1946, stoppage was reported to have stranded some New York City area commuters, effects in this respect were minimized by the circumstances that it occurred on Saturday afternoon and that many commuters, knowing that a stoppage had been scheduled, left their places of work or shopping early.

2. *Long-Distance Passengers*

The beginning of the 1946 nation-wide strike, according to newspaper reports, left thousands of long-distance passengers stranded at terminal points throughout the United States. A few of these remained on the stalled trains. It was reported that twenty-eight European war brides had spent the night of May 23 in their Pullman cars and that thirteen passengers had lived in a Pullman car in the Indianapolis yards throughout the strike, attended by a conductor and porter and fed by the dining-car crew. Passengers in the New York City area who sought refuge in hotels had no difficulty in obtaining rooms since their demands were matched by reservations canceled by travelers stranded elsewhere.

Those determined to continue their trips or starting out during the strike turned mainly to buses and airplanes as substitute means of transportation. On the second day, long-distance traffic on Greyhound lines running out of New York City ran 50 to 100 per cent over normal. Capacity of Eastern bus lines, at least, could not be increased quickly enough to handle promptly the augmented demand. Although by use of charter and other buses service was doubled and on some lines tripled, and each vehicle was packed to the limit, thousands of persons were turned away at Manhattan terminals on the second and third days even after the strike was called off. Persons who secured transportation in many cases did so only after considerable inconvenience. The *Times* reported that during the second day a person entering the New York Greyhound terminal could expect to wait three hours before reaching a reservations window and might have to wait six hours more before being able to board a bus.

On the second day the demand for reservations at La Guardia Field was 30 per cent above normal, and because almost all lines were already booked to capacity most of this demand remained unsupplied. Available passenger space on air lines was even reduced in the course of the strike; on the third day 164 passengers were "bumped" at La Guardia Field to make room for mail shipments.

A few travelers made their way across the continent, or portions of it, via the Canadian lines which enter the United States at such points as Seattle, Detroit, and St. Johnsbury, Vermont. One interesting aspect of this strike is that more persons could have traveled by American trains than did. There were reports of at least a dozen trains leaving or entering New York City during the strike with a large number of empty seats. One fourteen-coach train from St. Louis and Chicago arrived in New York City with only seventy-five passengers aboard. It was presumably the widespread publicity about the completeness of the shutdown and the irregularity of departures which prevented full utilization of the few passenger facilities which were kept running.

Among the suppliers of long-distance railway passengers who lost business because of the strike were the station porters. One porter in a New York terminal reported on the second day that he had not handled a piece of luggage since the strike began. Not all persons whose place of employment was a railroad station were thus affected, however. Restaurants and lunch counters in one New York terminal suffered no loss of business, since most of their clientele came from near-by office buildings.

During the 1951 switchmen's strike curtailment of long-distance traffic on the Pennsylvania, New York Central, and New Haven lines between the third and seventh days similarly left travelers stranded and increased air-line and bus traffic. Eastern bus depots were reported to be "swamped" as bus lines stepped up service. The brief May 18, 1946, strike which marooned 50,000 passengers in Grand Central Terminal alone and caused delays in railway traffic for twenty-four hours led to "jammed" bus stations and long delays in getting tickets in New York, Boston, Pittsburgh, Cleveland, Cincinnati, and Chicago. (Bad weather removed air travel as a rail substitute in the New York and Cleveland areas.) In the 1950 firemen's strike, which involved lines carrying more than 39 per cent of the total passenger traffic, air lines did a rushing business.

If it is difficult to arrive at an estimate of the number of prospective railroad passengers affected by a railway strike (the *Times* headlined its account of the first day of the 1946 nation-wide strike "Millions Discommoded"), it is equally difficult to generalize about the intensity of their affectedness. On the third day of the 1946 strike the *Times'* editorial column stated: "The effects of [the] strike ranged from the ridiculous—who cares if a commuter is late to dinner?—to the tragic; if it annoyed some it literally tortured others; if it was an adventure for some it was anxiety, sickness and even death for others." The editorial referred to people prevented "from getting to the bedsides of dying relatives," although the news columns of the same issue carried no accounts of such tragic occurrences but rather a report that "little actual hardship was experienced in the first twenty-four hours of the rail paralysis."[6]

3. Shippers of Mail

What snow and gloom of night have traditionally failed to do, the engineers and trainmen accomplished. Statements of postal officials made six days before the start of the 1946 nation-wide strike to the effect that there would be no interruptions in mail delivery "no matter how complete the tie-up" were not borne out, though the interruptions were relatively brief. From the beginning of the second day to

[6] The problem is how general was the hardship, not whether any occurred. One of the authors, traveling on a train from Providence to New Haven on the afternoon of May 23, 1946, encountered an elderly woman who spoke not a word of English and was going from Boston to Pittsburgh to attend her granddaughter's graduation exercises. Upon being put off the train at New Haven with the rest of the passengers, the woman insisted on continuing her trip and was taken to a jammed Greyhound station to wait—for hours— for a bus which would take her to New York City and connections for the West, if, with her extreme language handicap, she was indeed ever able to make connections.

6:00 P.M. on the third day intercity shipments of all mail except first class and air mail weighing sixteen ounces or less (daily shipments of which normally amounted to about 780 tons) were prohibited. This order halted all nonlocal movement of newspapers, magazines, books, and packages, around 10,000 tons of which normally passed between cities each day. In addition, in some areas at least, first-class mail dispatched before the strike was allowed to pile up for twenty-four hours in hope of an early termination to the stoppage. During the second twenty-four hours first-class mail was moved by air, with Army and other trucks distributing it to and from airfields, and by trains run by "volunteer" crews; in the New York area, at least, no more than negligible backlogs accumulated. Although during this second half of the strike the major portion of mail leaving New York City went by air, the volume of train service available for mail was so unexpectedly large that plans for the air movement of mail had to be curtailed and "officials were hard put to find mail to send to the Army, Navy, and commercial planes that had been made available." Just before the strike ended, bulk mail deposited before the embargo went into effect was being sent out of New York City, and the volume of railway mail service was great enough to have permitted the movement of all first-class mail by train.

There is little information on the extent to which customers of the postal service were inconvenienced by these interruptions in shipments. The Postmaster-General urged a moratorium on nonessential mail, especially business circulars sent at first-class rates. The *Times* reported that delays in the delivery of first-class mail on the second day had hampered the operations of New York banks, whose operations had widespread ramifications.

Embargoes on intercity shipments of other than first-class mail were also a feature of the 1951 switchmen's strike. At first (on the third day) limited to acceptance of bulk mail in ten cities, the embargo was extended to the whole nation on the fifth day. On the ninth day it was removed except for shipments within and across the region comprising Illinois, Indiana, and lower Michigan, and on the tenth day it was abolished everywhere. The *Times* reported that by the fourth day mail had piled up in New York City. On the third day of the 1950 firemen's strike mail shipments were reported to be slowed down but still moving.

4. Shippers of Express and Freight Cargo

When the 1946 nation-wide strike began, public officials were ready with plans to give certain essential categories of cargo priority in the use of remaining transport services. Trains still running were prohibited from carrying any cargoes other than food and feed, fuel, medical supplies, sanitary chemicals, newsprint, containers, and repair parts for transportation vehicles, and were required to give preference to items in the order listed. Trucks and air lines were ordered to move such priority cargoes (to the air lines' list mail was added) before accepting shipments of other goods. To supplement commercial carriers, 600 Army planes began carrying civilian cargo, and naval vessels were ordered into service wherever they could be of use. New York City officials established special express routes for the movement of food, medicine, mail, and other necessities by truck, with special police squads assigned to patrol these routes.

The arrangements set up apparently proved effective, for on the afternoon of the third day the Office of Defense Transportation announced that during the previous twenty-four hours all priority cargo backlogs had been eliminated. But the arrangements also prevented the full use of available transport. Complaints from air lines operating out of New York City that absence of cargo was forcing them to send out many partially filled planes were borne out by the ODT's statement that "The tremendous amount of air lift has not yet been used to full capacity. The demand by the shipping public has not made itself apparent." Probably the demand was not forthcoming because many shippers of nonessential cargo were discouraged from attempts to ship by the announcement of priority arrangements and by reports on the second day that air lines were accepting very little or no general merchandise.

Just what items of food were included in the priority lists is not clear; certainly not all food shipments were kept moving. The *Times* reported that by the third day "tons of perishable foodstuffs" were "spoiling in freight cars for lack of refrigeration." The situation was particularly acute in Pittsburgh; a concurrent strike of cold-storage and icing-house employees prevented the unloading of perishable items for temporary storage, as was done at many other terminal points. Railroad lines did succeed in moving some perishable cargo out of Pittsburgh to other points by means of volunteer crews. Livestock presented a special problem. Members of the volunter fire department of a Pennsylvania town were routed out of their beds at 4:00 A.M. on the second day to stretch sixty feet of hose from a factory to the railroad tracks and thus provide water for 2000 thirsty, stranded hogs.

Except for a deficiency in the supply of fresh-water fish, the strike apparently caused no noticeable shortages of food in the East. Although 75 per cent of the fresh fruit, vegetables, and eggs and virtually all of the meat, butter, and cheese consumed in New York City normally were brought in by rail, officials stated that existing stocks, replenished by trucked-in shipments, would prevent any serious food shortages for thirty days. In the days following the strike, however, the East's meat supply may have been lessened by virtue of the slaughtering in Detroit—which was said to have only a week's supply of food—of stalled shipments of livestock destined for the east coast. The strike was also said to have accentuated Pittsburgh's food shortages created by the tying up of 40,000,000 pounds of perishable foods owning to the aforementioned strike of storage-house workers.

In spite of official statements that food scarcity was not imminent, "stocking up" in many cities was reported. In New York City housewives' demands for additional supplies of food, especially canned goods, were reported 100 per cent above normal "in some extreme cases." Several grocery stores in Connecticut were forced to close because of a run on their stocks. According to the *Times*, the strike ended just in time to halt raids on the New York City area's food supplies, which might not have proved adequate "had reserve buying developed into panic buying."

The 1946 nation-wide strike had a perceptible effect on the output and distribution of industrial products. When the railroad strike began, industry was still laboring under the handicap of shortages of bituminous coal. Forty-two days of almost total shutdown of bituminous mines had been followed by eleven days of around 80 per cent of capacity production. The halting of coal-hauling services immediately caused the shutdown of many bituminous mines, and by the second day 4000 to 5000 anthracite miners were reported to have been laid off. The prospect of extended delays in the replenishment of already low coal stocks led several cities to impose or intensify dim-out conditions.

Bituminous shortages had reduced the steel industry's operations to around 48 per cent of capacity; the railroad stoppage reduced them further. The unavailability of railway services for the transportation of hot metal from blast furnaces to Bessemer and open-hearth furnaces caused Carnegie-Illinois to bank all of its still-operating blast furnaces in the Pittsburgh area, Bethlehem to shut down all blast furnaces and open hearths in its Bethlehem and Sparrows Point plants, laying off 6000 men at the former alone, and Jones and Laughlin to curtail operations at one of its plants. Some companies continued steel-making operations by using charges of cold pig iron, and most maintained some rolling-mill operations, stock-piling the finished products.

On the second day of the strike President Truman announced that "lack of fuel, raw materials, and shipping is bringing about the shutdown of hundreds of factories." Reports of specific shutdowns largely concerned automotive, agricultural implement, and steel-fabricating factories. On the second day shutdowns or curtailments at Studebaker, John Deere, and Nash-Kelvinator resulted in the layoff of some 30,000 employees; General Motors also "limited production." Steel fabricators in the Pittsburgh, Youngstown, and Wheeling areas were reported to be laying off workers "by the thousands." Some of this latter idleness, however, was probably the result of steel shortages resulting from bituminous strike-caused curtailments of steel output.

Customers of manufacturers were also affected. Several instances may be noted. The impeding of long-distance shipments gave New York City wholesalers and retailers of apparel a chance to get extra portions of New York City manufacturers' output, at the expense of faraway customers. (It should be remembered that this strike occurred during the reconversion period of "sellers' markets.") Temporary suspension of newsprint shipments led ten newspapers in six cities to omit advertising from their editions of the second day. Interruptions in the shipment of building materials gave the housing program "a serious setback," according to President Truman.

After the termination of the strike, the *Times* reported that "business observers" estimated "it would be many days, if not weeks, before business recovered from the 72-hour disruption in the flow of materials and semi-finished goods."

The 1951 switchmen's strike had an even more adverse effect on industrial output and employment. In the course of the ten days of stoppages 185 embargoes on freight and express were imposed by railroad lines. By the seventh day 250,000 mine and factory workers were estimated to be idle owing to curtailments in shipments of materials and finished goods; 66,000 were idle by the third day, 150,000 by the fourth day, 160,000 by the sixth. The automotive industry was most severely affected. The *Times* estimated that as many as 120,000 to 125,000 auto workers had been laid off during the strike. Not until eighteen days after the beginning of the stoppage were all of these re-employed. The industry as a whole fell behind in production to the extent of 75,000 vehicles. General Motors' losses alone amounted to 50,000 vehicles. Its officials announced that the firm would attempt to make up this loss within the next two or three months by overtime work—which, of course, meant increased costs.

In the course of the strike, at least 5500 anthracite miners, as well as 36,000 bituminous miners in West Virginia, Indiana, and Kentucky and an unspecified number in Illinois, were laid off. Curtailments in steel production caused losses of nearly 100,000 tons—50,000 tons by U.S. Steel alone—and by the fourth day steel shipments to Eastern industrial centers were reported to be almost at a standstill.

The five-lines 1950 firemen's strike was reported to have idled some 50,000 mine and factory workers by the sixth day. In the course of the strike at least 4500 auto workers were laid off and numerous others were deprived of opportunity for overtime work. At least 1750 employees of Pittsburgh basic steel or steel-fabricating firms, 7500 bituminous miners, and 500 Buffalo flour-feed mill employees were laid off. Officials of General Electric announced that the strike had done "irreparable damage" to the company's operations.

Among indirect suppliers suffering losses during this partial strike were those rail lines which remained operating. These roads stood to suffer losses due to a falling off in traffic which normally came to them over struck connecting lines. The Chesapeake and Ohio, for example, was thus affected. If railroads in this category are not operating at capacity they are able to recover some of the lost revenue in the weeks following the stoppage, but a significant amount of the traffic involved—that consisting of commuting passengers and goods which perished or that moved by alternative forms of transport, for example—is permanently lost.

Interruption of National Security Programs

Persons who linked American national security to postwar European recovery and rehabilitation may have been concerned by the fact that the 1946 nation-wide strike temporarily delayed UNRRA shipments to Europe of 100,000 tons of American grain, especially in view of relief officials' statement that "even a short delay will mean that thousands starve to death who might otherwise have been saved."

The 1951 switchmen's strike occurred during a crucial period in the Korean war. The Secretary of the Army's February 8 order that strikers must return to work or lose their jobs stated: "The interruptions in railway service are imperiling the national security, and holding up equipment for our fighting forces and are adversely affecting the support of our troops in Korea."

With this over-all view of how rail's publics are affected by its strikes, we turn now to rate—as we did in the case of coal—the total impact on the public of each of these strikes. We shall drop out of our analysis, however, the "unintended" 1946 stoppage which lasted for only a few hours, information on which is too scanty to make rating feasible.

CHAPTER 8

The Relative Impact of Three Rail Strikes

INVIDIOUS comparisons cannot be escaped, even in the study of strikes. We are concerned now with ranking the three major rail stoppages of 1946, 1950, and 1951 in order of their relative impact.[1] Which of these three strikes can be said to have been most serious, which least damaging? Can we ascertain—tentatively—some pattern which characterizes the effects of strikes on the railroads?

Nation-Wide Strike of 1946

In its short life of forty-eight hours this walkout paralyzed the railroad network of the nation as nothing else has ever done. It was as complete a stoppage as any union leader can reasonably hope for. In point of time, it came during the reconversion period which followed World War II and when the economy was still suffering from shortages of coal caused by the spring, 1946, bituminous strike.

The rating applies to the first twenty-four hours of the strike, that is, as of late Friday afternoon, May 24, the second day. Rating of effects at the end of the strike, which came on Saturday, would have understated the impact of the strike on commuters.

The total rating is 111.

The publics affected were as follows:

I. Direct Consumers. Score: 51.0

    A. Commuting passengers. Score: 19.8

       Urgency rating: 1.98

          1. Cultural necessity: 5. This was the first day that rail services were suspended. Under such a circumstance, dispensability of travel for shopping purposes is high; for working or

[1] We shall reverse the chronological order of the 1950 and 1951 strikes to facilitate comparisons in our ratings. For sources used and reasons for adopting an absolute rather than proportionate basis for the numbers affected, see note 1 of Chapter 5.

keeping business appointments travel is dispensable, but with "moderate" hardship; for keeping social appointments, its dispensability falls somewhere between these two. Deferrability for shopping is high, for working it is low, and for keeping appointments it is somewhere between these two. The average necessity rating would appear to be about 5, involving moderate hardship. This is somewhat higher than our cultural necessity of 4 for long-distance passengers on the first day of travel, since a much higher proportion of commuters are work-bound and their need is more immediate and less postponable.

2. Stock effect: 9.9. Passenger services cannot be stocked for use during a strike. Some railroad services were maintained, it is true, but at the end of the first twenty-four hours less than 1 per cent of all passenger traffic was moving. Consumption of railroad services by commuters was cut more than 99 per cent.

3. Substitutability: 4. Despite considerable variation, on an over-all basis buses, rapid transits, and private cars are relatively good. On the first day, however, the difficulty of arranging for car pools or adjusting travel schedules to alternative forms weakens their substitutability.

Number affected: 10

In April, 1946, total commuting passengers carried numbered 29,974,854, for a daily average of 999,162.

B. Long-distance passenger travel. Score: 31.2

Urgency rating: 2.4

1. Cultural necessity: 4. The day rated falls on a Friday, the beginning of a week end, when travel is normally heavier. Nevertheless, cultural necessity must be rated lower than for commuters for any one day, since a greater proportion of such travel is probably deferrable.

2. Stock effect: 10. So little long-distance passenger traffic was moving (less than one-half of one per cent) that we rate the stock effect at its maximum.

3. Substitutability: 6. Although long-distance bus lines expanded their facilities, there were long delays (much more so than in the case of commuter travel). Air lines were

unable to expand. Substitutes were therefore less adequate than for commuters.

Number affected: 13

Total noncommutation passengers for April, 1946, numbered 38,566,961, or a daily average of 1,285,565 (probably a low estimate for a Friday).

II. Indirect Consumers

The effect of the stoppage of freight and express shipments at the end of the first day is too small to measure. Milk deliveries continued throughout the strike. Some may choose to measure the effect on households of nondelivery of mail other than first class or air mail under sixteen ounces, but we consider it here to be *de minimus.* (For those wishing to include it, the following information is given: Cultural necessity would be low, stock effect high since more than 90 per cent of all types of mail was undelivered, substitutability high since alternatives were relatively inadequate for mail of the type not carried. Number affected might be estimated at 10,000,000, or 100 on our scale.)

III. Direct-User Producers. Score: 40.6

A. Heavy manufacturing. Score: 34.9

Urgency rating: .249

Transportation of inputs (urgency rating: .249)

1. Production necessity: 5.25. The situation here is highly similar to that faced by customers of coal-burning railroads on the first day of the freight embargo during the spring, 1946, bituminous strike, for which we estimated that about 60 per cent of employment was dependent on transport of inputs. However, there are two differences: (a) Here, by the day of rating, there had already been one day of almost total cessation of railroad transport of inputs; (b) here we are considering only firms engaged in heavy manufacturing, and these would be somewhat more dependent on transportation for securing materials than would manufacturers as a whole. The total deprivation of all forms of transported inputs on the day of rating (including stocks of inputs, into which transportation services had already been incorporated) would therefore have idled a larger proportion of heavy manufacturing's labor force than would have been the case for all manufacturing in the spring, 1946, bituminous strike.

We set the figure at 70 per cent. Recoverability would be the same as for this group in the spring, 1946, bituminous strike, namely, 25 per cent.

2. Stock effect: .5. Most manufacturing operations had stocks of materials, into which transportation services had already been incorporated, which permitted continuation of operations without need for self-rationing, at least on the first day of a railroad strike. However, there was some rationing in anticipation of a longer strike than actually developed. Moreover, even on the strike's first day some production operations were affected by nondelivery of new equipment, on which expansion of operations was dependent, while other firms were operating on a more hand-to-mouth basis in this postwar period of short supplies than is normally the case, so that nondelivery of materials by a given date meant loss of production. The steel industry was hard hit by lack of rail services for transporting hot metal from blast furnaces to Bessemer and open-hearth furnaces, so that there were mass layoffs at Carnegie-Illinois, Bethlehem, and Jones and Laughlin. A 5 per cent decline in the use of rail-transported materials by heavy manufacturers is estimated.

3. Substitutability: 9.5. Some small amount of materials may have moved by truck or air, but these would have been almost wholly ineffective to prevent the stock effect from materializing within the first twenty-four hours of a general railroad stoppage.

Transportation of outputs (urgency rating: 0).

Even in heavy manufacturing, with its bulky products, on the first day of a rail strike inability to store the product temporarily will have a negligible effect on operations. No layoffs can be said to have resulted from inability to move finished goods. In view of this, neither stocks nor substitutes were necessary to prevent cuts in production. For purpose of later comparison, however, the stock effect would have to be rated 10 (to the extent production was dependent on transport of outputs no rail services would have been available to meet the need) and substitutability 9 (possibilities of alternative forms of transport would have been restricted largely to water and truck transportation, for which first-day arrangements would be difficult).

The urgency rating for heavy manufacturing's use of rail freight services for receipt of materials is .249, for movement of output 0. The higher figure gives us the urgency rating for the category, in line with the procedure explained in the spring, 1946, coal strike rating (Chapter 5), under indirect-user producers.

Number affected: 140

In May, 1946, production employees in the categories of iron and steel products, all machinery, transport equipment, nonferrous metal products, and lumber products numbered 5,210,000. In 1947 on the average total employees in these categories were 120 per cent of production employees, so we estimate total employees in these categories in May, 1946, at 6,252,000. Conservatively, we judge three-fourths of these to be in operations depending on railroad transport, or 4,689,000, with two dependents each.

B. Mining. Score: 5.7

Urgency rating: .356

Transportation of inputs (urgency rating: 0)

1. Production necessity: 5.25. Transportation of inputs is virtually as necessary in mining as in manufacturing, even though volume is less. Explosives, for example, are indispensable and must usually be imported to the mine. Production necessity is therefore approximately the same as for heavy manufacturing, above.

2. Stock effect: 0. On the first day of a rail strike so little reduction in the use of such transported materials because of precautionary self-rationing can be expected that we see no point in distinguishing it from 0.

3. Substitutability: 2. Because of the lower volume of inputs, and in many cases because of their greater compactness, the possibilities of alternative transport of inputs are very good.

Transportation of outputs (urgency rating: .356)

1. Production necessity: .375. Owing to a shortage of coal cars stocks of coal at mine heads were larger than they would have been otherwise, with the result that one day of inability to move coal resulted in layoffs of about 4 per cent of pro-

duction employees. We estimate that if all forms of transport had been unavailable on the second day, about 5 per cent of employees would have been idle, with little likelihood of fill-in employment elsewhere on such short notice. Recoverability is assumed to have been 25 per cent.

2. Stock effect: 10. Since fuels were on the essential list for freight movement, some portion of the less than 1 per cent of traffic moving involved coal, but too small a fraction to measure. Obviously, there could be no "stocks" of rail freight services to draw on. Consumption of such services by mining operations virtually halted.

3. Substitutability: 9.5. Use of alternative forms of transportation is not feasible except on a minor scale.

The urgency rating for transportation of inputs is 0, for outputs .356. We adopt the higher rating.

Number affected: 16.3

For 1946, the average number of all employees in bituminous, anthracite, and metals mining was 542,300. We assume two dependents each.

IV-V. Effects on indirect-user producers and direct suppliers were too slight to rate.

VI. Indirect Suppliers. Score: 8.1

One-fifth of the total for III, according to our expedient method for giving some consideration to this group, since more precise information is almost impossible to obtain.

VII. Nonparty Members of the Struck Unit. Score: 10.9

A. Nonstriking employees. Score: 7.9

Urgency rating: .25

At the end of the first day of the strike relatively few nonstrikers would have received layoff notices. Many would have been retained to perform maintenance, clerical, and supervisory tasks if not a single train had been moving. Actually some trains did run, so that an even larger number of nonstriking employees was needed for both operating and nonoperating jobs. The available data indicate that only about 5 per cent of total nonstrikers had been laid off by the end of the first day. A negligible number of these could have so quickly procured employment in other industries. But since probably at least 50 per cent of strike losses were recoverable, permanent losses would have been only about 2.5 per cent or .25 on our scales.

Number affected: 31.6

Since there were 1,346,000 employees on Class I railroads in April, 1946, and about 293,000 strikers involved in this stoppage, 1,053,000 nonstrikers were affected each with two dependents.

B. Families of strikers. Score: 3

Urgency rating: .5

Strikers were of course totally without employment in the railroad industry and little alternative work could be procured on one day's notice. Recoverability of family losses through make-up operations is estimated at 50 per cent, but remaining losses are further reduced by 90 per cent because of the families' intimate involvement in the strike.

Number affected: 5.9

Two dependents each for 293,000 strikers.

Recapitulation of 1946 Strike Effects

Direct consumers	51.0
Indirect consumers	0.0
Direct-user producers	40.6
Indirect-user producers	0.0
Direct suppliers	0.0
Indirect suppliers	8.1
Nonparty members of struck unit	10.9
	110.6 (or 111 when rounded)

Switchman's Strike of 1951

This strike lasted ten days—over three times as long as the nation-wide strike of 1946. Centered in the yards of major railroad junctions, it was in no sense an industry-wide strike, but nevertheless it effectively impeded and even halted railroad traffic over large areas of the nation. The strike occurred during a period in which the railroads and most other industries were operating at or near to full capacity, and at a crucial stage in the Korean War.

Because the data indicate that the height of disruption of rail traffic was reached on the seventh day (Monday, February 5), this day was chosen as the day of rating.

The total rating is 161.

I. Direct Consumers. Score: 14.5

Although the principal effect appears to have been on commuter traffic in the New York City area, it is known that San Francisco was substantially affected and Chicago to a lesser extent. It is reasonable to assume that commuter traffic in other areas was also interrupted. Long-distance passenger traffic was definitely curtailed.

A. Commuters. Score: 6

Urgency rating: 2

1. Cultural necessity: 5.3. Some lines had been down since early in the strike. Others ceased operating for the first time on the day of rating. Commuters' need for transport on this day would therefore have been only slightly higher than after one day of no rail transport in the 1946 strike.

2. Stock effect: 9.5. Many of the lines involved were completely shut down and, of course, passenger rail services are not stockable. Alternative rail lines are seldom available to commuters. Thus consumption of rail services by those affected probably declined about 95 per cent.

3. Substitutability: 4. The lines chiefly affected in the New York City area served Connecticut and New York State, where bus service is not as readily available as in New Jersey. Here, and in any other struck area where such circumstances prevailed, this factor, making for poorer substitutability than in the 1946 strike, was offset by the better opportunities for more efficient use of alternative forms of transport afforded by the somewhat longer period of curtailment.

Number affected: 3

The *New York Times* estimated that 100,000 New York City area commuters were affected. In all the other struck regions combined there was a total of perhaps twice this number, or 200,000. Thus, altogether about 300,000 commuters were probably affected.

B. Long-distance passengers. Score: 8.5

Urgency rating: 1.74

1. Cultural necessity: 4.1. At the time of rating, traffic in some lines had been eliminated or curtailed for six days, on others for only one or two days. Regardless of this fact, for those

wishing to travel for the first time on the day of rating, the need—as in all our rail stoppages—is expressed by 4. For those whose desire to travel on the day of rating had been carried over from previous days, the importance of transport services became greater the longer the period they were forced to wait. On the whole, their need is probably well represented by a rating of 4.5. With the rating for each group weighted by the number affected in each group, the average cultural necessity rating is 4.1.

2. Stock effect: 8.5. Some traffic continued over the strike-bound lines. Some travelers could use alternative lines which were still operating. Consumption of rail services by long-distance passengers probably declined by about 85 per cent.

3. Substitutability: 5. In comparison with the 1946 rail strike, the longer period of shutdown afforded more opportunity to organize alternative forms of transport, and the lesser extent of this strike eased the traveler's task of finding them. Air and motor transport are less reliable substitutes in early February than in May, however. Altogether, substitutability was probably better in this strike than in 1946, perhaps about 5.

Number affected: 4.9

Though the data are inadequate, they suggest that this strike affected about one-third as many long-distance passengers as the 1946 strike. That is, on the day of rating about 433,000 persons wished, for the first time during the strike, to travel. Duration of the strike differed as between the lines involved, but for affected travelers as a group the strike may be regarded as going into its third day. Thus by the third day 866,000 persons had wished to travel on the two previous days. We estimate that about 7 per cent, or 60,620, of these had not canceled or indefinitely postponed their trips and still desired to travel at the first opportunity. The total number of long-distance passengers affected by lack of transport on the seventh day of the strike was thus 493,620.

II. Indirect Consumers

There was little effect on consumers due to nonshipment of freight. An embargo on all mail other than first class and air mail, imposed on the whole nation, was in its third day. As in the 1946 strike, we do not judge the effect to be appreciable enough to rate. For those who do, the data given under the preceding strike apply.

III. Direct-User Producers. Score: 113.5

A. Heavy manufacturing. Score: 105.1

Urgency rating: 1.44

Transportation of inputs (urgency rating: .72)

1. Production necessity: 6. A longer period during which firms were deprived of transport for inputs makes dependency higher than for the 1946 railroad strike. We estimate it at 80 per cent, recoverability at 25 per cent.

2. Stock effect: 1.5. Perhaps as many as 175 embargoes on freight and express shipments had been imposed by the seventh day. Freight traffic moving through Chicago had been reduced by 90 per cent as early as the fifth day. In 100 cities a total of fifty rail lines were not operating. Several hundred thousand employees were reported laid off. A reduction of 15 per cent in employment due to shortages of inputs, in consequence of either nonreceipt of materials or anticipatory self-rationing, seems conservative.

3. Substitutability: 8. Substitutes were probably more adequate than in 1946 owing to the fact that there were no priorities for essential movements and by the seventh day alternative arrangements could more readily have been made. Nevertheless, since this measures the extent to which inputs transported by alternative means were actually available on the seventh day to overcome deficiencies in stocks, the rating must still be high. Substitute transport over long distances would not always have been timely, except by air, which for heavy manufacturing is not very feasible. And many shipments were tied up in freight yards.

Transportation of outputs (urgency rating: 1.44)

1. Production necessity: 1.9. The physical possibility and economic desirability of storing additional output which could not be moved were diminishing by the seventh day. We estimate that, in the absence of transportation for out-shipments, about 25 per cent of employees in heavy manufacturing would have been idle. Recoverability is 25 per cent.

2. Stock effect: 9.5. Rail services for moving current output could not have been stocked. But some small portion of

freight was moving over the struck lines and over alternative non-struck lines. Its negligible amount is indicated by our rating of 9.5.

3. Substitutability: 8. Again, substitutes were probably somewhat improved over 1946, since the longer duration in some degree facilitated making alternative arrangements and the lesser extent of the strike meant that substitute transportation for fewer out-shipments was needed.

The urgency rating for freight services for outputs is higher, so we adopt it.

Number affected: 73

For December, 1950, all employees in the relevant categories numbered 6,406,000. We estimate, conservatively, that three-fourths of these were dependent on rail services in their employment (or 4,868,500), and that one-half of these relied on the struck lines, each with two dependents.

B. Mining. Score: 8.4

Urgency rating: .96

Transportation of inputs (urgency rating: .03)

1. Production necessity: 6. Again, a longer period of deprivation of transport for inputs makes dependency higher than for the 1946 strike.
2. Stock effect: .5. By the seventh day shortages of supplies may have forced a cut in employment of as much as 5 per cent.
3. Substitutability: 1. More adequate than in 1946, as explained under "Heavy manufacturing," above.

Transportation of outputs (urgency rating: .96)

1. Production necessity: 1.125. After several days without movement of finished product, stocks would have accumulated, making further additions to them both physically and economically less feasible. Thus the total lack of transport for outputs on the day of rating would have affected more people than on the day of rating in the 1946 strike. We estimate dependency at 15 per cent, recoverability at 25 per cent.
2. Stock effect: 9.5. For those affected there was close to a 100 per cent decline in consumption of transport services for output; only a negligible amount of their freight was moving over struck or alternative non-struck lines.

3. Substitutability: 9. As for inputs, more adequate than in 1946.

We take the higher of the two ratings (in this case, that for output) as applicable to the whole category.

Number affected: 8.73

Total employees in coal and metal mining numbered 582,-200 in December, 1950. We assume all to depend on rail services in their employment, and about one-half to depend on the lines involved in the strike, each with two dependents.

IV. There is no indication of any effects on indirect-user producers.

V. Direct Suppliers. Score: .3

A. Suppliers of coal to railroads. Score: .14

Urgency rating: .184

1. Market necessity: 5.25. Properly we should show here the proportion which purchases of coal by the struck railroads constituted of the total sales of coal by mines primarily engaged in supplying the struck lines, and this proportion would be applied to the *total* number of persons employed by such mines. But the necessary data are not available. We are thus forced to approximate the correct figures by using for number affected an estimate of the number of employees in all bituminous mines who are engaged in producing coal for the struck lines, and for market necessity a ratio representing the extent to which these employees are dependent on the struck lines for their employment.

As of a given day of the strike the extent of such dependency is a function of the extent to which purchases of the suppliers' goods have been continued prior to the given day and of the extent to which the suppliers have been able to avoid curtailment of operations by stocking their unpurchased finished product. In this case, where purchases of coal probably continued for some days after the beginning of the strike and where stock-piling of mined coal for short periods is feasible, we estimate that complete cessation of purchases and stocking on the seventh day would idle only about 70 per cent of all bituminous employees engaged in producing coal for the struck lines (the other 30 per cent continuing to be employed in supervisory, clerical, and maintenance jobs or finding temporary alternative work elsewhere).

We further assume that, while bituminous mines could expand output during the succeeding six months by enough to make up a substantial proportion of their lost output, owing to the continuing difficulties of unsnarling traffic and the high level of utilization of capacity preceding the strike railroads were more handicapped in expanding output of services, so that recoverability of strike losses by the bituminous industry would be limited to about 25 per cent. As always, this rough judgment of recoverability takes into account not simply the prospects of recapturing output lost during the strike but also the extent to which such recapture actually offsets strike losses, a figure impossible to calculate with precision but usually of lesser magnitude.

2. Stock effect: .5. We estimate that by the seventh day there were enough continued purchases of coal by the struck lines and enough stock-piling of coal to prevent output of coal from falling by more than 5 per cent.

3. Substitutability: 7. The coal industry is not so specialized to railroad specifications but that, in a time of high economic activity, some substitution of markets is possible. Nevertheless, on the seventh day the primary adjustment to a rail strike would come through the stock effect rather than a search for new sales outlets.

Number affected: .78

In 1951 railroad expenditures for coal were $277,012,000. As a rough means of estimating the total number of employees engaged in mining coal for the struck lines we first assume that the struck lines accounted for half of total railroad expenditures for coal or $138,506,000. We then divide this latter figure by the ratio of the number of total employees in all bituminous mining in 1949 to a figure representing total sales in 1949 of all bituminous mines (in this case "value of production at mines"). This ratio, which amounts to $5341, has been termed the "1949 bituminous employment divisor." The result indicates that the equivalent of 25,933 full-time employees were then devoted to producing coal for the struck lines. When the figure is multiplied by three (on the assumption of an average of two dependents for each employee) we arrive at an estimate of 77,799 persons affected by virtue of their relation to the mining of coal for the struck lines.

B. Suppliers of fuel oil and other fuels. Score: .02

Urgency rating: .184

Since dependency, recoverability, stock effect, and substitutability for suppliers of other fuels would be similar to those applying to suppliers of coal, the urgency rating computed for coal is used here.

Number affected: .114

In 1951 railroad expenditures for fuel oil and other (minor) fuels were $344,485,000. Taking half of this and dividing by the 1947 petroleum employment divisor of $45,428 gives the equivalent of 3792 full-time employees engaged in producing fuel oil and other fuels for the struck lines; with dependents, 11,376.

C. Suppliers of iron and steel products. Score: .05

Urgency rating: .056

1. Market necessity: ˙1.6. In the first seven days of the rail strike, steel suppliers of railroad needs were not seriously affected. Little unemployment on this account was evident. Therefore, we estimate that the absolute cessation of railroad purchases and of stock-piling by the steel industry on the seventh day would not have idled more than 80 per cent of affected employees. Since the nature of many of the iron and steel products used by railroads is such that the products must be bought regardless of their prevailing rate of operations, probably 80 per cent of the losses suffered by these suppliers was recoverable in the following six months.

2. Stock effect: .5. Probably no more than 5 per cent of the output of these suppliers was lost by the seventh day through discontinuation of purchases or inability to stock-pile the output.

3. Substitutability: 7. As for the suppliers of coal, on the seventh day adjustment to the strike-caused loss of markets would come primarily through the stock effect rather than through a search for new sales outlets.

Number affected: .81

In 1951 railroad expenditures for iron and steel products were $703,885,000. Taking half of this and dividing by the 1950 iron-steel employment divisor of $12,956 gives 27,164 employees affected; with dependents, 81,492.

D. Suppliers of forest products. Score: .03

Urgency rating: .056

Since suppliers of forest products would feel the loss of markets in much the same way that iron and steel firms did, the same urgency rating is applied to both.

Number affected: .45

In 1951 railroad expenditures for forest products were $188,-186,000. Taking half of this and dividing by the 1947 timber products employment divisor of $6211 gives 15,149 employees affected; with dependents, 45,447.

E. Suppliers of goods and services to employees of the struck units. Score: .06

Urgency rating: .015

1. Market necessity: 2.25. During only seven days (or less) of idleness purchases of goods and services by railroad employees would probably not have fallen off substantially. Therefore, total dependency by suppliers on these purchases or substitutes for them as of the seventh day would have amounted to only about 30 per cent of total output. Recoverability of what losses there were we estimate to be roughly the same as for the railroad industry (25 per cent).

2. Stock effect: .1. Services of retailers and wholesalers are not easily stockable, but by the seventh day the decline in sales to railroad workers had not been sufficient to have anything but a very minor effect on employment in the service trades.

3. Substitutability: 7. Local suppliers of goods and services are less specialized to railroad employees than in the case of coal. Although there are "railroad towns," in most cities railroad employees are a minor component of the total population. Suppliers are thus less dependent on them for sales revenue. On the other hand, although economic activity was high, postwar shortages had largely disappeared, making less possible the ready substitution of one customer for another that had characterized previous years. Price markdowns were a possible stimulant of trade. In the short

run, on the seventh day, a substitution of outlets was not very feasible.

Number affected: 3.76

Wages spent on goods and services in 1951 (estimated as two-thirds of total 1951 railroad pay roll) amounted to $3,557,778,000. Dividing 50 per cent of this by the 1950 retail trade employment divisor of $14,181 gives 125,442 employees affected; with dependents, 376,326.

VI. Indirect Suppliers. Score: 22.7

One-fifth the totals for III and V, above.

VII. Nonparty Members of the Struck Unit. Score: 9.5

A. Nonstriking employees. Score: 9.4

Urgency rating: .75

Of the lines involved in this stoppage, on the seventh day some had been struck for six days, others for only one day. Small amounts of traffic were moving over some. The longer a line had been struck and the less the amount of traffic moving over it, the greater would be the proportion of its nonstriking employees idled on the seventh day. Data suggest that as a whole about 10 per cent were so affected. About 25 per cent of the strike losses are estimated to have been recoverable.

Number affected: 12.6

For all Class I railroads in December, 1950, there were 1,277,000 employees. With 50 per cent of the railroad traffic involved in this strike, that number is cut in half. From this are subtracted the 11,000 strikers, giving an estimate of 627,500 nonstrikers involved. Then allowance is made for two dependents each.

B. Families of strikers. Score: .14

Urgency rating: .63

Strikers of course were entirely without employment except for jobs procured in other industries. Besides the difficulty of locating jobs after such a short passage of time, the nature of the strike—reporting "sick"—deterred search for alternative employment. Certainly not more than 10 per cent had obtained other jobs. Recoverability related to opportunities for make-up work is estimated at 25 per cent, related to families' intimate involvement in the strike at the usual additional 90 per cent.

Recapitulation of 1951 Strike Effects

Direct consumers	14.5
Indirect consumers	0.0
Direct-user producers	113.5
Indirect-user producers	0.0
Direct suppliers	0.3
Indirect suppliers	22.7
Nonparty suppliers of struck unit	9.5

160.5 (or 161 when rounded)

Firemen's Strike of 1950

This strike, which lasted for seven days, shut down operations almost completely on five railroad lines which carried more than 39 per cent of total passenger traffic and more than 24 per cent of total freight traffic. Two of the five lines served the major industrial areas of the nation. The strike occurred at a time when the general level of activity in the economy was rising. It is scored as of the last day of the strike, Thursday, May 16.

The total rating is 65.

I. Direct Consumers. Score: 11.1

    A. Commuters. Score: 3.4

       Urgency rating: 1.7

       1. Cultural necessity: 6. Commuters' need for transport is estimated to have been 5 on the first day of a rail stoppage (1946 strike) and to have reached a maximum of 9 after six weeks of curtailed transport services (winter, 1949-1950, bituminous strike). If it is assumed that need rises at a constant rate, then consumers' need for transport on the seventh day of a railroad strike would be about 6.

       2. Stock effect: 9.5. The affected lines had almost completely suspended, and their services could not be stocked. Little of the affected traffic could be provided for by expansion of alternative rail facilities, since commuting lines seldom duplicate.

       3. Substitutability: 3. By the seventh day, alternative arrangements for travel via buses and car pools were made by many.

Private travel was somewhat more feasible than in the 1951 strike, since the commuting areas affected were more closely knit.

Number affected: 2

The struck lines accounted for 39 per cent of gross passenger traffic, and there are about 1,000,000 railroad commuters daily. We cannot assume that these lines carried 390,000 commuters, however, because the Eastern seaboard, the region of greatest commuting, was unaffected. Chicago, Cleveland, Pittsburgh, Detroit, and other cities in the western New York-to-Illinois region were chiefly hit; probably no more than 200,000 commuters were affected.

B. Long-distance passengers. Score: 7.7

Urgency rating: 1.6

1. Cultural necessity: 4.4. Importance of transport for first-time travelers on the seventh day is 4, as in all other cases where rail services were curtailed. Importance of travel to the "carried-over" portion of travelers from previous days is for the seventh day estimated at 5. The weighted average of these is 4.4.

2. Stock effect: 9. Passenger transportation is of course not stockable. Non-struck rail lines, operating between the same points as were covered by the struck lines, together with the few trains running on the struck lines, could perhaps have supplied about 10 per cent of travelers' needs. This is a little less than in 1951 since in that strike more trains were operated on the struck lines.

3. Substitutability: 4. Substitutability was higher than in the 1946 strike or even the 1951 strike, both because by the seventh day passengers were in a better position to plan on such alternative transportation as buses and air lines and because the smaller proportion of total traffic affected eased the problem of finding alternative forms of transport.

Number affected: 4.8

Total passenger traffic for April, 1950, was 39,570,998, or a daily average of 1,319,033. With lines carrying 39 per cent of total passenger traffic shut down, some 514,423 persons, less 200,000 commuters, would have been involved each day. Thus on the seventh day 314,423 first-time travelers would have been faced with lack of transport services. A total of 1,886,538 would have been affected during the preceding six days; by the seventh day perhaps about 9 per cent or 169,788 of these, having failed to cancel or postpone indefinitely their trips, were still seeking to travel at the first opportunity. The total number affected on the seventh day was thus 484,211.

II. No indirect consumer effects were discernible.

III. Direct-User Producers. Score: 21.2

    A. Heavy manufacturing. Score: 19.3

    Urgency rating: .38

    Transportation of inputs (urgency rating: .14)

        1. Production necessity: 5.6. On the seventh day of this strike dependency would be about the same as for the seventh day of the 1951 strike (80 per cent), which, while more extensive, had not involved some areas until the third or fourth day. Capacity of the railroad industry was not so fully utilized, however, so that recoverability is estimated to have been 30 per cent.

        2. Stock effect: .5. Data suggest that curtailment in the use of transported inputs—and hence of employment—was substantially less than in the 1951 strike.

        3. Substitutability: 5. Better than for the 1951 strike because the lesser extent of the strike, by limiting the area of nondelivery of goods, limited the number of inputs for which substitutes were required.

    Transportation of outputs (urgency rating: .473)

        1. Production necessity: .875. Because the total volume of freight traffic involved in this strike was only half that of the 1951 stoppage, it was physically and economically more feasible to store output which was nondeliverable in the struck area or to divert it to other areas. However, for some areas the duration of that strike had been only three or four days. We estimate that dependency lies within a range of 10 to 15 per cent, and use the midpoint, 12.5 per cent, for the computation. Recoverability is 30 per cent.

        2. Stock effect: 9. The struck lines were running a few trains, and in some instances non-struck rail lines, operating between the same points as were covered by the struck lines,

could expand operations to supply some portion of the needs for the transport of outputs. Such rail services could probably not have met more than 10 per cent of needs.

3. Substitutability: 6. Slightly higher than for inputs since a smaller proportion of total freight traffic was affected, easing the problem of finding alternative forms of transport to customers in the struck area.

The urgency rating for freight services for outputs is higher, so we adopt it for the urgency rating for the entire category.

Number affected: 40.8

On April 1, 1950, total employees in the relevant classifications were 6,044,000. We assume three-fourths of these to be dependent on rail transport (4,533,000). Only 24 per cent of total freight traffic was affected, however. Because of the area involved (Pittsburgh to Chicago) the effect on freight traffic for *heavy* manufacturing operations—and by inference on employees engaged in such operations—was probably more than proportionate, perhaps amounting to 30 per cent. This gives 1,359,900 employees, with two dependents each.

B. Mining. Score: 1.9

Urgency rating: .44

Transportation of inputs (urgency rating: .007)

1. Production necessity: 5.6. For the same reasons as for heavy manufacturing this is like the 1951 strike except that recoverability is 30 per cent.

2. Stock effect: .25. Data suggest a lesser curtailment in the use of transported inputs than in 1951.

3. Substitutability: .5. Better than in 1951, as explained under "Heavy manufacturing," above.

Transportation of outputs (urgency rating: .44)

1. Production necessity: .7. The lesser extent but longer overall duration of this strike indicate that dependency would have been somewhat less than in the 1951 strike, probably about 10 per cent. Recoverability is 30 per cent.

2. Stock effect: 9. As for heavy manufacturing, we estimate that about 10 per cent of the needs for transport of mine products could have been met by expansion of operations on nonstruck rail lines.

3. Substitutability: 7. More adequate than in 1951 for reasons set forth for heavy manufacturing.

The higher urgency rating, .44, is adopted for the whole category.

Number affected: 4.3

Total employees in affected categories in April, 1950, numbered 592,800, all of whom we assume to be dependent on rail freight services. The reduction of 24 per cent in freight services is judged to have affected a proportionate number of mining employees, or 142,272, each with two dependents.

IV. No effects on indirect-user producers were discernible.

V. Direct Suppliers. Score: .15

The urgency ratings for each category of supplier are estimated to have been approximately the same as those for the 1951 strike. Basic expenditures and employment figures are similar enough for the two years to permit the use of the same figures for number affected for each category, except that the struck lines in this stoppage did not represent 50 per cent of total railroad expenditures. They accounted for 39 per cent of total passenger traffic and 24 per cent of total freight traffic. In 1949 for Class I railways, 39 per cent of total passenger revenue amounted to $335,690,160; 24 per cent of total freight traffic amounted to $1,691,577,600. The total of these shares of revenue amounted to 25.6 per cent of total combined passenger and freight revenue for Class I railroads. We assume that the struck railroads accounted for about the same proportion of total railroad expenditures on goods and services—say, 25 per cent—and that therefore a reasonably correct score for direct suppliers in this strike is represented by half the score for direct suppliers in the 1951 strike, where the struck railroads were assumed to have accounted for 50 per cent of all railroad expenditures.

VI. Indirect Suppliers. Score: 3

One-fifth of the totals for III and V, above.

VII. Nonparty Members of the Struck Unit. Score: 29.6

A. Nonstriking employees. Score: 29.4

Urgency rating: 3.5

At the time of rating, this strike had been going on for six days. Output of rail services had been close to zero. Thus most of the nonstrikers whose jobs depend on continued operations had been laid off. The nonstrikers still employed were those whose maintenance, clerical, or supervisory jobs must be performed—for a while, at least—even in the absence of rail traffic and those who had obtained temporary jobs outside the industry. Data suggest that on the seventh day about 50 per cent of all the nonstriking employees involved were idle—without jobs of any kind. Because capacity of railroads was not being as fully utilized at the time of this strike as in 1946 and 1951, chances of recovering strike losses would be somewhat better. We set it at 30 per cent.

Number affected: 8.4

In April, 1950, there were 1,188,000 employees on Class I railroads. We assume that 25 per cent of these were employed on the struck lines. Subtracting the 18,000 strikers gives 279,000 nonstrikers on the struck lines. With dependents, 837,000.

B. Families of strikers. Score: .23

Urgency rating: .63

The rating here includes an allowance of 10 per cent for fill-in employment, of 30 per cent for recoverability but with a deduction of 90 per cent of "nonrecoverable" losses to offset the party-oriented nature of this group.

Number affected: .36

Two dependents each for 18,000 strikers.

Recapitulation of 1950 Strike Effects

Direct consumer	11.1
Indirect consumer	0.0
Direct-user producers	21.2
Indirect-user producers	0.0
Direct suppliers	.2
Indirect suppliers	3.0
Nonparty suppliers of struck unit	29.6

65.1 (or 65 when rounded)

What do the ratings for these three rail strikes show? Our conclusions must be stated even more tentatively than in the case of coal, since our sample is so much smaller. Nevertheless, some interesting deductions are possible. For one thing, it is obvious that neither duration alone nor percentage of capacity shut down is a reliable indicator of a strike's severity. (The two-day nation-wide stoppage of 1946 had 70 per cent more impact than the seven-day partial strike of 1950, which affected five major lines, but about two-thirds the effects of the partial strike of 1951, also rated as of the seventh day.) This is a common-sense and commonplace conclusion which requires no elaboration. It does serve, however, to raise the more interesting question of just what is the relationship between the extent of a rail strike and its severity.

Unfortunately, the 1950 and 1951 strikes, though of approximately equal duration on the days rated, are not directly comparable, since different lines and even regions were involved. Even so, certain comparisons are possible. The percentage of total freight traffic halted by the 1951 strike was greater than in the 1950 strike, perhaps double, but its effects on direct producer-users (and on suppliers of such producers) were more than five times those of the less extensive strike. For these groups (and in this instance, at least,) the impact of a rail strike appears to increase more than proportionately to the increase in the amount of traffic halted. Why should this be so?

In the first place, even a small manufacturing firm draws its materials from many sources. A large firm depends on literally thousands of suppliers. Nondelivery of a few materials *may* not seriously interrupt production. Stocks may be sufficient, substitute materials available, one operation postponable in favor of another to keep the work force busy. But nondelivery of additional materials means that these alternatives are no longer as good an insurance against interruption of the work flow. There comes a point where there is *not* sufficient inventory on hand of some component which is strategic, for which no substitute is satisfactory; if further operations are shelved, soon the point is reached where the whole work force cannot be kept occupied. The safeguards against interference with production cannot be stretched to cover the contingency of many nondeliveries, even if they are adequate for a few. A doubling of nondeliveries means more than a doubling of the chances that the plant will not be able to keep busy. One can picture the production manager of a firm making shift for one missing shipment after another, each situation calling for more ingenuity than the last, until at some point improvisation is inadequate, his patience is exhausted, he gives up the struggle to keep operations going, the firm shuts down. This situation is reflected in the urgency ratings attached to transportation of manufacturers' inputs for the two strikes of approximately equal duration—.72 as against .14. It provides the explanation for the differing stock effects of the two strikes (three times greater in 1951 than in 1950) and for the differing substitutability effects. The higher urgency rating in the case of the more extensive strike means that the adverse effects on industrial users are more than proportionate to the numbers affected.

On the other hand, producers who are prevented from shipping their output to some customer by a rail stoppage in the customer's area can perhaps stock that output without difficulty or divert it to some other customer. But as the area in which delivery cannot be made widens, the possibilities of storing additional output or of diverting shipments to other areas diminish. Thus if a rail strike involves 25 per cent of freight traffic, a manufacturer who normally ships into the area affected might be able to store some portion of the output destined for that area or divert part of it to customers in unaffected areas. If 10 per cent of his shipments are affected, perhaps 5 per cent may be stored or diverted, so that output must be reduced by only 5 per cent. If the same manufacturer is faced with a rail strike involving 50 per cent of traffic, however, we may assume that—proportionately—20 per cent of his shipments will be affected. But the possibilities of storing and diverting will be no greater than in the first instance, thus requiring a 15 per cent cut in output. Consequently a doubling of the amount of traffic involved (the extent of the strike) leads to a tripling of the reduction of output—a disproportionate effect. This is reflected in our urgency ratings for the transport of manufacturers' outputs for the two strikes—1.44 as against .47.

The number affected in the category of industrial users in the two strikes is roughly proportional to the amount of traffic halted, if the assumptions underlying our ratings are correct. The proportionately greater disparity in effects is thus attributable almost solely to the higher urgency ratings of the more extensive strike. This suggests that the direct producer effects of the 1946 strike, which were much lower than in the partial 1951 strike, would have been much lower still except for the completeness of that strike. In view of its brevity—twenty-four hours, as of the day of rating—one might have expected producer effects to have been negligible. That they nevertheless racked up a score of 41 is probably attributable only to the fact that the paralysis of the rails was so complete.

As the descriptive materials on rail strikes in Chapter 7 show, producer effects increase rapidly with the duration of a rail strike. They are cumulative. Each plant that closes remains closed for the duration, and each day adds its quota of new closings. This is in contrast to direct consumer effects. Except for week-end declines, the number of commuters remains relatively constant from the first to the last day, and the number of long-distance travelers newly affected each day is not wholly additive to those affected from previous days, since the latter may have canceled their proposed trips or postponed them to the future. That is, each additional day of the strike does not keep from traveling all those affected for the first time on that day *plus* all those previously disappointed, since not all still want to travel, but each additional day does mean an income and employment loss for all those producers newly affected on that day *plus* all those who had experienced such losses in the earlier days of the strike. Thus producer effects may be expected to mount much more rapidly than direct consumer effects as the strike is prolonged.

This is probably the explanation for the more important role which consumer effects play in the brief 1946 strike than in the longer 1950 and 1951 strikes. In the former, consumers contribute close to half of the total strike rating, whereas in the latter two they account for approximately only one-sixth and one-tenth respectively. We may expect that if the 1946 strike had continued for only a few days longer producer effects would have increased enormously, while consumer effects would have risen only slightly until within a few days their percentage contribution would have fallen to a figure more comparable with either of the two seven-day stoppages.

Certainly it would appear that, as between strikes, any direct consumer ratings which indicate effects greatly disproportionate to the amount of traffic halted—the extent of the strikes—are probably spurious, the result of faulty data. The burden on the train-traveling public can be expected to be much more nearly proportionate to the extent of the strike than for producers. If our 1946 strike shows consumer effects somewhat exceeding what we would expect, this probably reflects largely the fact that in the nation-wide strike the number of consumers affected could be computed directly from national statistics of travel, thus scooping in everyone, while in the partial strikes they had to be built up from fragmentary reports, thus omitting some.

Finally, we may note that both the indirect and the supplier effects of these three rail strikes were negligible, falling within a range of from one-seventh to one-twentieth of the total rating for each category. The explanation for their relative unimportance lies in the brevity of all three strikes. A prolonged stoppage would lead to a different result.

What patterns, then, are discernible in strikes on the railroads? Again the warning should be made that any conclusions are tentative. It would appear, however, that the first day of a rail strike weighs more heavily on travelers than on producers. But this initial burden on consumers remains relatively constant as the strike continues, while the loss to producers mounts rapidly. An increase in the extent of the strike increases its impact on producers more than proportionately. Unless the strike continues for longer than recent experience suggests is likely, it will not seriously involve suppliers either of the railroad or of user industries.

CHAPTER 9

When the Mills Are Idle: Steel's Publics

———

THE three major stoppages in which the United Steelworkers of America (USA) has been involved between 1946 and 1952 have been more than industry-wide strikes. All three were centered on the basic steel industry, with more than 90 per cent of its productive capacity shut down in the 1946 and 1949 strikes and more than 85 per cent in the 1952 strike. All also included iron ore mines. The 1946 stoppage, a genuinely union-wide strike, involved the plants of a majority of firms with which the USA had contractual relations. At the peak of the strike some 700 firms which produced a variety of products ranging from rolling mills to hairpins and paper milk containers, as well as a number of aluminum plants, were shut down. The 1949 stoppage was more nearly confined to basic steel, including many fewer fabricators but somewhat more aluminum facilities than did the 1946 stoppage.

The potential magnitude of the effects of a steelworkers' strike, even if restricted to basic steel plants and steel fabricating plants, is suggested by the statement of the American Iron and Steel Institute that as of the end of 1945 "over 40 per cent of all the factory workers in the country earn their living by making steel into useful products for American life."[1]

Persons Affected Through Relationship to the Striking Employees

The 1946 stoppage, "the largest strike ever recorded in the United States" up to that time, began on January 21 and idled approximately 750,000 employees of struck companies for four weeks.[2] During the fifth

[1] *Washington Post*, December 13, 1945. Unless otherwise noted, all of the factual material pertaining to the effects of steelworkers' strikes has been taken from issues of the *New York Times*. In most cases the information appeared in the issue of the day following the date to which the information pertains.

[2] U.S. Bureau of Labor Statistics, *Work Stoppages Caused by Labor-Management Disputes in 1946* (Bulletin No. 918).

week settlements were reached with companies (mainly basic steel companies) which employed approximately 450,000; by the end of the sixth week the strike had ended for another 50,000 employees. Between the beginning of the seventh week and the end of the sixteenth week all but 28,000 employees had returned to work.

The 1949 stoppage, which began on October 1, originally involved about 500,000 employees in basic steel companies and iron ore mines. This number was eventually increased to 542,500 by 14,000 employees in fabricating plants who had joined the strike by the end of the first week, by 16,000 aluminum workers who struck on the sixteenth day, and by 12,500 basic steel employees who struck on the thirty-first day. On the thirty-second day, however, a settlement with Bethlehem Steel ended the strike for some 77,000 basic steel employees; by the thirty-ninth day settlements had been reached covering some 200,000 employees, and by the forty-second day some 400,000. By the forty-fourth day only 74,000 employees were still on strike, by the sixty-second this number had been reduced to 45,000 and by the seventy-fifth day only 5000 were still out.

The 1952 strike which began on June 2 and was settled on July 24 established a new record as the longest major steel strike in the nation's history. It idled some 600,000 steelworkers and 23,000 iron ore miners for almost eight weeks.

The duration of idleness coincides with the duration of a strike to a much smaller extent in basic steel operations than in bituminous coal or railroad operations. Substantial damage to coke ovens, blast furnaces, open-hearth furnaces, and Bessemer converters can be avoided only if the equipment has been specially prepared for a shutdown. These preparations require several days for their completion and cause the cessation of other operations. Thus in the 1946 and 1949 stoppages, which began on dates announced well in advance, layoffs of workers commenced four days before the beginning of the stoppages, and by the immediately preceding day almost all basic steel employees were idle. On the other hand, in the 1952 strike, which though anticipated by many was called on short notice, a number of union members were retained (by agreement with the union) for several days after the beginning of the strike to assist in the shutdown of facilities.

Correspondingly, considerable time is required before full-scale operation of basic facilities can be resumed. Not until almost a month after the termination of the 1949 and 1952 strikes in basic steel companies had all their employees been called back to work.

How many nonstriking employees of struck companies were made idle is uncertain. The estimates of total idle cited above include nonstriking nonsupervisory plant employees but exclude, at least for 1949, supervisory and office workers. In none of the stoppages have all of the nonstrikers been laid off. Many were retained for some time, and some supervisory, office, and plant maintenance workers were retained for the entire duration of each strike, although in some cases at salaries reduced by as much as 50 per cent.

One of the largest categories among publics affected by steelworkers' strikes consists of members of the families of idle employees of struck plants. If it is assumed that each idle employee had two dependents, then for the first four weeks of the 1946 strike some one and one-half million persons were affected by virtue of family relationship; 600,000 of these were affected for at least another two weeks, and 56,000 for a total of sixteen weeks. The 1949 stoppage affected some million members of steelworkers' families for a month, 300,000 of these for an additional two weeks, and 90,000 of these for a total of ten weeks. About 1,246,000 were affected for eight weeks by the 1952 strike.

As in the case of bituminous coal miners, the main impact of a strike on steelworkers' families is through the financial problems it creates, and the size of the financial problems depends largely on how full employment in the struck plants has been in the preceding months and how full it is expected to be in succeeding months. A preceding period of sustained high employment tends to permit the accumulation of reserves; steelworkers were best off from this point of view at the beginning of the 1946 strike when, according to union estimates, the five preceding years of war work had led to the accumulation of savings amounting to an average of $600 for each steelworker. If the estimate made by a top industry official that the "average" steelworker lost about $207 in wages during the first four weeks of the strike is correct, then it is apparent that on an over-all basis the bulk of steelworkers' families were able to survive the strike without undue privation (although at the cost of dissaving), but individual cases of hardship may, of course, have occurred. The 1949 stoppage came during a period when there was a substantial amount of unemployment in steelmaking and fabricating; workers were therefore not so well prepared financially. Lack of reserves was offset to some extent, however, by the fact that the part of the striking contingent who had been laid off prior to the strike and were drawing unemployment compensation were permitted in some states to continue to draw such compensation throughout the strike. The number of such persons amounted to "thousands" in Pennsylvania.

The 1952 strike occurred during a period of full capacity operations in the basic steel industry, although some wages had been lost during the preceding two months owing to a four-day strike and a closing-down period preparatory to a threatened strike. By the end of the eight-week stoppage the average steelworker had lost an estimated $600 in wages; as early as the eighteenth day, however, a Pittsburgh local was receiving requests from strikers for financial assistance, and by the forty-eighth day 3200 strikers in the Pittsburgh area had applied for public relief.

Whether the loss of wages during a strike represents a net loss depends on the extent to which forgone employment may be made up by employment greater than otherwise would have prevailed in the post-strike period. Apparently some small amount of employment was recaptured following the 1946 and 1949 strikes, both of which occurred during periods of operations at 80 to 85 per cent of total industry capacity; it was specifically stated that at one plant of Carnegie-Illinois "production will be stepped up over the pre-strike level for an indefinite period" by the use of hitherto idle blast and open-hearth furnaces. Whether the pay loss resulting from the 1952 strike was a net loss is not clear; the industry had been working at over 100 per cent of rated capacity; and such a level of operations would permit little recovery. However, reports that steel company officials had feared prior to the strike that a falling off of demand for certain types of steel would force a drop to operations at only 85 per cent of capacity in the fourth quarter of 1952 suggest that perhaps the idleness during the strike may have constituted to some extent a mere pushing forward in time of approaching unemployment.

Nevertheless, the existence of excess capacity does not always insure the recapture of strike-caused reductions in steel output and employment. Even with unutilized capacity in 1946 it was said that almost all of the loss of steel-using products resulting from the strike of that year would have "to be written off as irretrievable." Steel capacity is by no means wholly interchangeable. Capacity *for the kinds of steel needed* during the 1946 industrial reconversion program apparently was being utilized almost fully and for these steel types no slack existed. It was later asserted that the loss of steel production in that strike had been felt for more than two years.

Certainly all of the pay losses suffered by the families of strikers in steel fabricating plants and in iron ore mines during the strikes cannot be charged to strikes in these establishments, since had these workers not joined in the walkout many would have nevertheless become idle within two to four weeks as a result of layoffs forced by shortages of primary steel products or lack of demand for ore. However, losses due to layoffs would have been substantially less than those materializing from participation in the strike, since idleness would have occurred for a shorter period and in some cases would have been partially offset by unemployment compensation payments.

Like the bituminous miners, steelworkers' families have had to face strikes of considerable duration with little outside assistance. The strike relief payments which can be made when the national union's total strike fund ($5,000,000 at the beginning of the 1946 strike) is less than the wage loss of strikers for one day ($6,500,000 during the 1946 strike) are insufficient for general relief. Union funds were reserved for families that were "especially hard pressed." In some states nonstriking employees, strikers unemployed at the time of the strike, and in one state even strikers employed at the time of the strike are qualified to draw unemployment compensation, but in many cases only after waiting periods longer than the duration of the strike. A factor mitigating the immediate effects of wage losses in the 1952 strike was the advancing of vacation pay by many steel companies.

Whether families of strikers living in areas the economy of which is dominated by steelmaking and fabricating have fared worse than those situated in less specialized areas is a moot point. During the 1946 stoppage regular benefits to strikers were paid from the municipal treasuries of a number of western Pennsylvania towns, and some steelworkers in that area were exempted from alimony payments for the duration of the strike. In the 1949 strike, however, several chains of stores in western Pennsylvania were obliged to limit credit to strikers as early as the seventh day.

Suppliers to the Steel Industry

Steelworkers' strikes cannot avoid having a perceptible effect on the revenues of local suppliers of goods and services to steelworkers' families. The 1946 strike involved an estimated pay loss by steelworkers of some $35,000,000 every week for four weeks, weekly losses amounting to perhaps a third of that amount for an additional four weeks, and relatively small losses for another eight weeks. An estimate of a total wage loss of $285,000,000 for the 1946 strike would probably not be too high. The total wage loss of the 1949 strike has been estimated at $200,000,000, of the 1952 strike at more than $350,000,000.

How seriously pay losses of such magnitude are felt by the regional and local suppliers of workers depends partly on the degree to which the workers are geographically concentrated. If the idle workers are distributed thinly over the entire nation, the proportion which their purchases constitute of the total sales of any supplier will tend to be negligible. But if the idle workers are concentrated in a relatively few areas the burden of the impact will be borne by a smaller number of suppliers. Steelworkers tend to be more concentrated geographically than do bituminous miners or railroad employees. Of the 750,000 steelworkers made idle by the 1946 strike, some 350,000—almost half—lived within a 150-mile radius of Pittsburgh. Almost 200,000 lived in the four counties comprising the Pittsburgh district; 150,000 in the Youngstown-Erie-West Virginia area; 75,000 in the Chicago area and 50,000 more in Gary; over 35,000 in Cleveland; and 32,000 in Buffalo. Thus five fairly limited areas account for almost three-quarters of the total number of idle steelworkers, and consequently for roughly the same proportion of wage losses. It is not surprising that in both the 1949 and 1952 strikes retail sales in Pittsburgh and Wheeling had fallen by about 25 per cent by the end of the third week of the strikes.

As noted in the discussion of bituminous strikes, the loss of $350,-000,000 in wage payments would almost certainly have, through the multiplier principle, a perceptible effect on general income flows—an effect amounting to a fall in national income of more than $1,000,-000,000 provided the income multiplier had a value as great as 3.

Steelworkers' strikes are capable of having a substantial effect on the employment and revenues of transport lines. Because of the nature of the data available it is impossible to distinguish precisely the effects sustained by railroads in their capacity as direct suppliers of services to the basic steel industry (that is, as haulers of basic steel products) from those sustained in their indirect supplier capacity as suppliers of hauling services to other suppliers of the basic steel industry, such as the bituminous coal and iron mining industries, or as suppliers of carrying services to steel-using industries. However, the early layoffs and fall in revenues which occurred during the 1952 strike on Eastern district railroads such as the Pennsylvania, Baltimore & Ohio, Erie, and New York Central can probably be attributed to the loss of basic steel, coal, and ore loadings. By the fifth day such lines had furloughed 19,800 employees and had sustained decreases of as much as 25 per cent in freight revenues (New York Central) or 23 per cent in carloadings (Erie). By the sixteenth day, railroads' total loss in revenue (borne mainly by the Eastern lines) was put at $5,000,000 a week. By the thirty-seventh day the effects of the curtailments in steel-using industries were being registered in the form of additional layoffs on Eastern and other railroads. By the forty-fourth day freight car loadings had declined to their lowest level since the depression year of 1934, and 130,000 railroad workers (about 10 per cent of the railroads' total labor force) were idle, yet further layoffs were still being made. Two months after the end of the strike some of these workers had not yet been called back to work. By the end of the strike revenues of Eastern lines were 50 per cent below those of the previous year, though because of the cutting of labor costs through furloughing net income had not fallen proportionately.

A small part of the revenues and employment that railroads lost because of the strike was recaptured in the form of an increase in rail shipments of iron ore after the strike ended. The losses to the national economy during the strike were partially compensated also: equipment idled by the strike became available for the movement of a bumper winter wheat crop, which had been harvested during an unusually concentrated period of time, and some of which would otherwise have been lost.

Less drastic layoffs of railroad workers were reported in the 1946 and 1949 strikes. By the fifth day of the 1946 stoppage over 5000 had been furloughed; by the twelfth day over 6000 in the Pittsburgh area alone. By the seventh day of the 1949 strike 20,000 railroad workers were idle.

The effects of steel strikes can penetrate back to suppliers of railroads. The increased supply of available freight cars during the 1952 strike led railroad companies to cut their orders for new cars.

The closing down of ore mines in Minnesota and Michigan eventually brings to a halt shipments of ore on the Great Lakes, as stock piles at the docks dwindle away. The refusal of the union to permit unloading of ore at the mills during the 1952 strike caused Great Lakes shipments to fall 50 per cent by the end of the first week and 94 per cent by the end of the second week. By the forty-seventh day 220 of the total 275 Great Lakes ore carriers as well as all of Bethlehem's ten ocean-going ore vessels were laid up in harbor. Besides their crews, dock workers—some eighty-five at Marquette, for example—were idled. Since the ore lines operate mostly at full capacity during the open season on the Lakes in any case, not much of the lost employment could be recaptured after the end of the strike.

Every other form of long-distance transport except the air lines was also affected by the 1952 strike. By the end of the seventh week hundreds of workers on inland waterways had been laid off, and river barge companies, with traffic 20 per cent under normal, were losing thousands of dollars each week. Intercoastal shipping felt the loss of steel cargoes; crews of eight ships were laid off in New York City alone during the sixth week. During the seventh week the Defense Transport Administrator announced that the strike had "forced most highway steel haulers off the road." Layoffs of crews on Great Lakes ore carriers and river barges occurred also during the 1946 and 1949 strikes.

The direct effect of the three steelworkers' strikes on employment in one of steel's most important supplying industries, bituminous coal, has been varied. In the 1952 strike all the "captive" mines shut down on the first day, idling 50,000 miners for the duration of the strike and a smaller number for an additional week or so. Bituminous miners were less affected by the 1946 strike; 17,000 were idle by the fifth day, but a considerable number of these were soon called back to work, for by the tenth day only 7200 were idle and even by the twelfth and twenty-sixth days only about 8200 and 8900, respectively. Almost all of these were employees of "captive" mines. The main reason for the smaller number of layoffs among coal miners in 1946 was that many of the large basic steel companies, when barred from delivering coal to their picketed plants, leased space near their mines, continued to mine coal, and stockpiled it on the leased land. Nevertheless, the output of coal in the Pittsburgh area had by the eleventh day dropped about 15 per cent. The 1949 strike had almost no effect on employment of bituminous miners since from the beginning of the steel walkout until its fortieth day the miners themselves were on strike. By the fortieth day over 40 per cent of the basic steel industry's capacity was back in operation and by the forty-fourth day over 70 per cent.

The steel strikes have affected other suppliers of materials, fuels, and power for steelmaking. An unspecified number of workers in Pennsylvania, Ohio, and West Virginia limestone quarries and in Pennsylvania coke ovens were reported to have been laid off during the 1946 and 1949 stoppages. During the 1952 strike the fall in demand for zinc to be used in galvanizing steel led to a temporary fall in the price of zinc and to curtailments in the output of lead zinc mines in Oklahoma. Manufacturers of alloys also suffered a falling off of sales. Lack of the basic steel industry's consumption of a million barrels of fuel oil a week led to curtailments in the size of oil runs to refineries during the 1952 strike. Demand for electric power had dropped "drastically" in the Cleveland area by the sixth day of the 1952 strike. By the eleventh day of the 1946 strike the University of Pittsburgh's index of electric power output for the Pittsburgh area had fallen by more than 17 per cent.

The magnitude of the effects of a steelworkers' strike on the suppliers of goods and services to employees and firms in an area where such employees, firms, and suppliers are heavily concentrated is suggested by the fact that by the eleventh day of the 1946 strike business activity in the Pittsburgh area had dropped by more than one-third. The fall was even greater during the 1949 steelworkers' stoppage—over 55 per cent by the fourteenth day—but part of this decline must be attributed to the impact of the concurrent bituminous coal strike. The effects are also suggested by the fact that on the fifth day of the 1949 strike, leaders of Community Chest campaigns in two steel cities, Youngstown and Midland, Pennsylvania, decided to defer solicitation until after the strike had ended.

Users of Steel Products

Since at least two of the three steelworkers' strikes studied covered firms in many industries, each with substantially different types of users, user effects must be discussed in terms of each of the major categories of industries involved.

All three strikes were centered in the basic steel industry. In peacetime its major customers are the automobile and construction industries, each taking (as of 1951) about 17 per cent of the whole output. Machinery and tools consumed about 10 per cent, railroads and containers each about 8 per cent, oil and gas and appliances each about 3 per cent.

As in a bituminous strike, the extent to which the users of basic steel products are affected by a strike is mainly a function of the percentage of basic steel capacity shut down, the size of stocks accumulated prior to the strike, the rate of consumption during the strike, and, of course, these as they are affected by the duration of the strike. Unlike the case in railroad strikes, and to a lesser extent than in bituminous strikes, the availability of substitutes for the struck product is a negligible variable, for possibilities of substitution for steel in the short run are for most users slight. For that considerable number of steel-using firms which are under contract to the United Steelworkers, however, the major determinant of whether they are affected, *as members of the public*, by a steelworkers' strike is the union's decision as to their inclusion or exclusion in the strike coverage. Thus during the 1949 and 1952 strikes many steel-using firms were affected by a shortage of basic steel products who had not been so affected during the 1946 strike simply because during the earlier stoppage their plants, too, had been struck.

There has been little variation in the percentage of basic steel industry shut down during the hard core of each strike. In all three strikes it has fallen between 85 and 95 per cent. In addition, the 1946 strike was preceded by a week of relatively low operations—around 50 per cent of capacity. The period of almost total shutdown was longest, of course, in the 1952 strike, and somewhat longer in 1949 than in 1946. In the 1946 strike, firms representing 32 per cent of total capacity were operating by the fifth week, but only about 20 per cent by the same time in the 1949 strike. By the sixth week, firms representing 58 per cent of capacity were operating in 1946; only 40 per cent in 1949.

The ending of a strike does not bring an immediate full resumption of operations; recovery takes longer than in bituminous coal or railroads. Several weeks are usually required before the pre-strike level of operations in pig iron and steel ingots is restored and often several weeks more before the pre-strike amount of rolled-steel products are being shipped out to customers. Thus the real "pinch" on users may not develop until after the end of the strike.

As for current output during the strike, there has been little variation in the three stoppages in the effects among steel users, since a shutdown of 85 per cent or more of the industry's capacity stops almost completely the production of *all* types of primary steel products. The situation is quite different with respect to stocks and rates of consumption. Primary steel products are much more highly specialized and much less interchangeable than, for example, are the various types of bituminous coal. Structural beams are of no use to a washing-machine manufacturer, and container plate is of little value to a construction firm. Thus the over-all level of stocks and of consumption rates is of little significance; only the particular stock-consumption ratio applicable to each type of user is relevant to the matter of effects. Unfortunately, the data available are inadequate for the presentation of stock-consumption ratios for each of the major categories of steel users in each of the strikes and must be regarded as only suggestive.

The 1946 stoppage occurred during the early stages of reconversion from a wartime to a peacetime economy. The basic steel industry had been operating on a peacetime basis for only about three months. Production of many kinds of consumers' and producers' durable equipment and construction was just getting under way. Steel stocks were still subject to government control. No manufacturer was permitted to have more than a sixty-day supply. Because sheet steel, the main component of automobiles, refrigerators, washing machines, and other consumers' durable equipment, was especially scarce, a forty-five-day supply of this type was the maximum allowed. Actually, according to the head of the Civilian Production Administration, few manufacturers of domestic electrical equipment had more than a thirty-to-forty-day supply of sheet steel and many had less than a fifteen-day supply. Automobile producers customarily carried only a seven-to-ten-day supply of sheet steel, but some had increased their stocks in anticipation of the strike. Also in particularly short supply were malleable castings, structural steel, concrete bars, and rails. On the twelfth day of the strike the CPA reduced the maximum stock limits for all kinds of steel to a forty-five-day supply.

Besides users' stocks there are those belonging to the basic steel companies themselves and those held by independent warehouses. But the union has permitted the out-shipment through picket lines of steel from the basic steel companies' stocks only to military contractors or to customers who require it for uses related to public health and safety— that is, for use by public utilities, hospitals, railroads, food processors, and fire and police departments. During the 1946 strike some 11,000 carloads of steel were tied up in the yards of Pittsburgh steel plants. (Because some of it rusted beyond use, stocks available at the end of the strike were decreased.)

Moreover, during the 1946 stoppage the comparatively small stocks of warehouses were not available for the fabrication of products. On the first day of the strike governmental authorities instituted a program whereby all warehouse steel was reserved for uses necessary to public health and safety. However desirable in objective, this action, like similar ones taken with respect to coal stocks during bituminous strikes, may have hastened curtailment of output by nonessential users. Certainly considerable amounts of steel were withheld from use during the strike, for by the twenty-fourth day warehouse stocks had declined by only one-third.

In 1946 the circumstance of relatively small stocks of steel, especially sheet steel, opposed to a large demand was mitigated by the concurrence of strikes in the automobile and electrical manufacturing industries. The automobile plants of General Motors, which normally produce almost half of the total national output of passenger cars, and the electrical equipment plants of General Electric and Westinghouse were shut down by strikes during the entire period of the basic steel strike, and the electrical equipment plants of General Motors were shut down for its first three weeks. A sizable portion of the steel industry's market was thus out of operation.

The 1949 stoppage occurred at the beginning of a recovery after a period of mild recession in general business activity. Stocks of major steel users were said to amount to about a thirty-day supply. Many users, however, uncertain about price trends, had let their stocks fall below this level. Others had adjusted to the recession by sharply cutting back orders for steel and using up existing stocks. Now with increasing demand for their products, they found their steel stock piles severely depleted. Most important in this category were manufacturers of domestic electrical appliances, many of whom had supplies for only two weeks of full operations. Users of structural steel, on the other hand, started the strike with large supplies. For railroad lines the absolute level of their stocks could be low without causing hardship, for their rate of consumption of steel was abnormally low during the strike, owing to the circumstance that the establishment as of September 1 of a forty-hour week for nonoperating railway employees had prompted the completion of extensive (steel-using) maintenance projects a month before the steel strike began.

The 1952 strike occurred at a time when a rising demand for certain types of military goods was combined with a sagging demand for some types of civilian goods, especially consumers' durable equipment. The accumulation of heavy inventories of household appliances had caused some curtailment of output during the previous two months. Stock-consumption ratios of light steel products used for automobiles and home appliances were relatively high, at least high enough so that there had been no stepping up of demand for this type of steel even after the prospect of a strike and higher prices appeared. Stock-consumption ratios of heavy steel products used in construction, of oil and gas pipe, and of special alloy steel used for engines for military aircraft, ammunition, and atomic weapons were relatively low. To protect stocks needed for military purposes, the federal government placed an extensive embargo on exports of steel and froze warehouse inventories at the beginning of the strike. The latter action was presumably of limited value, for as one magazine put it, "The military is a custom orderer of steel goods"; it uses relatively small amounts of the shapes and forms ordinarily carried in warehouses.[3] As in 1946 the action probably accelerated the onset of layoffs throughout civilian steel-using industries in general. (In an attempt to hold down the number of layoffs the government on the forty-fourth day of the strike released from warehouses steel that was unsuitable for military production but useful for the manufacture of home appliances.)

Although the over-all levels of the steel stocks of many manufacturers of civilian goods were high in 1952, most of their stock piles were in a state of imbalance—too much of some kinds of steel, too little of other kinds. Since the item in shortest supply controlled the rate of operations, the possession of over-all high stocks was of small advantage.

In a particularly precarious position in all steelworkers' strikes are the 200,000 or so small steel-using manufacturers who maintain low stocks, operating on almost a hand-to-mouth basis.

Aside from these general observations, the user effects of basic steel strikes can best be appreciated by considering the effect of these three major strikes on each of the principal categories of steel users.

1. Automobiles and Agricultural Implements

At least in respect to employment effects, the major user impact of steelworkers' strikes has been on the automobile and agricultural implement industries. On the fifth day of the 1946 stoppage the Ford Motor Company laid off 15,000 workers in the Detroit area, and a few days later laid off 3000 more. By the seventh day a Detroit parts supplier had laid off 1500 employees. By the twelfth day the River Rouge

[3] *Business Week*, April 5, 1952.

final assembly plant was completely shut down and a total of almost 30,000 Ford workers in Detroit and other sections were idle, in addition to 600 employees of a Milwaukee auto frame manufacturer and 5200 employees of a Chicago agricultural implement company. By the fourth week of the strike at least a dozen Ford assembly plants had shut down, idling 40,000 employees, and some of them remained closed for six weeks. Altogether some 60,000 auto workers were idle. The Ford employees' idleness represents in part an indirect user effect, for the company gave as one reason for its layoffs a shortage of parts resulting from the inability of some of its parts suppliers to obtain steel.

The effect on the automobile industry might have been greater had it not been that General Motors was shut down by its own strike for the entire period of the steelworkers' strike and that other companies were already curtailing output because of shortages stemming from strikes in glass and parts plants.

The 1949 strike had a less drastic but still substantial effect on employment in the automobile and agricultural implement industries. On the sixth day shortages of steel impelled Packard and Briggs, who made bodies for Packard, to lay off 13,000 employees. On the twenty-fifth day an Illinois tractor company began a program of layoffs and shortened work weeks for its 25,000 employees. On the twenty-ninth day Chrysler and Ford announced the beginning of layoffs which would eventually lead to the complete shutting down of their plants and the idling of some 200,000 workers on the forty-fifth day.

The settlement with Bethlehem Steel, which occurred on the thirty-first day, came too late, according to an automobile industry executive, to prevent widespread curtailments of automobile output. Although the settlement created hopes for prompt termination of the strike among all the major steel producers, it was pointed out that the auto industry's steel supplies could not be replenished until from three to six weeks after the restoration of full operations in the steel industry. Ford did cancel its plans for more extensive layoffs but at the same time eliminated all overtime work. Chrysler, asserting that it could not expect to obtain any new supplies of steel for at least a month, proceeded on the thirty-fifth day to lay off 35,000 employees. By that time 14,000 Hudson employees had become idle, and several plants of General Motors were operating on a four-day week. In spite of further settlements with major steel producers, by the forty-first day two Nash plants in Wisconsin had shut down and a Toledo manufacturer of jeeps had closed down his assembly lines, idling 7000.

These effects were dwarfed by those eventually brought on by the 1952 strike. Initial layoffs were longer in materializing. As was the case with many other steel users, auto plants, rather than curtailing output early and thus conserving stocks, chose to operate at full capacity till their stocks of crucial materials were exhausted and then shut down. It was reported that this choice was prompted by a willingness to gamble on their stocks' outlasting the strike, by a desire to show a high output for a period which, it was believed, would constitute the basis for future government allocations of scarce materials, and by the knowledge that the period of the next few months was the peak season for sales of passenger cars. To keep production going, manufacturers adopted such costly expedients as altering steel stocks to fit emergency purposes or using higher-grade steel than called for in specifications. (At one Ford plant, for example, shortages of large steel sheets for tops and hoods were met by patching small sheets together.)

Thus no layoffs in the auto industry were reported until the twenty-sixth day of the strike. On that day 4500 employees of an auto body plant were laid off, and from then on idleness mounted rapidly. General Motors, Ford, and smaller companies began making sizable layoffs, joined on the forty-third day by Chrysler. Total layoffs of automobile workers caused by shortages of steel amounted to 60,000 on the twenty-ninth day, 75,000 on the thirty-first day, 250,000 on the thirty-seventh day, and 300,000 (about 45 per cent of all production workers in the industry) on the forty-fourth day. Idleness fluctuated somewhat after that date; some auto plants alternated weeks of limited operations with weeks of total shutdown. Because stocks had been so depleted, the resumption of steel operations after the settlement on the fifty-third day did not bring a quick recovery to the auto industry. Two weeks after the end of the strike most of the Ford, Chrysler, and General Motors operations were still shut down.

Idleness in the agricultural implement industry was also considerable. On the twenty-seventh day one plant laid off 3000; other plants laid off 2,000 more on the fiftieth and an additional 19,000 on the fifty-seventh day.

How much of this employment loss was recaptured is difficult to judge. Seven weeks after the end of the strike, operations were fully restored, but the major auto companies' attempts to institute overtime and week-end work were handicapped by shortages of labor.

The precise extent to which the ultimate consumers of steel in the form of passenger cars were affected by these strikes cannot be ascertained. By the end of the 1949 strike output of vehicles by the auto industry had declined about 23 per cent from immediately previous levels. By the end of the 1952 strike output was 60 per cent below that for immediately previous months. At that time 250,000 vehicles were said already to have been lost owing to the strike, and the level of operations was to remain low for several more weeks. After the restoration of normal operations a government official announced that $1,000,000,-000 worth of vehicles had been lost because of the strike.

As early as the forty-second day, shortages of some brands and models were reported causing an average falling off of sales amounting to 8 per cent. By one month after the strike, trade journals reported, stocks of new cars were at the lowest level since the end of the war. Some consumers would not be able to get new cars except after a substantial wait, and many of these would therefore postpone purchases until the following season. Between this tendency to postpone purchases and the difficulties of increasing output due to labor shortages the auto industry only partially recaptured the revenue and employment afforded by the 1952 models but lost because of the strike.

Curtailments of such magnitude as occurred during the 1952 strike could not fail to affect suppliers of goods and services to the auto industry. One supplier of parts to auto companies was forced to shut down on the fiftieth day and lay off 2200 employees, not for lack of steel with which to make parts but for lack of orders for parts from the shut-down auto plants. The decrease in the price and output of zinc, mentioned previously, was partly due to the falling off in the auto industry's market for zinc for die castings. By the forty-seventh day, according to the Defense Transport Administrator, highway auto carriers were "rapidly being taken out of service."

2. Domestic Electrical Appliances

Effects of the 1946 strike on the auto industry overshadowed those on the electrical appliance industry. The only specific report discovered was a statement that on the twelfth day an Indiana manufacturer of refrigerators had laid off 950 employees, though other instances must have occurred. However, it was the repercussion on the output of domestic electrical appliances which received most newspaper attention during the 1949 strike. As mentioned above, steel stocks of companies producing such goods were low and demand for the goods was high. On the fourth day Westinghouse reported that shortages of steel had forced it to begin rationing deliveries of refrigerators, kitchen ranges, washing machines, driers, vacuum cleaners, water heaters, and fans to its dealers. On the twenty-first day General Electric announced the beginning of "relatively light" layoffs at its Schenectady plant, and on the thirty-first day Hotpoint, one of its affiliates, laid off 5000 workers from a Chicago plant.

The 1952 strike also had considerable effect on the electrical appliance industry. Only a month before the strike General Electric, Westinghouse, and General Motors had curtailed production in an effort to reduce the inventories of appliances in which they were reported to be "wallowing uncomfortably." By the forty-fourth day of the strike, General Electric and Westinghouse were again curtailing output (laying off a total of 22,500 workers) but this time because of steel shortages. As late as the sixty-seventh day after the beginning of the strike General Electric was forced to lay off 2650 employees because of the continuation of the strike in the plants of its supplier of a special type of steel. Some portion of these layoffs may be considered as only a substitution for layoffs which might otherwise have come (in the absence of the strike) because of the sluggish movement of inventories.

According to reports at the end of the strike, buyers of home appliances could expect to feel the effects of the strike. Industry sources reported that owing to strike-caused curtailments "the last uncomfortable inventories were wiped clean," prices had been "strengthened," and the time at which a seller's market would become a buyer's market had been pushed into the future. A company official announced that as a result of the strike there would be temporary shortages of General Electric ranges, refrigerators, freezers, washing machines, clothes driers, and most models of water heaters.

3. Containers

The 1946 strike had a perceptible effect on the drug and cosmetic trade by interfering with the shift from cardboard containers used during wartime to the prewar type of metal (steel) containers. Drug wholesalers were affected through a continuation of the handling losses caused by the frequent breakage of cardboard containers. Manufacturers were affected through their inability to reintroduce products of "superior quality" which had been withdrawn during the war and the reappearance of which was awaiting the time when sufficient tinplate was available for their packaging in durable containers. Shortages of containers also necessitated some layoffs, as for example of 1200 employees of a coffee-processing plant in New Jersey.

To what extent a lack of containers was a result of the inclusion in the strike of container-fabricating plants rather than the stoppage of basic steel output is not clear.

The 1952 strike occurred during a season in which output of containers is greatly increased in order to supply the increased needs of the canning industry and caused considerable consternation among government and industry officials on that ground alone. On the thirty-eighth day, after reports that some small canneries had shut down for lack of containers, government authorities ordered the sole operating maker of tinplate to channel all its output to makers of cans for perishable foods and prohibited the use of tinplate for beer, coffee, and dog food containers. In spite or because of this action, a container plant in the New York City area shut down during the sixth week, idling 1500 employees. During the seventh week, officials of the National Grange said that serious losses of food were occurring because of shortages of containers, and after the end of the strike the National Association of Manufacturers stated that "approximately 2,000,000 cases of food were lost for the lack of steel for cans."[4]

4. Construction

Following the 1946 strike government officials stated that shortages of steel caused by the stoppage had retarded the building of residences. Particularly serious was the shortage of galvanized sheet steel for hot-air furnaces. The Commissioner of Public Works of the State of New York announced that the strike had necessitated deferring for as much as a year an extensive public works and permanent housing program. Construction of some $40,000,000 worth of state homes, hospitals, prisons, and schools, $80,000,000 worth of highways, and $100,000,-000 worth of low-rent housing had been postponed. The loss in employment to building trades workers and in revenues to suppliers of building materials of more than $200,000,000 worth of construction could be

[4] National Association of Manufacturers, *Who Lost the Steel Strike?* (September, 1952).

expected to be substantial even though these projects were simply postponed, since new jobs had to be found to fill in the period of postponement.

Because of the prior accumulation of large stocks of steel, apparently no more than scattered delays in large-building construction were experienced during the 1949 strike.

Probably the most serious effect of the 1952 strike on activity in the construction industry was the abandonment by the federal government of pledges to relax restrictions on the use of steel in the construction of houses and commercial buildings; several months after the end of the strike the government limited the use of structural steel for new projects to those essential to the defense program. Curtailments of construction activity during the strike were, according to the Commerce Department, "small and spotty." Construction of several water and sewer lines in Dallas was halted. Some 250 persons employed in the construction of a hospital in New York City were laid off. Work on various new television stations had to be postponed. The Department predicted, however, that more severe effects would follow the end of the strike, and an official of the American Automobile Association stated that the strike had caused highway construction and maintenance programs throughout the nation to fall about 100,000 miles behind schedules for 1952.

5. Miscellaneous Users of Basic Steel Products

Curtailment in production among miscellaneous steel-using manufacturers was reported later in the 1946 strike than in the 1949 stoppage. "Almost no curtailments" was the report at the end of the first week of the 1946 strike. Reduction of production schedules by "dozens," and expectation of immediate closing by "scores," of manufacturers was reported at a similar juncture of the 1949 strike. At the end of the fourth week of the 1946 strike, however, lack of steel had forced many users to reduce operations.

As in the case of the auto and home appliance industries, curtailments of operations by miscellaneous steel-using industries occurred relatively late in the course of the 1952 stoppage but they were continued for a long time after the end of the strike. On the twenty-seventh day the beginning of curtailments by New England manufacturers was reported. During the sixth week some 15,000 employees in New York State plants were laid off and another 1400 put on part-time work.

Three weeks after the end of the strike a basic steel company was forced to lay off 4000 employees of one of its fabricating plants for lack of steel, and many New England steel-using plants were still shut down. Seven weeks after the end of the strike steel shortages were causing lay-offs by Philadelphia manufacturers.

Reports of effects on specific types of steel-using manufacturers indicate that output of freight cars was curtailed as early as the twenty-fifth day, a locomotive plant was shut down on the sixtieth day, and the total loss of railroad rolling stock due to strike-caused steel shortages was 300 diesel locomotives and 20,000 freight cars. Layoffs in machinery and tool plants had been instituted by the twenty-seventh day. Lack of steel for tire rims forced layoffs of 1000 Akron employees of Goodyear and Firestone on the thirty-second day. A printing press manufacturer laid off 200 workers, and a radiator and sanitary company shut down during the sixth week. During the second and third months following the start of the strike steel shortages prevented the inauguration of production work on barges with a consequent fall in employment of one-third in one shipyard and 45 per cent in another. The catalogue of steel-using plants affected could be extended to include representatives of virtually every major industry.

Having been on a hand-to-mouth basis with respect to steel supplies at the beginning of the 1952 strike, the oil industry (which as a supplier also suffered from loss of the basic steel industry's market) was among the most severely affected of the steel-using industries. Chemical companies were said to have been hard hit also, not by lack of steel but as a result of the shutdown of the basic steel industry's coke ovens, from the by-products of which some of the companies derived as much as 80 per cent of their supplies.

As was the case with the auto industry, curtailments of output by other steel users during the 1952 strike had effects on the suppliers of goods to these users. Such curtailments were contributory causes of the cutbacks in the output of petroleum products and of a 20 per cent drop in the prices of industrial diamonds, reflecting a decline in demand from diemakers and drillers.

How much of this lost production was recoverable by subsequent make-up operations is problematical, but unquestionably the amount of such postponable output was substantial, despite the continuing high-level utilization of manufacturing facilities. Nevertheless, we are not entitled to assume that—at least from the standpoint of wage earners attached to the affected firms—postponed income is an exact equivalent for current income. There are hardships attending a current loss of receipts for which subsequent earnings do not always compensate.

6. User Effects of Strikes at Nonbasic Steel Plants

As noted previously, both the 1946 and 1949 steelworkers' strikes included companies other than basic steel companies, but since there is no reason to believe that this is a necessary pattern for a steelworkers' strike it is desirable—but, unfortunately, also difficult—to discuss separately those user effects which are attributable to strikes against nonbasic steel companies. The extent to which reduction in output of automobiles and containers was due to the inclusion of parts plants and container plants in the steel workers' strikes, rather than to a shortage of basic steel products, is not easily ascertained. The entire matter of the user effects of steelworkers' strikes in nonbasic steel plants is extremely complicated, because the 700 companies struck in 1946 were distributed among more than forty different industries, and as between industries there were great variations in the percentage of total capacity shut down, levels of stock-consumption ratios, and duration of the strike.

The sort of user effect which can arise, however, out of a union-wide steelworkers' strike which includes nonbasic steel companies is suggested by the 1946 case of a milk container plant. The USA's contractual relationship with the American Can Company included a plant in Brooklyn which manufactured one-half of the total number of paper milk containers used in the New York metropolitan area. Packaged milk (sold mainly in stores and restaurants) accounted for about one-quarter of all milk sold in the area. Thus when the Brooklyn plant was shut down by the strike, the area was deprived of containers for about 12½ per cent of its daily milk supply. As of the first day of the strike milk distributors were reported to have in no case more than a three-day supply of paper containers. Most distributors' supplies of glass bottles, a relatively satisfactory substitute, were totally inadequate to fill the gap, as were supplies of the necessary accompanying wooden cases. Proposals for the sale of milk in stores in bulk, with the customer providing her own container, were rejected by city authorities as being too hazardous to health.

By the third day of the strike, one major distributor had cut deliveries of packaged milk by 20 per cent, the other major distributor had cut deliveries to restaurants but had maintained deliveries to stores through the use of glass bottles, and the small distributors (supplying stores only) had cut deliveries by 30 to 50 per cent. The city's health commissioner estimated that New York consumers were being deprived of 500,000 quarts of milk daily because of the strike. By the twenty-ninth day supplies of milk were still reduced; on the forty-second day the strike was terminated at the Brooklyn plant.

The proportion of basic aluminum capacity shut down by steel-workers' strikes has been much less than the proportion of basic steel capacity. In the 1949 strike, in which nine of the Aluminum Company of America's twenty-five plants were struck, about 25 per cent of the country's total basic aluminum capacity was closed down. Company officials stated that the strike would have little effect on output or employment at the sixteen unstruck plants, since two of them produced basic aluminum, which together with accumulated stocks would provide primary metal for the fourteen fabricating plants. At the most 1000 fabricating workers might be laid off.

According to newspaper reports, in neither the 1946 nor the 1949 strike was there any curtailment of airplane production due to aluminum shortages. The 1946 strike, however, was said to have caused the loss to consumers of a million aluminum pots and pans. Whether this was due to strike closings of basic aluminum or fabricating plants is not clear.

Household Consumers

There are no reliable estimates of the over-all effects of steel stoppages on members of the public in their capacity as consumers. Statements were made that by the twenty-seventh day of the 1946 strike a total of 6 million tons of raw steel or 4.2 million tons of finished steel products had been lost, that the 1949 strike cost more than 10 million tons and the 1952 strike 17.5 million tons of raw steel, that during the hard core of the 1946 strike the amount of steel lost daily was sufficient to have made 195,000 automobiles, 2,350,000 refrigerators, 14,700,000 typewriters, and so on. The latter sort of estimate, of course, gives no idea of what combination of autos, refrigerators, and typewriters actually failed to be manufactured during the strike because of steel shortages.

There is no question that some amounts of consumers' goods (and intermediate producers' goods) were lost during each of the strikes. To what extent losses were permanent and to what extent they were merely temporary is less certain. At the end of the 1952 strike those authorities who believed that, had the strike not occurred, the rate of operations in basic steel would have fallen to around 85 per cent of capacity by the end of the year apparently also believed that this situation meant that all the losses in civilian output suffered during the strike and subsequent period of reduced operations would *eventually* be made up. This belief neglects the fact that delays of several months may mean permanent losses to many consumers, in the form of having to do without the services of desired equipment or having to make do with faulty or inadequate equipment. Moreover, a postponement of a purchase may mean a postponement of each subsequent replacement; this may continue indefinitely into the future, so that the loss suffered both in consumer satisfaction and in producer income is never fully made up. And the loss of income sustained by members of the public in their capacity as producers—the annual rate of personal income fell off by $2,500,000,000 during the second month of the 1952 strike—may lead them, in their capacity as consumers, to cancel intended purchases.

National Security Programs

The 1946 strike occurred at a time when considerable amounts of American resources were being devoted to European rehabilitation. The 1949 strike came during the early stages of European rearmament, and the 1952 strike while the United States was engaged in hostilities in Korea. No mention was discovered of any effects on national security programs caused by the 1946 and 1949 strikes, but considerable attention was given to the effects of the 1952 strike on the output of military goods. As noted previously, stocks of the types of steel used in the production of aircraft engines, ammunition, and atomic weapons were said to be low at the beginning of the strike. Governmental authorities made various efforts to keep military production going throughout the strike. They reserved all warehouse and mill stocks for military production and funneled top priority defense orders into the basic steel plants still operating.

Such measures were of limited value since warehouses generally do not carry, and the unstruck plants were not equipped to make, the specialized kind of steel necessary for military goods. Moreover, seeing that military contractors get priority on steel supplies is a task of enormous complexity. As one reporter pointed out, a plant turning out B-29 airplanes is supplied by 18,000 other plants, and *each* of these is supplied by many subcontractors, *each* of whom depend on many other subcontractors. "Somewhere in the maze a supplier fails to produce a tenth part of a vital part because he depended on a supplier who depended on another supplier who ran out of stuff and didn't give warning because he had been expecting a shipment of raw materials and suddenly it turned up missing."[5] Apparently believing that the available stocks were insufficient to support continued production, governmental authorities on the eighth day secured an agreement on the part of the companies and union to permit the production in certain struck plants of essential military material. But details of such a project could not be worked out and the plants remained closed.

The first report of curtailments in the output of military goods came on the eighteenth day of the strike with the announcement that an Ohio plant making mortar and artillery shells had gone on a three-days-a-week working schedule. The next day a plant making 4500 mortar shells daily shut down, and another shell plant laid off 500 employees on the thirty-second. Nevertheless, on the thirty-fourth day Army officials said the production of ammunition had not yet been affected.

On the forty-seventh day Air Force officials announced that they had "a long list of reports of partial stoppages," due to steel shortages, in the production of Air Force material. On the fifty-first day the Army's largest shell-making plant was shut down, with 2600 idled, and on the fifty-ninth day it was announced that the plant would remain closed for three weeks more. The day before the strike was terminated the Secretary of Defense stated that during the seventh week twenty-nine manufacturing facilities supplying the Navy had shut down, and that "in recent weeks" manufacturers of Navy rocket motors and heads, 20 mm. projectiles, mine sweeper generators, proximity fuses, torpedo parts, soldiers' helmets, and parts for gas masks had ceased operations. Moreover, the 57 mm. recoilless cartridge was now being turned out at a rate slower than that at which it was being fired by American soldiers in Korea. Subsequently Defense Department officials reported that during the second month of the strike military truck production had been sharply curtailed and production of jet engines "slowed down to a walk." Output of military aircraft, however, was "on schedule."

There appeared to be some disagreement about the strikes' ultimate effects on output of military goods. The day before the strike ended the

[5] *New York Times*, August 17, 1952.

Secretary of Defense stated that "No enemy nation could have so crippled our production as has this work stoppage. No form of bombing could have taken out of production in one day 380 steel plants and kept them out nearly two months." He estimated that the strike would result in the loss of "between 20 and 30 per cent of all armaments scheduled for delivery during the calendar year." (Subsequently, he said that there had been losses in aircraft production amounting to 20 per cent, and 37 per cent in ammunition.) Some three weeks later Defense Department officials announced that the full amount of the strike-caused loss could not be made up until late 1954 at the soonest and probably not until 1955 or 1956. To illustrate the nature of the difficulties ahead the officials cited the case of a forging plant which forged 60 per cent of projectiles for a major artillery weapon. It had been closed throughout the strike. Since it and "all other forging companies" had been "running night and day" before the strike "just to keep up with the defense program," no expansion of output to compensate for losses incurred during the strike could be expected.

On the other hand, a business journal[6] stated that "very little arms output" had been lost due to steel shortages.

Losses of another sort of military material were reported. On the fifty-first day the Red Cross reported that the industrial layoffs in the Detroit area had caused a falling off in blood collections made by the mobile units which visited plants.[7]

Regional Concentration of Effects

A discussion of the over-all effects on the public of steel strikes neglects the important consideration that these effects tend to be concentrated in certain geographic areas. The result is to focus a given impact on a smaller public. The concentration of effects which stems from the geographical concentration of the basic steel and steel fabricating industries has already been noted. It is illustrated by the fact that on the forty-second day of the 1952 strike one-half of the *total labor force* of Youngstown, Ohio (an important basic steel and steel-using center), was idle either through participation in the strike or through strike-caused layoffs. But it is also noteworthy that the idleness which occurs not only in the steel industry itself but also in its user and supplier industries tends to be concentrated in certain areas.

[6] *Business Week*, August 16, 1952.
[7] *Detroit Free Press*, July 20, 1952.

The Pennsylvania was among the railroads hardest hit by the 1952 steel strike. A substantial portion of its maintenance and operating employees live in Altoona, and this portion constitutes a large majority of the city's labor force. Thus a substantial proportion of the Pennsylvania's total layoffs during the 1952 strike fell on Altoona employees, and these Altoona layoffs (amounting by the end of the strike to 12,000, or half the city's total labor force, and lasting, in part, until two months after the end of the strike) could not fail to have had a pronounced effect on suppliers and public relief facilities in the area. To cite another example, about 160,000 of the 300,000 auto workers idle by the forty-fourth day of the 1952 steel strike lived in the Detroit area, a situation which produced many kinds of effects on members of the Detroit public, including a falling off of 25 per cent in the daily alimony collections made by the Detroit courts and a rise of 26 per cent in complaints registered by ex-wives.

The experiences of early April, 1952, indicate that even the *threat* of a strike against basic steel companies may have perceptible effects on members of the public. The USA announced in March that a strike against basic steel companies would begin at 12:01 A.M., April 9. The stoppage was averted at that time by government seizure of the industry late on April 8, but by the time of the seizure 400,000 employees of basic steel companies and 55,000 employees of captive mines had been laid off—some of them five days previously. Not until sometime after April 11 were all of these steelworkers and miners recalled to work. More than 900,000 tons of steel were lost as a result of the slowing down of operations. The loss of certain kinds of high-alloy steel during this period was expected to "slow up output of some military end-products two or three months hence." Sales of consumers' goods—especially durable equipment—had been falling off steadily for the past month in many areas dominated by steelmaking and steel-using plants. Although steel-using plants were not included in the strike coverage, many employees expected that they would be laid off "within a week" because of steel shortages. With such expectations, they tended to conserve income by postponing or eliminating purchases. Again the effect of their pessimism was regionally concentrated.

In this chapter we have seen how a steel strike can be expected to make itself felt on consumers, industrial users, and suppliers. We shall sharpen such a general impression, however, by attempting to quantify the impact of each of these three stoppages.

CHAPTER 10

The Relative Impact of Three Steel Strikes

A S IN the case of coal and railroads, strikes in the steel industry can be expected to have some characteristic pattern. By rating the impact of the three major walkouts of 1946, 1949, and 1952, we shall have a more precise basis for discerning that pattern.[1]

Strike of 1946

During the first four weeks of this, the largest strike till then recorded in the United States, around 93 per cent of the basic steel industry's capacity was shut down. Basic aluminum and about 700 steel-using firms were also included in the strike call. The fifth week was marked by resumption of most basic steel and some fabricating operations. Plant openings continued until by the sixteenth week only about 28,000 workers were still idle.

The stoppage occurred during the early stages of the reconversion period which followed World War II. Stocks of sheet steel, the main component of most consumers' durable goods, and of malleable castings, structural steel, and rails were relatively low. Federal authorities early in the strike restricted holdings of all kinds of steel. One significant factor was that the rate of steel consumption during the strike was lower than it otherwise would have been because of the concurrence of strikes in the automobile and electrical manufacturing industries.

The day chosen for rating is the twenty-eighth day (February 17), coming at the end of the hard core of the strike.

The total rating is 167. This incorporates the effects of the union's inclusion of steel-using companies and aluminum producers in the walkout. The score for the twenty-eighth day, if confined to effects of the basic steel strike only (but including iron ore mining) is 109. In the

[1] For sources used see note 1, Chapter 5. The reader is again reminded that because of limitations of the data the results must be regarded as approximate and tentative.

computations below, basic steel has been rated first, and the additional impact of the accompanying stoppages has been calculated separately, at the end.

I-II. Direct and Indirect Consumers. Score: 0

Household consumers were probably lightly affected by the twenty-eighth day by lack of availability of products such as wire fencing made by basic steel companies and of fabricated goods made by steel-using companies. There is little direct evidence, however, in view of which we enter an urgency rating of 0, and a consequent score of 0.

III. Direct-User Producers. Score: 66.6

Those affected by the shutdown of basic steel plants can be classified in two major categories: (1) "fabricators," which represents firms which in 1947 consumed 44 per cent of all steel tonnage and which includes employees listed in the Bureau of Labor Statistics' classification "Iron and Steel and Their Products" minus those listed in the subclassification "Blast Furnaces, Steelworks, and Rolling Mills"; and (2) "machinery makers," which represents firms which in 1947 consumed 41 per cent of all steel tonnage and which includes employees listed in the BLS classifications, "Machinery, Except Electrical," "Electrical Machinery," and "Transportation Equipment."[2] Those affected by the shutdown of iron ore mines were almost exclusively the basic steel firms, nearly all of which were shut down themselves by the strike and therefore not in a position to sustain effects.

A. Fabricators using basic steel products. Score: 26.3

Urgency rating: 1.35

1. Production necessity: 6. Steel stocks were such that most fabricators continued full-scale operations for the first two weeks of the strike before output began falling off. By the twenty-eighth day perhaps 80 per cent of the employment of fabricators depended on the availability of steel. That

---

[2] The basic steel industry is of course a multi-product industry, turning out many different types of primary steel products which cannot be substituted for one another. Thus strict adherence to the procedure set forth in Chapter 3 for rating the effects of strikes in multi-product industries would require that user effects be classified in terms of each of the major types of primary steel products. However, because the available data are furnished in terms of effects on a few major *industries using* steel products, it has been necessary to classify effects in terms of broad user groups, assuming for purposes of rating that the effects of "typical" industries within these groups represent roughly the over-all effects on the entire group.

is to say, had there been no stocks of steel or substitutes for steel on the twenty-eighth day about 80 per cent of the labor force would have been idle, the 20 per cent still employed being supervisory, maintenance, and clerical workers whose services would still have been needed plus those who could have found temporary work elsewhere. Recoverability was substantially curtailed by the limited opportunity of post-strike make-up operations in the basic steel industry during this reconversion period. It is estimated to have been about 25 per cent, yielding a production necessity of 60 per cent.

2. Stock effect: 2.5. The fact that some stocks of steel did exist, however, prevented employment from declining to the full extent indicated by the production necessity. Stocks of steel were low at the beginning of the strike, however, and less than 10 per cent of the basic steel industry was operating. Many fabricators were reported to have reduced operations. It is probably conservative to say that on the twenty-eighth day consumption of basic steel had declined by at least 25 per cent owing to dwindling stocks.

3. Substitutability: 9. The use of substitutes for the struck product also prevented employment from declining on the twenty-eighth day. Here we judge that use of substitutes contributed only 10 per cent toward the prevention of the full decline, for in the short run the possibilities of substituting other materials for steel are poor.

Number affected: 19.5

The total number of employees in steel fabricating in December, 1945, is calculated to have been 947,276. But some 250,000 employees of steel-using companies were included in this strike, hence must be classed as parties rather than affected publics. (Some of these struck companies probably fall into our machinery classification, but all are included here for purposes of rating.) The subtraction of these strikers leaves 697,276. The strike closed down some 93 per cent of basic steel production, and we therefore assume that the fabricating group was normally 93 per cent supplied by the struck steel firms, reducing the number of employees subject to strike effects to 648,467. Assuming that each employee had two dependents, we arrive at the figure of 1,945,401 persons affected by virtue of their relationship to steel fabricating, or according to our unit of account (100,000), 19.5.

B. Machinery makers. Score: 40.3

   Urgency rating: .4725

   1. Production necessity: 5.25. Steel is not so large a component of total value of product in this category. Other materials are important, and some operations can continue longer without steel. Thus after four weeks of dwindling stocks and about two weeks of gradual curtailment of output in consequence, if on the twenty-eighth day machinery makers had been deprived of their stocks of steels and all substitutes for them, we estimate that only 70 per cent of the labor force would have been idled, the other 30 per cent including not only those obtaining temporary jobs elsewhere, and supervisory, clerical, and maintenance workers, but production workers who could still be given employment, on that day at least, on phases of operations which did not immediately depend on the consumption of steel. Recoverability (in the sense of the extent to which strike losses—not simply lost output—could actually be offset by operations in the six months following the strike) is put at 25 per cent.

   2. Stock effect: 1. Stocks of sheet steel, a major component of consumers' durable equipment, were especially low. Some idea of curtailment of consumption of steel is provided by the fact that on the twenty-eighth day about 16 per cent of total production workers in the auto industry were idle. But apparently other machinery makers kept larger stocks than did the auto industry and were thus less adversely affected. An estimated 10 per cent decline in consumption of steel by the twenty-eighth day due to dwindling stocks would seem conservative.

   3. Substitutability: 9. In the short run, adequate substitutes are poor.

   Number affected: 85.3

   Total employees for December, 1945, numbered approximately 3,055,925. Assuming that 93 per cent of them were supplied by the struck plants and that each had two dependents, we get a figure of 8,526,030 persons affected.

IV. Indirect-User Producers. Score: 0

It seems more than likely that some production operations were curtailed because firms were unable to obtain necessary components from other firms which in turn relied on steel. We have so little information regarding such consequences, however, that we are forced to enter a rating of 0, recognizing that this must surely understate effects on indirect-user producers.

The total score for producer-users of basic steel products probably does not understate too seriously the *combined* effects on direct and indirect producer-users, however. Some of the employees of fabricators and machinery makers whom we have counted as direct-user producers undoubtedly worked for firms whose supplies came not directly from basic steel companies but from other fabricators and machinery makers. Thus part of our score for effects on direct-user producers consists of effects which actually fell on indirect-user producers, and to that extent our score of 0 in this category simply reflects the difficulty of separating out the indirect effects from the direct effects.

One point should be made. If direct-user firms had *not* been included in the strike call, the fall in steel output would nevertheless have forced some reduction in their operations and hence —by transmitted effects—in their customers' operations. This latter consequence would then have had to be counted as an effect on indirect users of basic steel. But when some steel-using firms themselves were struck, the situation was changed. Their customers become involved not as indirect users of steel but as direct users of the fabricating firms' products. They would not have been much less affected had there been no strike at all in basic steel. Under the circumstances, some repercussions which otherwise would have shown up in the basic-steel rating must be taken account of in the separate rating for the steel-using firms included in the strike, a rating which follows that for basic steel. Thus the only indirect-user effects omitted *here* (for lack of information) are those which fell on customers of *unstruck* steel-using firms.

V. Direct Suppliers. Score: 6.9

   A. Suppliers of bituminous coal to the struck basic steel plants. Score: 1.9

Urgency rating: 1

1. Market necessity: 5.25. As in the bituminous coal and railroad strikes, we use for number affected the equivalent of the number of employees in all bituminous mines who are wholly engaged just in producing coal for the struck basic steel plants, rather than the correct but unavailable figure of all those employed by such mines. For market necessity we then use a ratio representing the extent to which such employees are dependent on the market afforded by the struck plants for employment, rather than the correct but unavailable figure showing the proportion which purchases of coal by the struck plants constituted of total coal sales of those mines actually supplying the steel industry.

   As of a given day of the strike, market necessity depends in part on the extent to which the coal mines have been able—on previous days of the strike—to sustain operations either because of continued purchases by steel or through stock-piling their output. In this case, at the beginning of the strike about one-third of employees engaged in providing coal for the struck steel plants had been idled, but in a few days many of these plants began buying coal again and stock-piling it themselves, so that by the day of rating only about one-sixth of the employees were idle. Thus if all coal purchases or stock-piling had been halted on the twenty-eighth day, fewer coal employees would have been laid off than if output had been lower since the beginning of the strike. More nonproduction work would remain to occupy at least a portion of their time. We estimate dependency as of the twenty-eighth day at 70 per cent, recoverability (limited by that of the basic steel industry) at 25 per cent.

2. Stock effect: 2.4. We have said, above, that 70 per cent of the miners supplying bituminous to the steel industry would have been idle if their normal coal output had been reduced 100 per cent. Actually, only about 17 per cent of such miners were idled. This means that their normal coal output had been reduced only 24 per cent.

3. Substitutability: 8. The level of economic activity was high, somewhat facilitating the substitution of other markets, but

this fact is more than offset by two other considerations: (a) The degree of specialization of bituminous suppliers is high, owing to the inclusion of the steel-owned "captive" mines, and (b) the short-run price elasticity of the demand for coal is probably fairly low.

Number affected: 1.9.

As a rough means of measuring the total number of employees engaged in mining coal for the struck plants, we first divide the total 1946 sales of all bituminous mines (in this case, "value of production at mines") by the total number of employees in bituminous mining in 1946. The resulting figure ($4694), which we term the 1946 bituminous employment divisor, is taken as indicating the value of output attributable to each mining employee. We divide the total 1946 expenditures for bituminous coal made by the struck steel firms (estimated at $300,000,000) by this employment divisor. The result indicates that the equivalent of 63,911 full-time employees were devoted to producing coal for the struck plants. When this figure is multiplied by three (on the assumption of two dependents for each employee) we arrive at 191,733 persons affected by virtue of their relation to the mining of coal for the struck firms.

B. Suppliers of transportation services. Score: 2.1

Urgency rating: .53

1. Market necessity: 3. Stock-piling of rail services is impossible, and the union did not in general permit the out-shipment through picket lines of basic steel firms' stocks of steel. However, some purchase of rail services for the movement of stocks of steel considered necessary for public health and safety continued throughout the twenty-eight days. We estimate that complete cessation of steel hauling on the twenty-eighth day would have idled about 40 per cent of employees (the others continuing to be engaged in supervisory, clerical, maintenance, and nonoperating jobs or finding temporary work elsewhere). If the basic steel industry could have expanded operations within the following six months sufficiently to make up something more than one-fourth of the tonnage lost, and if the steel-hauling railroad lines were

capable of at least an equal expansion, the idled employees could have recovered perhaps 25 per cent of their strike losses. Thus 30 per cent measures the extent to which all employees of steel-hauling railroads were dependent on the basic steel industry for markets for their services.

2. Stock effect: 2.5. Available data suggest that output of transport services had declined about 25 per cent by the twenty-eighth day.

3. Substitutability: 7. Alternative markets are not generally available in the short run.

Number affected: 3.7

In 1946 expenditures of the struck plants for transport services are estimated at about $700,000,000, which divided by the 1946 railroad employment divisor of $5612 and adjusted for dependents gives 370,199 persons affected.

C. Suppliers of ferrous scrap metal. Score: 0

Urgency rating: 0

Because the demand for scrap by steel mills was high at this period, we assume that the struck plants either continued all of their normal purchases throughout the strike or that (where this did not happen) scrap producers maintained output, stock-piling their product because they expected that steel mills would purchase the accumulated stocks at the end of the strike. In either case, no loss was suffered, and the urgency rating thus is 0.

D. Suppliers of goods and services to employees of the struck units. Score: 1.35

Urgency rating: .63

1. Market necessity: 3. During the first twenty-seven days of the strike output of services of retail employees would have been partially sustained as steelworkers continued to buy essential items on the strength of credit, savings, gifts, and relief payments. Thus a complete falling off of steelworkers' expenditures on the twenty-eighth day would have brought idleness to only an estimated 40 per cent of the labor force. Recoverability is approximately the same as for the basic steel industry (25 per cent).

2. Stock effect: 3. On the twenty-eighth day output of suppliers' services had declined by perhaps 30 per cent.

3. Substitutability: 7. Alternative customers would be somewhat more available in steel areas than in coal towns, but the chance of offsetting loss of steelworkers' trade with sales to new customers is still not great.

Number affected: 2.15

Wages spent on goods and services by steelworkers and iron ore miners (estimated as two-thirds of the struck firms' total wage bill) amounted to $793,949,356 in 1946. Dividing by the 1946 retail trade employment divisor of $11,101 and adjusting for dependents gives 214,560 persons affected.

E. Other suppliers. Score: 1.56

Scores for the suppliers of other materials, fuels, and power, computed in the above manner, may be summarized:

Item Supplied	Score
Fluxing materials	.490
Electric power	.660
Fuel oil	.055
Alloys	.091
Nonferrous metals	.260
Total	1.556

The purchase of natural gas did not decline because of its use to keep the idle furnaces from cooling off.

VI. Indirect Suppliers. Score: 14.7

One-fifth the total for III and V, above, in accordance with the formula of expediency which we have adopted.

VII. Nonparty Members of the Struck Unit. Score: 20.8

A. Nonstriking employees. Score: 14.3

The total cessation of steel production does not eliminate the need for maintenance, clerical, and supervisory employees. Even after twenty-seven days of no output of steel, perhaps 20 per cent of the total number of nonstriking employees would have been retained. Of those laid off, only a small proportion —probably not more than an additional 10 per cent—could have found employment in other industries. (Alternative employment in steel areas is likely to be more available than in coal towns, but steel employment is geographically concentrated, and in absolute numbers is higher than for bituminous coal, with the result that probably no greater proportion of steelworkers could find alternative employment.) But some of the losses represented by the idleness could have been recovered during the next six months. Because shortages of raw materials and noninterchangeability of steel products made make-up operations in the basic steel industry less likely than in the bituminous industry during this period, we estimate recoverability at 25 per cent in contrast to 50 per cent for bituminous.

Number affected: 2.7

There were about 90,000 nonstrikers involved; with two dependents, 270,000.

B. Families of strikers: Score: 6.5

Urgency rating: .68

Since strikers' only opportunity for employment was in other industries and only about 10 per cent are estimated to have procured such jobs by the twenty-eighth day, unemployment amounted to 90 per cent. Since strike losses are judged to have been 25 per cent recoverable and of remaining losses 90 per cent are offset by the closeness of the association of strikers' families with the strike, the urgency rating becomes .68.

Number affected: 9.5

About 475,000 workers in basic steel mills and iron ore mines were directly involved. On the assumption that each, on the average, had two dependents, 950,000 of such dependents were affected.

Effects of Concurrent Strikes at Fabricating Plants.[3] Score: 50

Some 250,000 employees of 700 fabricating firms making products classified in forty different industries were involved in this strike on the twenty-eighth day. Because of the diversity of industries represented and the lack of specific data, it is impossible to rate the effects on the public of stoppages in the individual plants. But to ignore the effects of the fabricator strikes would understate the total

[3] By common usage most of the nonbasic steel companies under contract to the United Steelworkers of America have come to be called "fabricators." It is in this sense that the term is used in the following paragraphs, and in corresponding sections of the 1949 and 1952 strike ratings. That is, as used in these places the term "fabricators" is inclusive of the kind of firms which we have called machinery makers and that we distinguished from fabricators in our ratings of the direct producer-user effects of the basic steel portion of the strikes.

effects of the 1946 steelworkers' strike. The only alternative appears to be to hazard a rough estimate of the probable effects of the fabricator strikes, based on impressions, casual fact, and logical reasoning. Thus, because fabricators' products are nearer, in the stages of production, to final consumers' markets, stoppage of their operations is more likely to affect ultimate consumers. Moreover, union organizational lines are blurred, so that a general steelworkers' strike includes even some nonferrous fabrication. Thus the 1946 strike closed down a plant manufacturing paper cartons for packaged milk in the New York City area, depriving that city of more than 10 per cent of its supply of such milk. Under the circumstances a score of 20 for all direct and indirect consumer effects appears to be conservative —the New York City case alone would almost give such a result.

Because of their place in the stages of production, fabricators stand in a somewhat less fundamental position than do basic steel firms as suppliers of products to producers, and therefore we allow for the direct and indirect product-users relying on their outputs a score somewhat less than one-fifth that computed for the effects of the strike in basic steel on producer-users, or 12. On the other hand, fabricators' more forward position in the stages of production tends to give them greater importance as users of other firms' products. For this reason effects on fabricators' suppliers should have been proportionately greater than effects on basic steel's suppliers. But because the principal supplier of fabricators, basic steel, was itself shut down by the strike, the effects on fabricators' suppliers should be less than—say, half—the score computed for basic steel's suppliers, or 3.5. One-fifth of the combined score for producer-users and direct suppliers gives a score for indirect suppliers of 3.1. Finally, the application to nonparty members of struck fabricating units of urgency ratings similar to those for nonparty members of struck basic steel plants yields a score of about 11 for this category. A total score of about 50 thus represents our estimate of the effects of that portion of the 1946 steelworkers' strike which was concerned with plants of fabricators.

Effects of Concurrent Strikes in the Aluminum Industry. Score: 8

It seems likely that about 10,000 aluminum workers were involved in this union-wide walkout. By the same kind of rough calculation employed above in the case of fabricating plants, we arrive at a score of 8 as an estimate of the effects of that portion of the 1946 steel-workers' strike which was concerned with the aluminum industry.

Recapitulation of Effects of the Basic Steel Portion
of the 1946 Steelworkers' Strike

Direct consumers	0.0
Indirect consumers	0.0
Direct producer-users	66.6
Indirect producer-users	0.0
Direct suppliers	6.9
Indirect suppliers	14.7
Nonparty suppliers within the struck unit	20.8
	109.0

Strike of 1949

The hard core of this strike also lasted for about a month. During all or part of this time about 90 per cent of the basic steel industry, about 25 per cent of basic aluminum capacity, and a small number of steel-using plants were shut down. Resumption of operations in some plants began on the thirty-second day and continued until by the eleventh week only 5000 workers were still on strike.

The strike occurred at the beginning of a recovery after a period of mild recession both in general business activity and in the steel industry. Over-all steel stocks amounted to about a thirty-day supply but many fabricators, especially manufacturers of electrical equipment, had let their supplies fall to lower levels. Just as the concurrence of automobile and electrical manufacturing strikes with the 1946 steel strike temporarily removed from among steel's publics a large segment of its normal users, so did the concurrence of the first part of the 1949-1950 bituminous strike remove the possibility of the 1949 steel strike's affecting one of its most important suppliers.

The day of rating, the thirty-first (October 31), occurred at the end of the hard core of the strike.

The total rating is 128. Excluding fabricators and aluminum producers involved in the strike, the rating for basic steel, including iron ore mining, is 115.

I-II. Direct and Indirect Consumers. Score: 0

Because after thirty-one days household consumers were affected lightly, if at all, by shortages of steel products, we consider the urgency rating for them, and therefore the score, to be 0.

III. Direct-User Producers. Score: 72.8

As in the 1946 strike, we rate two categories—fabricators and machinery makers—which together consumed approximately four-fifths of all steel tonnage.

A. Fabricators using basic steel. Score: 26.7

   Urgency rating: .756

   1. Production necessity: 5.6. Since the length of time during which operators had been curtailed is similar to that for the 1946 strike, fabricator dependence on supplies of steel is the same, 80 per cent. However, because supplies of raw material were more available in 1949 than in 1946 chances of making up lost steel tonnage in the following six months were better, so that recoverability is estimated at 30 per cent rather than 25 per cent. (Use of a higher figure than 30 per cent seems unwise in view of the limits to make-up operations set by the noninterchangeability of steel-finishing equipment.)

   2. Stock effect: 1.5. The curtailment in the use of steel by fabricating firms, occurring on the thirty-first day of this strike, was less than the estimated 25 per cent reduction of the 1946 strike.

   3. Substitutability: 9. In the short run possibilities of substituting other materials for steel are poor.

   Number affected: 35.3

   Because number of employees in steel fabricating alone is not available after 1948, we use an estimate of total employees in fabricating classifications (chosen as explained in the 1946 strike) for September, 1948, of 1,324,546, of which about ninety per cent are assumed to have been dependent on the struck plants, or 1,192,091. Subtracting the 14,000 employees of fabricating plants on strike and adjusting for dependents, we get 3,534,273 persons affected.

B. Machinery makers. Score: 46.1

   Urgency rating: .44

   1. Production necessity: 4.9. Again the similarity of duration makes dependence 70 per cent as in the 1946 strike. This is lower than the dependence estimated for fabricators because,

since steel is not so large a component of total value of product, machinery makers can continue some operations longer without steel. Recoverability, 30 per cent, is limited by the possibilities of the basic steel industry's making up lost output, and (as for fabricators) while higher than in 1946 it is still low because of the noninterchangeability of steel-finishing equipment.

2. Stock effect: 1. By the thirty-first day the effect on the auto industry was less, on the electrical appliances industry greater than on the twenty-eighth day of the 1946 strike. The cut in the use of steel is estimated to have been about the same as for the 1946 strike.

3. Substitutability: 9. Little can be done in the short run in the way of substituting other material for steel.

Number affected: 104.7

Estimated total employees in the relevant classification in September, 1949, were 3,489,151; with dependents, 10,-467,453.

IV. Indirect-User Producers. Score: 0

As for the 1946 strike, insufficient information prevents the computation of a rating for indirect-user producers. Again, however, some portion of the employees of fabricators and machinery makers which we have counted as direct-user producers undoubtedly belong in the indirect-user category. Their firms used not basic steel products, or not only such products, but products already processed by other fabricating or machinery firms. Thus part of the direct-user score really represents effects on indirect users. In the 1946 strike, it will be remembered, the amount of our understatement of basic steel *indirect*-user effects was reduced by the fact that concurrent fabricator stoppages transformed some portion of those into fabricator *direct*-user effects. The number of fabricators involved in this strike, however, was too small to have been of much significance in this respect.

V. Direct Suppliers. Score: 5.8

Because the duration of the strike and percentage of the basic steel industry shut down (in terms of the day of rating) are approximately the same in this as in the 1946 strike, the urgency ratings for each category of direct supplier involved should be approximately the same as those computed for the 1946 strike, except in so far as the somewhat lower level of activity in basic steel and supplier industries makes recoverability of losses greater, and thus market necessity less. Improved make-up possibilities in the basic steel industry are the chief factor contributing to a recoverability estimated at 30 per cent for every supplier category except ferrous scrap metal.

A. Suppliers of bituminous coal. Score: 0

The bituminous coal industry was itself shut down by a strike during the entire period of the hard core of this steel strike; therefore, effects on the bituminous industry as suppliers can be disregarded.

B. Suppliers of transportation services. Score: 2

Urgency rating: .49

Number affected: 4.17

In 1949 expenditures on transportation services are estimated to have been about $1,000,000,000, which divided by the 1949 railroad employment divisor of $7197 and adjusted for dependents gives 416,841 persons affected.

C. Suppliers of ferrous scrap metal. Score: .143

Urgency rating: .36

1. Market necessity: 2. Because scrap was still much in demand, though not constituting the serious bottleneck to operations it had been in 1946, purchases of scrap undoubtedly continued for some time after the beginning of the strike. If on the thirty-first day all such purchases had ceased, no stockpiling had been possible, and no substitute markets had been available, perhaps about 50 per cent of scrap companies' employees would have been idled. Steel mills, eager for scrap, would have presumably taken a substantial portion of that scrap not purchased during the strike, so that recoverability of strike losses was perhaps double that of other suppliers.

2. Stock effect: 2. In view of the considerable demand for scrap in 1949, current purchases or stock-piling for future purchase would probably have prevented output of scrap from declining by more than 20 per cent by the thirty-first day.

3. Substitutability: 9. In the short run there are few markets for ferrous scrap which could be substituted for that provided by the basic steel industry.

Number affected: .397

In 1949 expenditures are estimated at $600,000,000, which

divided by the 1948 waste materials employment divisor of $45,125 and adjusted for dependents gives 39,788 persons affected.

D. Suppliers of goods and services to employees of the struck units.
Score: 1.68
Urgency rating: .588
Number affected: 2.86
Wages spent on goods and services by steelworkers and iron ore miners (estimated as two-thirds of the struck firms' total wage bill) amounted to $1,353,216,760, which divided by the 1950 retail trade employment divisor of $14,181 and adjusted for dependents gives 286,275 persons affected.

E. Other suppliers. Score: 2
Scores for the suppliers of other materials, fuels, and power are as follows:

Item Supplied	Score
Fluxing materials	.741
Electric power	.836
Fuel oil	.074
Alloys	.142
Nonferrous metals	.238
Total	2.031

VI. Indirect Suppliers. Score: 15.7
One-fifth of totals for III and V, above. This, it will be remembered, is our arbitrary method of allowing for effects on those who supply goods or services either to the users of steel or to the suppliers of the steel industry, adopted in view of the extreme difficulties of any more precise method of calculation.

VII. Nonparty Members of Struck Units. Score: 21
A. Nonstriking employees. Score: 14.7
Urgency rating: 4.9
As in the 1946 strike of approximately the same duration, by the thirty-first day about 30 per cent of nonstrikers would still have been retained to perform maintenance, clerical, and supervisory tasks which had to be done even though no output of steel was forthcoming, or if laid off would have found other jobs. But because the steel industry was in a somewhat better position to expand post-strike output, recoverability of strike losses would have been better. We

estimate it at 30 per cent in contrast to 25 per cent for the
1946 strike.

Number affected: 3

There were about 100,000 nonstriking employees involved;
with two dependents each, 300,000.

B. Families of strikers. Score: 6.3

Urgency rating: .63

This takes account of the possibility of alternative employment and of recoverability of strike losses, including our
special allowance for the party orientation of this group.

Number affected: 10

Two dependents for each of 500,000 strikers.

Effects of Concurrent Strikes at Fabricating Plants. Score: 3

In 1949 only about 14,000 employees of fabricating companies
were included in the steelworkers' strike (in contrast with the 250,000
fabricating employees who participated in the 1946 strike). A score
of 3 seems to be a reasonable estimate of the effects produced by the
shutdown of fabricators' plants by the 1949 strike.

Effects of Concurrent Strikes in the Aluminum Industry. Score: 10

Somewhat more aluminum workers (about 16,000) than in 1946
were involved in the 1949 strike. We estimate the effects of their
participation in the strike to be represented by a score of 10. This
score, relative to the number of workers involved, is much higher
than that for fabricating plants, because the proportion of the
aluminum industry closed down by the strike of 16,000 aluminum
workers was much larger than the proportion of fabricating facilities shut down by the strike of 14,000 fabricating plant employees.

Recapitulation of Effects of the Basic Steel Portion
of the 1949 Steelworkers' Strike

Direct consumers	0.0
Indirect consumers	0.0
Direct producer-users	72.8
Indirect producer-users	0.0
Direct suppliers	5.8
Indirect suppliers	15.7
Nonparty suppliers within the struck unit	21.0
	115.3 (or 115 when rounded)

Strike of 1952

Whereas the 1946 strike was the largest in terms of number of strikers involved, the 1952 strike was the longest major strike of steelworkers in the nation's history. For about eight weeks more than 85 per cent of the basic steel industry's capacity was shut down. Unlike the other two strikes, this one did not include aluminum and metal fabricating plants. It occurred at a time when a rising demand for certain types of military goods, caused by rearmament programs and engagement in the Korean War, was combined with a sagging demand for some types of civilian goods, especially consumers' durable equipment. These demand conditions partly explain the fact that stock-consumption ratios of the light steel products used for consumers' goods were relatively high, while ratios of the heavy steel products used in construction, and of pipe, and of special alloy steel needed for military goods were relatively low. At the beginning of the strike federal authorities embargoed exports of steel and restricted deliveries from warehouses.

The fifty-third day has been chosen for rating because it was the last day of the hard core of the strike.

The total rating is 315.

I. Direct Consumers. Score: 0

As in the two previous strikes, there is little indication that household buyers were unable to obtain such consumer items made by the basic steel companies as nails or wire fencing, though this may have happened in isolated instances. We enter an urgency rating and score of 0.

II. Indirect Consumers. Score: 1.1

Household consumers may also have been affected on the day of rating by shortages of products utilizing the output of basic steel companies, but the only evidence relates to the case of new passenger automobiles.

A. New passenger automobiles. Score: 1.06

Urgency rating: .25

1. Cultural necessity: 5.

The dispensability and deferrability of a car is largely a function of the use for which the car is needed and of whether the purchaser already owns a car, and if so, what condition it is in. If taking a vacation trip during the summer or being able to accept a job depends upon the acquiring of a new car by a certain date, the dispensability and deferrability of its purchase will be low. If, however, a would-be purchaser wants a new car only for uses of marginal importance or already has a car which, while outmoded or worn, is still in working condition, forgoing of immediate purchase causes little hardship. Generalization is therefore difficult, but in American society and on an over-all basis, a cultural necessity of 5 seems reasonable.

2. Stock effect: 1. By the forty-second day of the strike, over-all sales of new passenger cars had reportedly fallen off by 8 per cent, as a result of shortages of new cars in dealers' hands. By the fifty-third day the decline must have amounted to 10 per cent.

3. Substitutability: 5. For many people, used cars are more or less satisfactory substitutes for new cars.

Number affected: 4.25

Registrations of new cars in May, 1952, were 422,217; in June, 1952, 423,655. We assume that registrations approximate sales of new cars. Since slightly more cars are normally sold in July than in June, we estimate potential purchasers of new cars during July (the period for which automobile production was curtailed owing to dwindling stocks of steel) to have numbered about 425,000.

III. Direct-User Producers. Score: 208.4

  A. Fabricators. Score: 73.4

    Urgency rating: 2.3

    1. Production necessity: 6.38. The longer period of curtailment of operations raises dependency of fabricating employees on supplies of steel as of the day of rating from the 80 per cent estimated for 1946 and 1949 to 85 per cent. Because the steel industry was operating at more than 100 per cent of rated capacity in 1952, lost output could not so easily be recovered (unless, indeed, the rate of operations would have dropped in the absence of the strike, as was frequently claimed). In any event, to give the recoverability figure of 25 per cent, which we use here, a make-up within the succeeding six months of something more than one-fourth of the tonnage lost would have been necessary, an achievement which was not likely to be exceeded.

2. Stock effect: 4. Data regarding layoffs suggest that reductions in the use of steel by fabricators was at least this much greater than in the 1946 strike, when it was figured as 2.5.

3. Substitutability: 9. As mentioned before, in the short run the possibilities of other materials for steel are poor.

Number affected: 31.9

Estimated total employees in the relevant categories in May, 1952, were 1,250,000. Probably about 85 per cent were supplied by the struck firms; with two dependents each, 3,187,500.

B. Machinery Makers. Score: 135

Urgency rating: 1.35

1. Production necessity: 6. Again the longer period of curtailment of operations raises dependence, perhaps from 70 per cent to 80 per cent. Recoverability is 25 per cent.

2. Stock effect: 2.5. The fact that on the forty-fourth day about 44 per cent of all production workers in the auto industry had been laid off suggests how sizable were the cuts in consumption of steel. On an over-all basis they probably amounted to as much as 25 per cent.

3. Substitutability: 9. Short-run possibilities of substitution are very limited.

Number affected: 100

Total employees in the relevant categories in May, 1952, were 3,921,990, of which 85 per cent are estimated to have been supplied by the struck units, or 3,333,692. With two dependents, 10,001,076.

IV. Indirect-User Producers. Score: 0

As in the 1946 and 1949 strikes, lack of information prevents us from computing a rating showing the effects of the stoppage of basic steel production on customers of fabricators and machinery makers. However, it remains true that some of the firms counted in our direct-user ratings were undoubtedly indirect users. That is, they depended on fabricated steel products rather than (or as well as) primary steel products. Though the over-all rating thus takes account of some indirect-user effects, others are probably not represented. The understatement of indirect-user effects is greatest of all for this steelworker stoppage, since there were no concurrent fabricator strikes to claim as their own direct effects the impacts on fabricators' customers, which in the absence of such strikes must be counted as indirect effects of the basic steel closings.

V. Direct Suppliers. Score: 27.3

  A. Suppliers of bituminous coal. Score: 8.5

    Urgency rating: 3.4

      1. Market necessity: 6. If, after approximately a month of suspension of basic steel operations, total cessation of coal purchases and stock-piling would have idled 70 per cent of miners (as in 1946), then after almost two months of basic steel shutdown the effect would probably be to idle 85 per cent. Recoverability of strike losses in coal, largely limited by the possibility of making up lost output in steel, was probably about the same as for steel, which has been estimated at 25 per cent.

      2. Stock effect: 7. On the fifty-third day of the strike at least 50,000 bituminous coal miners were idle because the steel mills were shut down. This represents an idleness figure of 60 per cent of the equivalent full-time employees engaged in supplying coal to the steel industry and a consequent cut of 70 per cent in the output of coal for steel (since a 100 per cent reduction in coal output leads to 85 per cent idleness).

      3. Substitutability: 8. As in the 1946 strike, the degree of specialization of bituminous suppliers to the basic steel market and the low short-run price elasticity of demand for coal would have severely limited the possibilities of finding substitute markets for the coal not taken by the steel mills.

    Number affected: 2.5

    In 1952 expenditures for bituminous coal are calculated to have been about $750,000,000. Dividing by an estimated bituminous divisor for 1952 of $9000 gives 83,300 miners dependent on the shut-down portion of the basic steel industry for markets for their services. Adjusting for dependents gives a total of 249,900 persons affected.

  B. Suppliers of transportation services. Score: 11.7

    Urgency rating: 2.6

      1. Market necessity: 4.5. While not permitting general outshipment of basic steel firms' steel stocks, the union, as in

1946, did allow special shipments—in this case, of steel for use in the manufacture of military goods. So, although the stock-piling of rail services is impossible, there was some continuation of purchases of steel-hauling services. But after almost two months, the amount of employment which such purchases could sustain was dwindling, so that total cessation of the purchases on the fifty-third day would have idled perhaps 60 per cent of those transport workers dependent on basic steel for markets. (This compares with a figure of 40 per cent for the one-month basic steel stoppage in 1946.) The possible recovery of strike losses in the six months following the strike is set at 25 per cent.

2. Stock effect: 9. According to the estimate below, about 150,-000 transport workers were dependent upon the struck portion of the basic steel industry for employment. By the fifty-third day at least 140,000 transport workers were idle because of curtailment of output of basic steel products and of products using basic steel. Probably between 80,000 and 85,000 of the 140,000 had been employed on basic steel-hauling operations. Thus we estimate the curtailment in employment of this direct supplier group at 55 per cent. If the number of employees who would have been idle with no output of services on the fifty-third day amounted to 60 per cent and the actual idleness was 55 per cent, then output of services must have declined by 90 per cent owing to lack of purchases and inability to stock output.

3. Substitutability: 6.5. Some of the facilities idled by the strike were used to help transport a suddenly accumulated bumper crop of wheat. Thus substitute markets for rail services were somewhat improved over what they had been in the other steel strikes.

Number affected: 4.5

In 1952 expenditures for transport services are estimated to have been about $1,500,000,000, which divided by a 1952 railroad employment divisor of $10,000 and adjusted for dependents gives 450,000 persons affected.

C. Suppliers of ferrous scrap metal. Score: .32

Urgency rating: .65

1. Market necessity: 2.4. Because of the much longer period

during which the scrap companies' chief market was shut down, dependency is estimated at 60 per cent on the day of rating in this strike as compared to 50 per cent in the 1949 strike. Recoverability is put at 60 per cent as in the 1949 strike.

2. Stock effect: 3. By the fifty-third day employment in scrap companies would have been curtailed perhaps about 30 per cent.

3. Substitutability: 9. In the short run there are few markets for ferrous scrap which could be substituted for that provided by the basic steel industry.

Number affected: .5

In 1952 expenditures for scrap are estimated to have been about $1,000,000,000, which divided by an estimated waste materials employment divisor of $60,000 and adjusted for dependents gives 50,000 persons affected.

D. Suppliers of goods and services to employees of the struck unit.
Score: 3.7
Urgency rating: 1.05

1. Market necessity: 3.75. As in the 1946 strike, output of services of retail employees would have been partially sustained throughout the strike by continued purchase of "essential" items by idle steelworkers. But the savings and credit which permitted these purchases would have become largely exhausted before the fifty-third day, so that some retail employees would have been already laid off. Thus a complete termination of steelworkers' expenditures on the fifty-third day would have brought idleness to perhaps 50 per cent of the labor force as compared to 40 per cent on the twenty-eighth day of the 1946 strike.

2. Stock effect: 4. We estimate that as of the twenty-eighth day output of retail suppliers' services had declined by about 40 per cent.

3. Substitutability: 7. The chance of offsetting loss of steelworkers' trade with sales to new customers is not great.

Number affected: 3.56

Wages spent on goods and services (estimated at two-thirds of the struck firms' wage bill) amounted to about $1,900,-000,000, which divided by an estimated retail trade employment divisor of $16,000 and adjusted for dependents gives 356,250 persons affected.

E. Other suppliers. Score: 3.11

Scores for the suppliers of other materials, fuels, and power are as follows:

Items Supplied	Score
Fluxing materials	1.247
Electric power	1.020
Fuel oil	.114
Alloys	.220
Nonferrous metals	.508
Total	3.109

VI. Indirect Suppliers. Score: 47.1

One-fifth of totals for III and V, above.

VII. Nonparty Members of the Struck Units. Score: 31.5

A. Nonstriking employees. Score: 23

Urgency rating: 6.4

Presumably after almost two months of complete suspension of production the maintenance, clerical, and supervisory work force of the struck mills would have been reduced below the level maintained at the end of one month of shutdown. Thus on the fifty-third day perhaps as many as 85 per cent of nonstriking employees had been laid off and had not been able to find jobs elsewhere. Probably not more than 25 per cent of the losses caused by the idleness would have been recoverable.

Number affected: 3.6

About 120,000 nonstriking employees were involved, with two dependents each.

B. Families of strikers. Score: 8.5

Urgency rating: .68

Alternative work opportunities probably provided employment income to no more than 10 per cent of strikers' families. Recoverability is set at 25 per cent, as for nonstrikers, and 90 per cent of the remaining losses are considered to have been compensated for by the fact that this group, unlike any others of the affected public, were joined in interest with one of the parties.

Number affected: 12.5

Two dependents each for 625,000 strikers.

Recapitulation of Effects of the 1952 Strike

Direct consumers	0.0
Indirect consumers	1.1
Direct producer-users	208.4
Indirect producer-users	0.0
Direct suppliers	27.3
Indirect suppliers	47.1
Nonparty members of struck unit	31.5

315.4 (or 315 when
rounded)

What generalizations emerge from these ratings concerning the effect of steel strikes? Is it possible to discern some pattern characterizing strikes in this industry, as we have identified strike patterns in coal and railroads?

Of the three strikes rated, that of 1952 registered the greatest total impact (315), the one of 1946 ranked second (167), with the stoppage of 1949 coming last (128). The 1946 strike, however, included the effects of concurrent strikes in steel fabricating and aluminum firms, with these accounting for one-third of the total score. If such concurrent effects are eliminated from the 1946 and 1949 ratings, we find that the basic steel stoppages of those two years have remarkably similar scores (109 and 115 respectively). It is these scores which should be compared with the dispute of 1952, since the latter was confined almost exclusively to the basic steel industry.

The strikes of 1946 and 1949 were rated as of approximately equal duration (twenty-eight days and thirty-one days respectively).[4] Their ratings for each of the various categories of consumers, producers, and suppliers were in close agreement. For purposes of comparison with 1952, then, we can treat these two as one. Thus the interesting question emerges: Why should the basic steel strike of 1952 have had an impact more than two and one-half times greater than the basic steel strikes of 1946 and 1949?

The explanation clearly does not lie in the consumer category. No

[4] Since the 1949 strike is rated somewhat higher than that of 1946, then we can all the more treat these two as of approximately the same duration, since the fact that the 1949 walkout was slightly longer than that of 1946 is offset by the fact that it has a slightly higher score.

direct-consumer effects were present in any of the three basic steel stop-pages, and indirect consumers were affected only to a minor extent in 1952 by inability to obtain new cars. The major disparity arises in the direct-producer category—which in all three strikes produces the larg-est component score, but a score which in 1952 was three times that of the two earlier years (more than 200 in contrast to 67 and 73). It is true that the 1952 direct-supplier effects are four times those of the previous stoppages, but the absolute size of the score is small (27 in 1952, 7 in 1946, and 6 in 1949). The 1952 score for indirect suppliers is also three times that for the prior strikes, but this is only a reflection of the primary impact on direct users. Finally, the rating for nonparty members of the steel industry in 1952 is increased over that of 1946 and 1949, but not significantly in absolute terms. Thus only one conclusion is possible. The much greater impact of the basic steel stoppage of 1952 is attributable principally to the increased effects on industrial users of steel.

Our inquiry must then be pursued further. What is it that explains why direct producers were more seriously affected in 1952 than in the earlier years?

It is not in the numbers affected that the explanation lies. More direct producers were involved in 1952 than in 1946, it is true, but fewer than in 1949. We must look elsewhere for the reason.

The 1952 strike ran for fifty-three days, in contrast to four weeks for the previous disputes. Duration would thus appear to make the difference. But duration, as we know, is significant only in so far as it influences production necessity, or the stock effect, or substitutability. Production necessity was somewhat higher in 1952, in consequence of the longer duration, but not markedly higher. The greater length of the strike meant that more employees of steel-using firms were dependent on resumption of the flow of steel for employment, but not so many more as were similarly dependent after a four-week shutdown in steel as to explain the great disparity of effects. The possibilities of substi-tuting other materials for steel are estimated to have been roughly the same in all three strikes. It is the stock effect which almost by itself ac-counts for the vast difference in effects. By the fifty-third day of the 1952 stoppage the reduction in employment and output of steel-using firms due to inadequacy of stocks was at least twice as great as in the two prior disputes.

The data of the preceding chapter support the strike ratings in the conclusion that the effects of a steel strike on direct producer-users tend to make themselves felt rather slowly at first and then to mount at a rapid rate, as stocks are exhausted. After thirty-one days in 1949 industrial-user effects stood at 73 on our ratings. After fifty-three days in 1952 (twenty-two days longer, a duration 170 per cent of 1949) these effects mounted to more than 200 (roughly 300 per cent of 1949).

The effects of duration on stocks are further shown if we compare the 1952 strike with the total steelworkers' strike of 1946, the latter embracing not only basic steel but a large number of fabricators and part of the aluminum industry. The total 1946 stoppage involved 125,000 more strikers, shut down a greater percentage of the basic steel industry's capacity, and offered poorer prospects of recovery of lost production. Nevertheless, despite these factors intensifying the 1946 effects, their impact was only 53 per cent of that of 1952. Longer duration far more than offset greater extent.

Other characteristics of strikes in the basic steel industry should be noted. Supplier effects are consistently more significant than in coal or rails. In all three they contribute a little more than one-third of the total rating. In the two shorter strikes almost half of supplier effects are attributable to nonparty members of the steel industry itself (nonstriking employees and the families of strikers), but in the longer strike nonparty members contribute less than a third of total supplier effects. Apparently as a strike stretches beyond a month, affecting more and more producers, the repercussions on industrial firms which supply them goods and services increase markedly relative to the effects on those who are most intimately affected through supplier relations with the steel industry, the nonunion employees and the families of unionists.

Indirect effects—on consumers, industrial users, and suppliers—were comparatively slight in all three instances. They are, however, somewhat understated by the fact that some repercussions on indirect producers are in our ratings lumped with those bearing on direct producers, because of inability to separate them out. There is also reason to believe that our data are especially incomplete with respect to the indirect-producer category. Moreover, with a steel strike of longer duration than any we have experienced, there is every indication that all the indirect effects would mount at a rapid rate.

Finally, the interesting and suggestive conclusion appears to emerge that while the concurrence of strikes in steel-fabricating firms (as in

1946) increases the rating for the total steelworker stoppage, it decreases the rating for basic steel considered by itself. The direct-user effects of fabricators are indirect-user effects of basic steel. Inclusion of fabricators in the strike call thus reduces basic steel's indirect effects by transforming some portion of these into fabricator direct effects, which are excluded when computing the score for basic steel alone. This is not simply a figure-juggling matter; it carries a significance of its own. It suggests that, at least in some instances, the concurrence of strikes reduces the total effect on the public over what it would have been if they had been called at different times. If basic steel alone were struck, its indirect effects would extend in some degree to the customers of steel-using firms. If fabricators were then subsequently struck, these customers would be affected for a second time, and the steel industry itself would again be involved as a supplier of the struck fabricators. If basic steel and fabricators were struck simultaneously, however, steel would not be twice involved (once as a party and once as a supplier) and fabricators' customers would likewise not be twice affected (once as steel's indirect users, once as the fabricators' direct users).

What can we say, then, about the pattern of strike effects in steel? It appears (on the strength of our admittedly imperfect data) that household consumers, both direct and indirect, are likely to be affected to a degree so slight that they can well be disregarded. Steel-using producers bear the brunt of the burden. With average stocks on hand, distributed (as they usually are) in uneven fashion, the influence on them begins to make itself felt after one or two weeks and then mounts rapidly. After four weeks, as steel stocks become depleted, these effects become more and more telling. They widen (blanket in more firms) and deepen (reduce output more drastically) and suck in as well the suppliers of such firms. Because of the size of the industry the effects on its nonstriking employees and the members of strikers' families are important. The impact of any steel strike is thus almost wholly on employment and income rather than on consumer needs.

CHAPTER 11

The Price of Strikes

W E HAVE examined the effects of seventeen strikes of national extent occurring in three industries. By comparing the results we shall be able to arrive at some significant conclusions regarding the impact of strikes.

When the seventeen strikes are ranked in terms of their hardship on members of the public, as in Table 4, coal stoppages appear at both

TABLE 4. RANKING OF 17 STRIKES ACCORDING
TO TOTAL EFFECTS ON THE PUBLIC

	Total Effects
Coal, winter, 1949-1950	492
Coal, spring, 1946	338
Steel, 1952	315
Coal, fall, 1946	306
Steelworker, 1946	167
Rail, 1951	161
Steelworker, 1949	128
Steel, 1949 (basic steel only)	115
Rail, 1946	111
Steel, 1946 (basic steel only)	109
Coal, spring, 1948	101
Rail, 1950	65
Coal, spring, 1939	62
Coal, summer, 1947	34
Coal, spring, 1941	26
Coal, spring, 1947	23
Coal, summer, 1949	12
Coal, fall, 1941	10
Coal, spring, 1949	10

the top and the bottom of the array. The two most severe and the seven least severe strikes occurred in coal. The differences between these bituminous stoppages have been marked, the most serious having had almost fifty times the impact of the least affecting.

No steel strike has approached the worst bituminous strike in severity. That of 1952 carried less than two-thirds the impact of the coal strike of winter, 1949-1950. But steel strikes have been more consistently severe than those in coal. The three rated fall within the top seven strikes when the concomitant effects in the aluminum and fabricating industries are included, and within the top eight when only the basic steel portions of these walkouts are considered.

Since railroad stoppages are often regarded as entailing consequences serious enough to warrant special preventive measures, it is interesting that the most affecting rail strike was exceeded by two Steelworker[1] and three coal disputes. The least severe railroad stoppage was exceeded by all except seven relatively insignificant shutdowns in coal. The railroad effects were, however, accumulated after much shorter strike duration than any of the strikes which precede them in the rankings.[2]

Total effects of the seventeen strikes range from 10 to 492. If a range of 0 to 500 is divided into ten equal intervals, and the total rating for each strike is placed within the appropriate interval (as in Table 5, column 1), the following relationships appear: In the top (tenth) interval there is only the bituminous stoppage of the winter of 1949-1950. In the top five intervals (50 per cent of the range) there are only three coal and one steel strikes. All rail strikes fall in the lower 40 per cent of the range. Six bituminous are included within the bottom (first) interval.

The effects on the various categories of the public can be separated

---

[1] In this chapter the term "Steelworker strike" includes all stoppages called concurrently by the United Steelworkers, not only in basic steel but also in aluminum and fabricating establishments.

[2] We repeat the caution previously given, that it is not strictly correct to speak of the severity of these *strikes*, but only of the day of the strike rated. In some instances the two may not be the same. Each day of a strike would have to be rated and summed to determine whether the relative rankings of the effects of the whole strike were the same as the relative rankings of the one day rated, and the data necessary are not available. In some cases the effects of the day rated may reflect substantially the whole of the impact of a strike. This is notably true of the brief nation-wide rail stoppage of 1946. But in other instances the effects of the days rated are not so good an indicator of relative total impact. If the strike had been of some duration and if on the days preceding the day rated lack of stock and poor substitutability had led to significant effects, the one-day rating would be a weaker indication of relative total strike effects. The coal strike of fall, 1946, is a good example of a stoppage of which this is true. By and large, we believe that our rankings are a sufficiently close approximation of the *relative* total impact of these strikes to permit the generalizations we have made. The rail ratings, however, are probably overstated relative to the major coal and steel strikes, since—because of such short duration—they reflect more completely the total effects.

TABLE 5. RELATIVE IMPACT OF 17 STRIKES ON THE PUBLIC AND ITS COMPONENT GROUPS

Interval	Col. 1 Total Public	Col. 2 Consumers	Col. 3 Producers	Col. 4 Suppliers	Col. 5 Users
10	Coal, '49-'50				Coal, '49-'50
9					
8					
7	Coal, spring '46 Steel, '52 Coal, fall '46	Coal, '49-'50	Steel, '52 Coal, spring '46		
6					Coal, spring '46 Coal, fall '46
5					Steel, '52
4	Steelworker, '46 Rail, '51		Coal, fall '46		
3	Steelworker, '49 Basic steel, '49 Rail, '46 Basic steel, '46 Coal, '48	Coal, fall '46	Steelworker, '46 Rail, '51 Coal, '49-'50 Steelworker, '49 Basic steel, '49 Basic steel, '46	Steel, '52	Rail, '51 Steelworker, '46
2	Rail, '50 Coal, '39	Rail, '46	Coal, '48 Rail, '46 Rail, '50	Coal, spring '46 Steelworker, '46	Rail, '46 Steelworker, '49 Basic steel, '49 Coal, '48 Basic steel, '46
1	All others	All others	All others	All others	All others

out of the totals and ranked separately. Which of the seventeen strikes were most injurious to consumers? Which worked greatest harm on producers? Most consumer-affecting was a coal strike, which in terms of our ten intervals placed at the top of the seventh interval (Table 5, column 2). The next most serious, from the consumer's viewpoint, was another coal strike, but its impact was very much slighter, rating only the third interval. The most consumer-affecting rail strike barely makes the second interval. The other fourteen strikes all fall in the bottom interval, as far as their repercussions on consumers are concerned. Six bituminous and the basic steel portion of two Steelworker strikes had no measurable effects whatsoever on consumers.

The strike which most hurt producers (including suppliers as well as user firms) was the steel strike of 1952. It and a bituminous strike place in the seventh interval (Table 5, column 3). All other coal, steel, and rail strikes fall in the lower 40 per cent of the range, with six bunching in the third interval.

Two of the three most supplier-affecting strikes were in steel, as is evident from Table 5, column 4. One of these falls in the third interval, and one is joined in the second interval by a coal strike. All other stoppages belong in the lowest tenth of the range.

If we separate out the effects on all users, both industrial and household, in distinction to suppliers, three bituminous stoppages head the list, as is shown in Table 5, column 5. The impact of one was very great indeed, placing in the tenth interval. Two others fall in the sixth interval, and are followed by the 1952 steel strike in the fifth interval. All others belong in the low 30 per cent of the range.

Thus, in the experience of these three industries over the period 1939-1952, it has been two or three strikes in coal which have brought greatest hardship to consumers, to users as a group (both household and industrial), and—close after steel—to producers as a group (both users and suppliers). In addition to carrying the greatest impact on producers, steel strikes have also led in effects on suppliers (including both firms and nonparty individuals attached to the struck industry).

These conclusions apply to the relative effects of our seventeen strikes on various groups composing the public, when the ratings themselves are compared. There is another method of comparison. We can ask what proportion of the effects of any strike or of all strikes have fallen on the variously situated members of the public. Which strikes have been, for example, primarily consumer-affecting? Which have been predominantly producer-affecting?

Because of the basic nature of the three industries examined, we might reasonably expect that for the strikes as a whole producer effects (loss of income) would outweigh consumer effects (loss of goods and services). The extent to which this has been true is surprising, however. Of the total number of points registered by all the strikes, almost three-fourths come from producers and only one-fourth from consumers. In only one strike—in coal—were consumers more seriously affected than producers. In thirteen of the seventeen strikes consumer effects accounted for less than one-fifth of the total. (Three of the exceptions were in coal, one in rails.)

The proportionate impact on suppliers and users may also be compared. Of the total points for all strikes, three-fourths are attributable to users and only one-fourth to suppliers. In seven of the strikes supplier effects were greater than or equal to user effects. These included all the minor bituminous and one rail stoppages.

Only in coal did indirect effects—on consumers, industrial users, and suppliers—show up significantly. In four strikes in that industry, however, such effects accounted for 30 per cent or more of all effects, and in three strikes they were responsible for more than 100 points of the total.

Two conclusions of some importance may be drawn from this summary of our analysis. First, in some strikes, at least, the income effects outweigh the consumption effects. A strike may be serious not because it withholds final products from consumers but because it deprives employees in related industries of employment income. In recent years there has been a tendency to judge the impact of a strike in terms of the hardship it inflicts on ultimate consumers. This emphasis is probably attributable to an understandable desire to limit the area of strike controls; to the extent that the flow of vital goods or services is not shut off, a strike may be allowed to run its course. If this view were followed consistently, however, it might permit a general strike throughout the automobile industry to be continued for months without government intervention, while a stoppage at a local utility would not be allowed to finish out a day. Such an approach overlooks the fact that loss of income can be as serious to some individuals as loss of goods is to others.

Second, our analysis suggests that one common approach to governmental limitation of the right to strike—that of drawing up lists of industries in which strikes are forbidden or in which the state is accorded the right to intervene—is of limited value. This classificatory approach is usually based on the importance of certain products or services to ultimate consumers, and suffers from the defects of that position, as noted above. It is thus sometimes argued that strike restrictions should apply only to "essential" industries, such as public utilities and transportation. Seldom is the steel industry included in such a list, and often coal is omitted. As our ratings show, however, the most serious of the rail strikes analyzed had less of an impact than two of the Steelworker strikes, and less of an impact, too, than three bituminous stoppages. The least affecting rail strike—and this was one that for seven days shut down lines carrying 39 per cent of the nation's passenger traffic and 24 per cent of its freight—was exceeded in total effects by all the strikes rated except for seven in coal. It had only one-seventh the impact of the most severe bituminous strike and one-fifth that of the most severe steel strike. This is not to argue that rail strikes are unimportant, for had these strikes continued the effects would have mounted rapidly. It does suggest, however, that *any* major strike on the railroads is not necessarily more public-affecting than any strike in coal or steel, so that the case for treatment by category is weakened.

We have been concerned in this study with strikes of national extent, but the manner in which the importance of producer effects casts doubt on the utility of the special-categories approach to strike-control legislation can be briefly illustrated with reference to local situations as well. Beginning April 21, 1951, a sixty-day walkout of operating employees brought to a halt all local transit service in the Detroit area. Beginning January 25, 1950, a strike by Chrysler employees shut down the company's operations for more than 100 days. The first of these falls in a category which is frequently recommended for strike control. The second is seldom mentioned for similar treatment. Let us briefly compare the effects of these two strikes on members of the Detroit public as of the sixtieth day of each strike.[3]

Consumer effects in the Chrysler closing were negligible. For many the purchase of a car was deferrable. Some stocks of cars existed, and —Chrysler advertising notwithstanding!—good alternatives in the form

[3] Data on the transit strike were obtained from the *Detroit News*; on the Chrysler strike from the *Detroit News, New York Times, Automotive Industries, Fortune,* and *Business Week.*

of other makes were available. Shortages of parts may have created more of a problem for those wishing to have Chrysler-made cars serviced. Even so, the urgency rating of local transport after sixty days was presumably greater. Its use was less deferrable, stock effect was at a maximum, and substitutes—while available in the form of car pools and thumb-a-ride programs—were probably less adequate than for Chrysler cars. Altogether, then, the Detroit bus rider was more affected by the lack of transit service on the strike's sixtieth day than was a Detroit car buyer by the lack of Chrysler-made cars after a similar passage of time. And since the number of persons wishing to use buses was greater than the number of persons wishing to buy Chrysler-made cars, the total impact of the transit strike on Detroit consumers was much heavier than the impact of the Chrysler strike.

When we consider the comparative effect of the two strikes on Detroit producers as of the sixtieth day, the situation is quite different. Whereas around 16,000 nonstriking transit employees, members of their families, and the families of strikers were experiencing a loss of income, the equivalent group in the Chrysler stoppage locally numbered 158,000. The $4,000,000 of wages lost by transit employees must have seemed small to Detroit merchants who had felt the effects of a loss of $60,000,000 in wages by local Chrysler workers, within an equivalent duration, plus $14,000,000 in wages given up by idle employees of Detroit parts suppliers to Chrysler. The largest decline in sales reported for downtown Detroit stores during the transit strike was 30 per cent; during the Chrysler strike, 50 per cent. Whereas local suppliers of gasoline, oil, and electric power had lost a maximum of $900,000 in sales by the sixtieth day of the transit strike, local parts suppliers had lost $140,000,000 in sales by the sixtieth day of the Chrysler closing. Supplier losses in the transit strike caused relatively few layoffs, certainly no more than one or two thousand. Losses suffered by local parts suppliers had caused layoffs of 33,000 by the sixtieth day.

This cursory survey suggests the extent to which local producer effects—in this case, supplier effects more particularly—of an automobile strike can overshadow the producer effects of a transit strike of equal duration. The difference remains, we think, even after account is taken of the greater possibility of recovering income lost in a strike involving a durable good, in contrast to a service. Though sketchy, the data suggest that the impact of the Chrysler strike on Detroit producers was perhaps ten times as great as the impact of the transit strike. It seems unlikely that the effects on Detroit consumers were enough greater to cancel out this considerable differential effect on producers. In any event, one might reasonably judge that the total impact of the Chrysler strike on members of the Detroit public was at least as great as that of the transit strike. If the correct criterion for determining the desirability of government intervention in a strike situation is the total impact of a strike, as we believe it to be, then the local transit situation is no more inherently deserving of special treatment than is the automobile industry, at least in Detroit. We make out no case for inclusion of the automobile industry in a strike-control classification, nor for the exclusion of the transit industry from such a classification. It is the classificatory approach itself which appears to be faulty.

One other conclusion of some significance emerges from the analysis of the preceding chapters. It is sometimes suggested that the concurrence of strikes increases the impact on the public. A wave of strikes occurring simultaneously is said to intensify hardship. There are circumstances under which this judgment is justified, but there are also conditions under which the opposite is true. To clarify analysis we must first clarify the problem. It is always the case, to be sure, that two strikes occurring together occasion more inconvenience *at that time* than if only one of them were called. The real question is whether the concurrence of two strikes works greater total hardship on the public, over time, than if one follows the other.

The 1946 Steelworker strike is instructive in that respect. That stoppage shut down not only the basic steel industry but some 700 steel-using firms and a portion of the basic aluminum industry. This concurrence of strikes resulted in a lesser total impact on the public than if they had been called serially, as we know from Chapter 10. If basic steel had first gone down by itself, steel-using fabricators would have been affected and in some degree their customers would also have been involved as indirect users of steel. If later the union had struck the fabricators, these firms would have been closed promptly and their closing would have been felt by basic steel, as a supplier, and by their customers, as direct users of their products. Thus a serialization of strikes could have affected basic steel, steel-using manufacturers, and the latter's customers twice, whereas with simultaneous strikes they are all affected but once.

We may generalize from this experience. Where firms are related to each other in complementary fashion—as suppliers and customers, in an integrated production chain—the concurrence of strikes will generally lead to a smaller total impact on the public than if these firms were struck in succession. When down together, one cannot pass effects to the other. When down separately, each transmits the repercussions to the other. Some of the difficulties of the 1945-1946 wave of stoppages were occasioned precisely by the fact that firms were hard pressed recurringly, as one after another of their suppliers were closed down, causing repeated interruptions of the production process. Examples are to be found in our own analyses. In 1946 steel was closed down— the basic industry for about a month, its fabricators for longer periods; subsequently the coal industry was struck for almost two months; the day after the government had seized the mines to force a resumption of coal deliveries the railroads were hit by the first nation-wide stoppage in their history. All three of these industries are important suppliers to numerous manufacturing firms, and each of these strikes brought its own fresh interruption to manufacturing operations across the nation, as our strike ratings reveal. Other stoppages of the period —that of General Motors, for example, lasting from mid-November to mid-March—added to the difficulties to the extent that the products involved were ingredients of other firms' output. On the other hand, some of the losses of the period were reduced by the fact that certain strikes overlapped. Thus steel was down for at least part of the same period as two of its chief users, General Motors and the electrical appliance industry. In this case supplier and users were affected together, instead of supplier first involving users and then users involving supplier. In the same manner, as our ratings show, the coincidence of the steel 1949 and coal 1949-1950 strikes mitigated the losses which would have been suffered had they been shut down sequentially, since coal is so important a supplier to steel.

The situation is different, however, when strikes run concurrently at firms which produce similar products—substitutes for each other. In this case, a strike at only one firm is not likely to be seriously felt by users of that firm's goods, since there are competitors who are able to expand output to supply their needs. Suppliers are likewise less affected, since the expanded output of the producers of substitutes will furnish alternative markets. Where substitute products are involved, then, the simultaneous closing of firms lessens the availability of goods for users and of markets for suppliers and makes the impact greater than would have been the case had the strikes been called in different periods. This is the same kind of effect which makes industry-wide strikes more serious to the public than a serial closing of firms in that industry. The effect is not limited to firms in a single industry, however. Concurrent strikes on the railroad and bus lines, for example, or in coal and oil, will work more hardship than strikes in these industries if separated in time, since one important substitute product to which the user might have turned is withdrawn.

Similarly, the effect of strike concurrence is to increase public hardship when the struck units provide substitute—alternative—markets for suppliers. Thus simultaneous strikes in the automobile and appliance industries will work more hardship on the steel industry (as a supplier), since each of these is in some measure a substitute market for the other. If one strike had followed the other, steel could have been diverted from the one struck to the one still operating.

Where firms are complementary to each other, then, concurrent strikes reduce the impact on the public, but where firms are in some respect substitutes for each other (whether for users of their products or suppliers of their materials) the coincidence of strikes increases the effects on the public.[4]

This conclusion suggests that public policy might profitably be directed to encouraging the negotiation of collective bargaining agreements of complementary producers at the same time, where these are

---

[4] The question may be raised whether the fact that inclusion of the 700 fabricators in the 1946 steel strike lessened the impact on the public was due only to the circumstance that the number of such firms, while high in absolute terms, was small as a percentage of the total number of fabricators. There was no concentration in any one industry—more than forty different industries were said to be represented among the 700. Their closing thus did not mean a complete withdrawal from the market of the kinds of products they were making—competitors not unionized and still operating were able to supply users with substitutes. If *all* steel-using fabricators had been included in the strike, it might be argued, then no longer could it be said that the concurrence of these strikes lessened the impact on the public, since such complete coverage would have made substitute products unavailable to users.

This conclusion does not follow, since the contrast which it makes is not the pertinent one. We would have to say that if all fabricators had been organized by the union and had been struck simultaneously, but at a different time from basic steel, then the effect of making the fabricator and steel strikes concurrent would be to lessen their impact. For an independent fabricator-wide stoppage would have withdrawn substitute products, in any event, and it does no more when linked with the basic steel stoppage. The linkage does, however, prevent the repetition of effects on steel, fabricators, and fabricators' customers, as previously discussed.

On the other hand, if all fabricators had been organized but normally would have been struck at different times, then the inclusion of them in the same strike call—whether or not linked with basic steel—would have been more public-affecting, because withdrawing substitute products.

now negotiated at different times, as long as this is not made the basis for increasing the number of competitors who are negotiating simultaneously. Thus coal and steel and General Motors might be urged to hold their wage conferences during the same period, and other firms not competitive with any of these but complementary to them might similarly be encouraged to negotiate at the same time. Such breakdowns as occur would thus occur simultaneously, and the total effect would be reduced over what it would be if breakdowns occurred serially. But neither Ford nor Chrysler, for example, would be urged to bargain during the same period, since these are producers of substitutes for General Motors' products and offer alternative markets to steel should General Motors be struck.

The restriction on including competitors in that group which would be encouraged to conduct their bargaining at the same time limits the value of such a policy, to be sure. Nevertheless, to the extent that certain negotiations are recognized as key bargains and set patterns for others in the same or related industries, this limitation may not be serious. Even if General Motors were the only representative of the automobile industry negotiating during the period, the terms of its agreement might be generalized to other automobile firms, or in any event might serve as a guide to subsequent settlements in the industry.

We undertook this investigation to answer the question of whether the impact of strikes on the public was so damaging as to warrant firmer strike-control measures, or whether, as has sometimes been contended, the effects of strikes are exaggerated and only in rare instances are serious enough to call for governmental intervention. The primary conclusion which emerges from our detailed examination is that to the extent the latter view relies on the consumer effects of a strike it vastly underrates the problem. Because of the integrated nature of the American economy a strike has consequences far more ramifying than are revealed by consideration of whether consumers can get along for a time without the final product. Producers who rely on the struck product, and other producers who depend on goods made with the struck product, as well as suppliers of the struck unit, and other firms who supply not only the suppliers of the struck unit but also the directly and indirectly affected producers are all caught in the backwash of a stoppage. In many instances these repercussions are minor and work no substantial hardship, but in other instances they constitute the most important effects of a strike.

Recognition of the widespread ramifications of a strike does not in itself, of course, establish a case for government intervention. Even with such a network of consequences it may still be true that the really serious stoppages are so few that no general control program is necessary. But the case is not so simple as it appears when one concentrates on the consumer effects of strikes, and an analysis which runs only in terms of the importance to direct users of the final product of the struck firm is clearly no basis for public policy.

How serious a strike must become before the government is warranted in intervening is not a question that can be answered solely by statistics—it depends on the public's willingness to pay the price of a strike. In our cultural system of values there is a presumption that the government should not intervene in private affairs. When "private" affairs have public ramifications, however, then public demand for nonintervention must be balanced against the public cost of nonintervention, and there is no assurance that demand will sustain the price which some strikes ask.

But if the public is unwilling to pay the price of some strikes, then some means of measuring their cost—of more precisely ascertaining the price of strikes—must be discovered. Otherwise we shall be unable to distinguish between those strikes which the public accepts as "reasonably" priced and those whose cost must price them out of our culture. The issue is an important one, but difficult to resolve. If, because our inclination is to limit the area of government intervention, we restrict the right to strike in certain obvious situations only, without consideration as to whether in other situations the consequences—while more subtle—are no less telling, there remains this danger: a public which is still reluctant to pay the price of some strikes which are still unrestricted may, in the absence of better guides, become impatient with the strike itself, making blanket condemnations.

It is *because* it is desirable to most of us to limit the area of government control that it is so necessary to appraise accurately the impact on the public of particular kinds of strikes. There is probably little to be gained and perhaps much to be lost by misleading ourselves into dismissing the strike problem as inconsequential on the ground that rarely has the public been forced to go hungry, rarely has it been permanently injured, rarely have any lives been lost as a result of labor stoppages. Public policy is not commonly based on so Spartan a view. A general desire to keep government intervention to the minimum does not permit keeping it at less than the minimum which is publicly acceptable.

This should not be construed as a plea for greater restrictions on the right to strike. It is simply a conclusion that the classificatory approach to identifying strikes which should be controlled is not likely to accomplish what we seek. It will blanket in some strikes which entail far less public hardship than others which are left without restriction. It will leave uncontrolled some strikes which can be seriously injurious to the public.

It is clear that any satisfactory strike-control program must allow a large measure of administrative flexibility, simply because strikes cannot be classified in advance by degree of public effects, because even within the same industry or firm the nature of effects varies with underlying conditions. It seems no less clear, however, that we should work to provide adequate guides for the exercise of administrative discretion, simply because the nature of strike effects is as complex as our economy. We offer the strike rating procedure which has been applied in this study as an example of the kind of analysis which might aid the executive office in its decisions, not with any conviction that it provides the best guide, and certainly not the only guide, but with the belief that it provides a better guide than is now available.

INDEX
